A BEACHCOMBER IN THE ORIENT

HARRY L. FOSTER

Dixon-Price Publishing
Kingston, Washington

First Edition printed in 1923 in New York, New York

This edition follows most of the conventions of the original edition, but some punctuation has been revised to reflect modern usage. Illustrations used in the first edition have been excluded from this edition. Volume arrangement and editorial changes are copyright© 2005 by Dixon-Price Publishing, Kingston, Washington.

No part of this book may be copied as is for commercial use without the permission of the publisher.

Library of Congress Cataloging-in-Publication Data

Foster, Harry L. (Harry La Tourette), 1894-1932.
   A beachcomber in the Orient / Harry L. Foster.
      p. cm.
   Originally published: New York : Dodd, Mead, 1923.
   ISBN 1-929516-09-6 (alk. paper)
   1. Asia, Southeastern--Description and travel. 2. East Asia--Description and travel. 3. Foster, Harry L. (Harry La Tourette), 1894-1932--Travel--Asia, Southeastern. 4. Foster, Harry L. (Harry La Tourette), 1894-1932--Travel--East Asia. I. Title.
   DS522.4.F68 2005
   915.04'41--dc22
                                        2005017565

ISBN 1-929516-09-6

Printed in the U.S.A. by Lightning Source Inc., LaVergne, Tenn.

Dixon-Price Publishing
9105 Leprechaun Lane
Kingston, WA 98456

CONTENTS

CHAPTER ONE
   THE FOOL-KILLER STRIKES 5
CHAPTER TWO
   IN THE PARIS OF THE JUNGLE 11
CHAPTER THREE
   UP THE MEKONG TO PNOM PENH 24
CHAPTER FOUR
   THROUGH CAMBODIA BY SAMPAN 38
CHAPTER FIVE
   HITTING THE TRAIL WITH HENRI 48
CHAPTER SIX
   OVERLAND THROUGH SIAM 63
CHAPTER SEVEN
   THE CITY OF THE GREAT WHITE ANGELS 76
CHAPTER EIGHT
   BY FREIGHT CAR TO THE MALAY STATES 93
CHAPTER NINE
   ON THE BEACH—IN SINGAPORE 114
CHAPTER TEN
   IN A WATERFRONT GROG-SHOP 128
CHAPTER ELEVEN
   BY CARGO BOAT TO THE PHILIPPINES 148
CHAPTER TWELVE
   A TOURIST IN JAPAN 170
CHAPTER THIRTEEN
   SING-SONG AND OPERA IN SHANGHAI 194
CHAPTER FOURTEEN
   THE NIGHTMARE CITY OF CANTON 217
CHAPTER FIFTEEN
   BACK TO HONG KONG 233

CHAPTER ONE

THE FOOL-KILLER STRIKES

I

I drifted westward about a year ago—drifted until the West became the East—until my tramp steamer dropped me one day at the waterfront of Hong Kong.

There, upon the wharf, I met a prophet.

He sat upon a cotton bale—a burly son of the sea, with a wooden leg and a red nose, a strong breath, and a Cockney accent.

"Where bound, me lad?" he inquired.

"I don't know."

"Got any work 'ere?"

"No."

"Got any money?"

"A little."

"Then go 'ome while you got it. S'no plyce 'ere for an 'igh class white man like you'n me. S'elp me, bob, it ain't! S'no work to be 'ad in the East—not even if you look for it. Tyke it from me, s'the worst bleedin' plyce in the 'ole bloody world. What you doin' 'ere any'ow?"

"Just knocking about."

A broad grin spread across his unshaven face.

"Good," said he. "That's 'ow I got *my* start."

Then he bummed me for the price of a "square meal," and still grinning, stumped his way through a crowd of Chinese stevedores toward a waterfront grog-shop.

II

I was a tramp, so far as occupation and destination were concerned, but in my own estimation a decidedly aristocratic, respectable sort of tramp, for I had money in my pocket, a suitcase full of decent clothing, and a typewriter wherewith to justify my vagrancy by writing about it.

Two years earlier, when the wanderlust first attacked me, another seafaring man had similarly warned me against South America, but I had disregarded the warning, and during those two years of wandering I had found employment whenever I needed it—at mining, clerking, selling shoes, playing the piano, at any sort of work that presented itself, but always at something; I had written stories of my experiences, and had finally sold them; with enough cash to keep me for several months, I had struck out for the Orient, confident that my luck—which I conceitedly called "success"—would continue. After my tramping in South America, I was ready to make a comparative splurge.

The best opportunities for employment, of course, would have been in the large cities of Japan or China, but something inside of me—perhaps the migratory instinct which summons the birds and the hoboes southward in winter—was calling toward the tropical lands where life was abundant, where alluring brown-skinned maidens frolicked beneath the palm trees, where oriental rajas rode upon their sacred elephants and worshiped the sacred ox, where yellow-robed priests performed strange heathen rites in barbaric temples.

I struck farther into the East, farther away from home, buying passage on another steamer to Singapore, choosing the destination for no particular reason save that it was situated near the equator and its name sounded romantic. And while this second steamer carried me southward across the blue waters of the China Sea, with the hazy outline of Indo-China just visible in a greenish blur upon the horizon, I sat upon the deck beneath an awning that flapped lazily in the soft breezes of the tropics, talking to myself about the future.

"You've always been a lucky sort of tramp," I told myself. "You'll never be up against it like that beachcomber in Hong Kong."

Whereupon the Goddess of Fortune, chancing to overhear me, summoned her servant, the Fool-Killer, who selected his largest and hardest club, girded up his loins, limbered up his muscles, and prepared to tap me gently but firmly upon my over-confident young head.

III

Upon the steamer, I met a poet.

At least, if he were not a poet, he should have been, for he was an Italian, he had a pair of soulful dark eyes, he was slender of body, and temperamental of soul, he needed a haircut, and he had just been disappointed in love.

He sat at the stern, gazing sadly at the foaming wake that trailed behind us toward the rim of the sea, drinking French cognac and telling me his troubles. Ah, but she had been a wondrous creature, that girl! Not only beautiful, but talented! She danced in an American cabaret in Shanghai, and no other dancer in all the cabarets of the East could kick so high or so gracefully.

"*Mon dieu!*" he exclaimed, mixing French with his English. "How I have make the love at that girl! I have to tell her that I love her like the wind love the mountain, like the sea love the seashore, like the everything love the everything! Sentimental fool that I am, I have make the love at her like the true *artiste!*"

But the girl lacked appreciation of real art, and having spent the poet's money, had run away with another man.

He was young, that poet—as young as myself—and even more foolish. He, too, was a vagabond author, without employment or destination. He, too, had just broken into the magazines with his first writings, and his check could be awaiting him in Singapore. He called for more cognac, and his imagination soared skyward toward the silvery stars that were beginning to dot the heavens. If I would join him, we would wander up through the Malay States, perhaps to Siam, and live like a pair of kings in the jungle, with turbaned attendants to kowtow to us, and dancing girls to jingle their brass anklets at our command. We would forget that cabaret dancer in Shanghai. We would—

There we sat upon the deck, two vagabonds in white linen, two prospective adventurers with a combined height of eleven feet and a combined weight of two hundred and forty pounds, with the capital of young authors and the ambitions of millionaires, planning our kingdom. We worked out every detail. When we reached Singapore—

And we didn't even reach Singapore.

Our steamer, a French mail packet, called on the way at the French Indo-Chinese port of Saigon. At midnight it crept up a winding river between swampy, jungle-grown banks. The air was breezeless. The edge of a tropical moon, peering above the ragged palm-tips, traced an unbroken path of gold across the placid surface of the stream. The palms themselves hung motionless, as though painted upon a canvas.

The heat was intense, and neither the poet nor I could sleep. We watched by the rail as we slid alongside a wharf. A few coolies in conical straw hats and little else—Annamite relatives of the Chinese—appeared from somewhere to seize the ropes and tie the ship fast; then they faded into the night as mysteriously as they had appeared. A sleepy French official in a sun helmet came aboard. A drowsy steward slouched from the bridge to the gangway to post a notice that we would sail at daybreak for Singapore.

We read the notice with disappointment. Somewhere beyond the wharf and the motionless palms lay the city of Saigon, the little French capital of Cochin-China which previous writers had described as a Paris hidden in the jungle. The very name of Paris attracted us as would a magnet. We glanced cautiously about. There was not an immigration official in sight. The only evidence that Saigon was inhabited consisted of a slowly forming line of half-naked rikisha coolies at the other end of the wharf. They squatted between the shafts of their night-going vehicles, their brown bodies glistening under the rays of an arc-light, their faces staring toward the gangway in search of night-going passengers.

"Come on," I exclaimed.

As we reached the dock, a thunder of bare feet sounded upon the boards, and the whole swarm of runners dashed toward us, shouldering one another aside, bowing to us in the oriental fashion and rubbing their hands together, beseeching us in mixed Annamite and pigeon-French for our patronage.

"Where do we go?" demanded the poet.

"Wherever they take us."

We climbed into two of the carriages and away we went—past dim warehouses and shops, past stucco homes and government offices. There was a delightful fascination about galloping through a strange city in the early hours of the morning, led by guides who could not tell us whither they were guiding us. The coolies jogged steadily along, chattering together in an undertone, giggling occasionally like a couple of mischievous boys. Wherever they were going, it became evident that they were not going into town; the road became a path and finally a mere trail, the trees became a tangle of palms and banana trees. The golden moon, seeping though the jungle growth, shed an eerie light in mysterious patches upon the glistening bodies of the Annamites, and still they trotted, untiring, turning corners until we had lost all sense of direction, to pause finally before an atap-shack half-hidden among the profuse vines, where they indicated by gesture that we were to dismount.

"*Bien*," said the poet, a trifle doubtfully. "We see what is this place."

From the shack came the sound of music—the faint tinkle of some weird stringed instrument. Entering through a dark hallway, we found ourselves in a bare room with a small platform in one corner, upon which several natives were seated cross-legged before all sorts of odd musical contrivances. There was a species of banjo with an extremely long neck, with three bulky pegs to hold the cords, and with a sounding board as big around as the head of a keg. There were three or four squeaky Chinese fiddles, several gongs and tomtoms, a sort of zither built like a barrel chopped lengthwise, and a crude, homemade xylophone.

A woman advanced to welcome us. She was old, withered and wrinkled, with the features of a Chinese but with the darker complexion that proclaimed her an Annamite: her skin was tightly stretched across skull-like cheekbones; her lips were stained red from the juice of the betel-nut which she chewed; she wore black pajamas.

She led us into a second room—a chamber elaborately hung with silken draperies in red and black, with lettered designs of gold. Along the wall were large divans with silken cushions. Over the entire place there was a peculiar aroma, somewhat like that of joss in a Chinese temple, yet different—an aroma that was sweet, almost nauseating, yet subtly pleasing. And the woman stood before us, smiling and bowing, rubbing her aged hands together in an oriental obeisance.

"What you like?" she inquired in pigeon-French. "Smokee?"

"*Bien!*" decided the poet. "We see what is this opium."

She brought us two bloated-looking pipes, extracted a gooey substance from a tube of tinfoil and smeared it with a stick upon the bowls. She brought us a funny little lamp, and showed us how to heat the substance and draw its fumes into our lungs with slow, deep puffs.

I felt like a regular devil as I seated myself upon the divan. The poet, too, was affecting nonchalance.

"*Mon dieu!*" he exclaimed. "All we lack is our harem."

As though she understood, the woman clapped her hands.

The silken draperies parted, and into the room came a troupe of Annamite girls, tiny little creatures, scarcely sixteen or seventeen. Each perfect little figure was clad in silken pajamas; the jacket, not quite connecting with the trousers, showed a slight expanse of bronze skin. They circled about us with mincing yet graceful step. But their teeth, like those of the old woman, were black, and their lips discolored with betel juice.

Even the poet shuddered.

"*Mon dieu!* What an ugliness!"

"Come on," I exclaimed. "Let's get out of here!"

We dropped our pipes and strode out into the dark hallway. But as we stepped from the light, something happened. The roof seemed to fall on my head, but it may have been that oriental banjo. As a musical instrument, I could not endorse it favorably; as a weapon, I shall always respect and remember it. For the world faded out from before my eyes, and darkness reigned—darkness punctuated, so it seemed, by visions of red and gold draperies, and smiling, betel-stained lips.

And at daybreak, the little French mail packet felt its way cautiously down the river between the swampy, jungle-covered shores of Cochin-China, toward the open sea and Singapore, carrying my baggage and the poet's to our destination, but leaving us behind.

The Fool-Killer had made a double killing.

CHAPTER TWO

IN THE PARIS OF THE JUNGLE

I

I awoke in a rice field, whither some one had very considerately dragged me. It was a damp, soggy field, bordering upon a mangrove swamp. Daylight was breaking, and from the wet ground there was rising the morning mist of the tropics, enveloping the land with a thick, poisonous-looking vapor.

Beside me sat the poet, his clothing awry and stained with mud, his long hair disheveled, a peculiar hazy expression in his eyes, as though he had not fully recovered his senses and was figuring out how he had chanced to awake in such an unattractive place. With one hand he was stroking a large bump on his forehead, a companion bump to the one which I found upon my own.

We were stranded, and our cash was gone, but we were not altogether down and out—not yet. For, searching through our pockets, the poet found the stub of his steamer ticket, a damp box of matches, a lace handkerchief, and two cigarettes, while I found my American passport, a key to my suitcase, and—this final discovery inspired us to rise and essay a jig upon our exposure-stiffened legs—nothing less than a travelers' check for one hundred dollars. Not so bad!

Rejoicing at our luck, we made our way out of the rice field until we came to a path. It was bordered by palms and banana trees, like the one we had traveled the night before, but the thatched houses hidden among tropical vines, each resembling the opium-joint, gave us no clue to our whereabouts.

We trudged slowly and painfully along the path until we reached a road—a broad, dusty thoroughfare upon which the newly risen sun was already beating down with a promise of stifling heat to come. A stream of ox-carts, drawn by queer cattle, by humpbacked zebus and cloven-footed water buffaloes, was lumbering along evidently toward the city, laden with produce and driven by a motley assortment of brown Annamites in cone-shaped straw hats.

A few coolies, naked save for a loincloth, walking slowly along between the shafts of their rikishas in search of customers, passed us without noticing we were white men, so stained with mud was our once-white clothing. A stout Frenchman in immaculate linen, his eyes peering out from between a sun helmet and a bushy black beard, went rattling along on the box of a funny little old-fashioned coach, crackling a long whip over the heads of two tiny little ponies, without favoring us with a single glance. Only a group of old native women in black pajamas, with white handkerchiefs tied over their heads, recognized us as belonging to the dominant race, and chattered loudly among themselves, telling the rest of the neighborhood all about us and laughing shrilly at our unkempt appearance.

At length, however, we came to a canal filled with the rounded palm-thatched roofs of sampans and houseboats, and found ourselves in the region of the docks. Where our steamer had been, several coolies were bringing up mail bags from a pile at the edge of the wharf, but there was no steamer in sight—only a few native sailing vessels, drifting slowly along the brown river, while their crews chattered together in raucous Annamite that came to us clearly but unintelligibly across the water.

The poet sighed.

"So this," he said, "is Paris."

II

We cashed my check at the bank, receiving "piastres" at a rate which seemed to double the hundred dollars.

The money gave us a new feeling of respectability, and forgetting our bedraggled attire, we climbed into a pair of rikishas—which in the

French provinces have been rechristened with the name of "pousse-pousse"—and instructing the runners to take us to a hotel, we sat up and dared the world to snub us.

The rikisha has that effect. On your first ride, you feel rather like a fool, galloping along behind a fellow human being; on your second ride, you feel like an inhuman slave-driver, making a draft animal out of the poor coolie; on your third and succeeding rides, you feel like a potentate drawn in style through the streets by one of his vassals.

But when we challenged the world, it accepted the challenge. As we drew up before the leading hotel—a truly French hotel with wide verandas, and tables upon the sidewalk before it—the manager came out expectantly, but after one contemptuous glance at our mud-stained persons, informed us that his rooms were all occupied.

Saigon was truly Parisian in the number of its sidewalk cafés. From place to place we went, seeking lodgings, along wide boulevards, past houses and government buildings of French architecture, all of them yellow stucco and surrounded by pretty walled gardens, through an avenue lined with shops whose plate glass windows displayed jewelry or perfumes or gowns, and whose doorways bore such familiar inscriptions as "*Le Bon Marché*" or "*Le Paradis des Dames.*"

Many years ago, when the native city of Saigon was destroyed by fire, the French conquerors rebuilt it in imitation of their own beloved capital, and only the people remained unchanged. Its Parisian boulevards were thronged with Annamites in black pajamas, the men in straw hats sometimes conical in shape, sometimes broad and flat like the head of a barrel; the women with their long black hair tied in a chignon and wrapped with a handkerchief, or braided in a pig-tail, which was inserted into a species of umbrella wrapper and then coiled around and around the top of the head.

With them mingled a throng of Chinamen, and Hindus, and Japanese, a heterogeneous mixture that looked out of place against the background of French cafés and shops—as though someone had picked up a handful of all the strange natives of all the strange countries of Asia, and had dropped them in a conglomerate mob upon the Champs Elysées.

We finally found a hotel—a small hotel—whose manager was not so particular about his guests, and were escorted to a room where countless little green lizards, crawling about the walls and ceiling in search of bugs, cocked their heads at an angle and chirped a welcome to us.

"When does the next boat leave for Singapore?" the poet inquired in French.

The manager shrugged his shoulders.

"*Je ne sais pas, monsieur.* Perhaps next week, perhaps the week after next, perhaps the week after that."

We sat upon the bed, like the Hall Room Boys in the comic supplement, and while the manager sent our clothes to the laundry, we smoked the poet's two damp cigarettes and made faces at the lizards. But in the evening, once more immaculate, we swung out into the boulevards with jaunty step. With the coming of nightfall, French officialdom was issuing from the shade of home and office to recapture the city from the Asiatics. The ox-carts in the streets were giving way to pony carts driven by chic mademoiselles and to automobiles filled with bemused and bewhiskered Frenchmen. Stocky little poilus from the garrison, their slovenly khaki uniforms supplemented with sun helmets, were promenading the broad sidewalks or loitering at the numerous sidewalk tables, quite as though at home in their own Paris. At the leading hotel, in fine defiance to the tropical heat, a French orchestra was grinding out jazz, while a headwaiter who looked like Carpentier was bowing the guests toward tables that fairly gleamed with white napery and resplendent silverware, and French gentlemen in white uniforms whirled about the floor with French ladies whose silks and satins were cut to the latest model from Paris.

We stood outside, gazing with fascination at the brilliant spectacle; then, remembering that our hundred dollars was to take us a long way, we adjourned to the cheapest restaurant we could find, and dined upon ham and eggs. The breeze died down, the palms again drooped as they had drooped the night before, the same tropical moon appeared and shed its silver light upon a scene as devoid of motion as a painting, and the feeling of unreality settled upon us once more. Here we were, in the steaming heat of one of the hottest regions on earth, sitting at a typical Parisian restaurant, in a city surrounded by jungle, a thousand miles from anywhere else, with lizards chirping at us from the eaves of the roof, stranded—two near-bums, looking like wealthy young tourists, and dining upon ham and eggs.

Two little French mademoiselles at the next table eyed us mischievously from under the brims of their Parisian chapeaux, and rising with a beckoning nod, climbed into a pousse-pousse, displaying two pairs of rather heavy but neatly stockinged ankles.

The poet sighed again.

"Saigon," he mused, "is not so bad place."

III

Indo-China exists mainly as a happy hunting ground for the French office-seeker.

It seems that every high official in Paris, whose relatives wish a comfortable government appointment, uses his influence to have a new bureau of some sort created in Hanoi or Saigon, and sends them off to the Asiatic provinces.

We met most of them upon the following day. Our hotel manager had required us to fill out a long form, giving our life histories, our ages, our condition of marriage or bachelorhood, our occupations, our reasons for being in Saigon, our ultimate destination, and countless other details required by the local French government. But this was merely the beginning. We had to call at the passport office to explain how we had landed without a French visé. The poet had the gift of gab, and spoke French fluently; his white suit was of Chinese silk, cut by the most fashionable tailor in Shanghai; we made an impression of flawless respectability, and the passport officials were very sorry to learn that our steamer had sailed away while we were merely taking our morning constitutional around the block, but our case was most unusual, and they would have to refer us to higher authority.

They led us from one government office to another. Since practically every white man in Saigon, or anywhere else in Indo-China, is a government official, there were plenty of offices. It appears that every structure in the city which is not a millinery shop or a café is a *bureau des postes* or a *bureau d'administration* or a *bureau de* some kind of *autre chose*. They line all the principal boulevards, ornate structures as a rule—the *Palais duGouvernment* alone cost twelve million francs—until the visitor begins to wonder what all the various governors can find to govern.

The truth is that there are more governors than government. According to one authority whom I later met, himself a Frenchman, the average official comes out to Indo-China with no preparation for his duties, and with little knowledge of economics or administration, and once arrived in the already over-officialed provinces, spends most of his time at the sidewalk cafés, wishing he had never left his own gay homeland.

Indo-China, until very recent years, has been a burden to the French government, and has served little purpose except to gratify the national pride by making France a colonial nation. The officials have built roads and beautified the cities with splendid government buildings and cathedrals and opera houses, but instead of encouraging commerce and business, have discouraged promoters and shippers with heavy port charges and taxes and restrictions, which, instead of providing the funds for the roads and the buildings, have sometimes been insufficient to pay the salaries of the great army of office-holders engaged in collecting the taxes.

Each official instead of doing something worth while, seemed to be conscientiously engaged in performing the same trifling, inconsequential duties which his fellows were performing, chief of which—it appeared to me—was securing from the infrequent visitors the same complete information which the poet and I gave upon the printed form at the hotel. From office to office they kept referring us, each new office appearing a trifle more ornate than the previous one, and each now official a trifle more important, and at each place the poet rehearsed our convincing story. And finally, when we had reached a large structure with several armed sentries at the gate, and had been inspected by about the tenth bemustached official—all with flattering French politeness which, instead of annoying us, had begun to give us a feeling of immense importance—the Director of Security at length bowed us from his office with permission to remain in Indo-China.

"Ah," exclaimed the poet hopefully. "Then we can leave?"

"No," replied the Director. "As there is no boat for three weeks, monsieur, it would have been impossible to leave, anyway."

IV

The steamship agent confirmed the report.

He would honor the poet's stub of a ticket; he was very sorry that he could not give me free passage until he communicated with higher authority at Singapore or Hong Kong; he was very sorry, extremely sorry, but he was sure everything would be all right; it was merely a matter of sending the cable and awaiting the answer.

We settled down at a sidewalk café to wait, trying for the sake of economy to make one bottle of beer last all the afternoon, and to give

Carpentier, the headwaiter, the impression that we did so not for economy, but because of our natural habits of abstinence.

Day after day passed, and we still sat there.

We talked until bored with each other's conversation, after which we sat and didn't talk until bored with each other's silence. When the poet spoke, it was usually to tell me additional details about the cabaret dancer in Shanghai. She was a sweet, guileless creature, it seemed, but terribly extravagant. One day she would come to him, for instance, with tears in her girlish blue eyes because she had seen a mandarin coat in a window at the ridiculously cheap price of five hundred dollars, and it broke her heart to see such a bargain when she had just spent the last five hundred dollars the poet had given her. He would give her the money——e happened, at the moment, to be vice-president of a swindling concern run by a fellow Italian, and had more money than he usually earned as an author—but the next day she would be back again with tears in her eyes because she had seen some other bargain.

Having told me these details of her innocent extravagance, he would lapse again into silence. His dark eyes, surrounded by premature wrinkles like those of the fellow in the advertisement who is pounding away his life at every step because he doesn't wear rubber heels, would stare away into space, filled with a dreamy expression. Presently he would recover long enough to pour the dregs of our beer into my glass with the exclamation of "Take," or to reach for another of my cigarettes with an exclamation of "Give."

Then Carpentier would come and stare at us in an accusing manner, as though to inquire whether we intended to monopolize the table all day for sixty centimes, and we would rise with dignity, feeling somewhat as Charley Chaplin looks when he walks deliberately away from a suspicious policeman.

We were forced, of course, to make some purchases—a safety razor and such things—and were tempted finally to buy a camera, a somewhat battered relic of a kodak, which it took us an entire afternoon to secure at a reasonable price from a Chinese pawn broker, since, according to the rules of such transactions in all Asiatic countries, we were forced to examine it casually and contemptuously, haggle over the price, start to walk out five or six times, but return with an air of indifference when the price was reduced, examine it again and turn up our noses at it, and finally, after gradual compromise upon both sides, accept it at a fourth the original price—and probably at twice its actual value.

Thus armed, we set out in search of interesting sights, and found none. Saigon, being off the tourist run, has no sights for tourists, which is probably why it is off the run. The Annamites were interesting enough—particularly the women in their black pajamas, walking very erect and swinging the arms back and forth with the hand flapping loosely at the end of the swing, tiny little creatures with the most beautiful figures I have seen anywhere in the world, but with potentially attractive faces marred by the inevitable betel-discolored mouths—but the French had rebuilt Saigon so thoroughly that one could not photograph its people without getting an incongruous Parisian background.

We tried "pousse-pousse" coolies as guides, but the only places of interest which they knew seemed to be the brothels and the opium dives, and we felt we were already sufficiently acquainted with such places. The French are not puritanical, and are not noted as reformers, so that these resorts seemed scattered throughout the suburbs. It has even been said of Saigon that not a few of its white exiles take to opium, although I ran across no evidence of this statement. Certainly, they make no strenuous effort to suppress the Asiatic vice.

Saigon, at first glance interesting, soon palls upon the man who has to remain there, and particularly upon the French, than whom no race is less suited to the dull task of colonization. The officials would sit in groups at the sidewalk cafés, as silent as ourselves, staring at the golden bubbles rising through their amber glasses of cognac and soda, or watching their cigarette smoke drift upward through the breezeless night to hover beneath the palm leaves overhead. Or another group would become noisy, pounding upon the marble top of the table and calling for service—using, strangely enough, the English word "Boy," pronouncing it "Boi-ee," and repeating it in varying tones, first in a normal key, then in deep bass, then in falsetto—finding amusement here even in such small diversions. Or the child of some sallow-faced French couple might try to romp with the Annamite beggar children that hung about the tables; his parents, to maintain racial distinctions, would call him back, and he would obey with reluctance, as though he, too, were lonesome and discontented in this faraway port.

Only once did the poet rouse himself from his ennui to grow enthusiastic about anything. That was when he discovered that an Egyptian princess, touring the world, happened to be stopping at Saigon's principal hotel. She was rather stout, and of middle age, but she seemed to be vastly wealthy, for she was accompanied by a retinue of servants and wore much jewelry.

"And what you think, my friend! She no is marry! She no has the husban'! Perhaps we can make the marry with her and—"

"We?"

"Perhaps! Can the royal princess not have so many husban' like she want? She have plenty money, and we shall travel like the prince!"

"Well, I have no objection to *your* marrying her."

But he shook his head. It seemed too great a task for a one hundred pound poet who couldn't write poetry.

"No," he decided. "I think I like bettair the girl in Shanghai. I send her one cable, I think. I tell her, 'Come to Singapore, all is forgive.'"

And he lapsed again into silence.

V

Days passed.

We began to concoct various schemes for increasing our capital. The poet inserted an advertisement in the local French newspaper, informing the public that Professor ——, the celebrated Italian master of foxtrot and one-step, accompanied by Mr. Harry L. Foster, the famous American pianist and jazz artist, had arrived in Saigon and would be glad to call upon young ladies at their home and give instruction in the latest ballroom steps direct from the capitals of Europe and America.

The only response came from a wealthy, English-speaking Chinese merchant, who was about to send his daughters to England, and wished them to be fully trained in European accomplishments, but he had no piano in his house, and Carpentier refused to let us use his hotel ballroom as a studio.

I hit upon another idea. Since we had no reason to go to Singapore, why not write to the steamship company to forward our baggage, while we hiked overland through the jungle to meet it in Siam? The poet was not enthused.

"No is railroad," he said.

"But we'll walk."

"No is road to walk."

I dragged him around to the American consulate, a neat stucco-walled building on a quiet street. The consul, a pleasant and obliging young man, not much older than ourselves, had a map, the best map published, but there was only a vague, dotted line to indicate a trail. It began at a town called Battambang, situated a few hundred miles up the River Mekong, and it stopped at the Siamese border; beyond that point, so far as any one in Saigon knew, there might be nothing but jungle.

The consul was enthusiastic about our project.

"Just the thing for writers to do," he said. "They never go into the interior in these countries. Of course, it will be expensive—guides, servants, carriers, ponies, ox carts, provisions, weapons—you'll want a big caliber gun for tiger or rhinoceros."

"Good-bye," said the poet. Wild animals, he always maintained, should be kept only in menageries.

We continued to wait.

In outward appearance we might have been a pair of wealthy young tourists, and Saigon accepted us as such. On our first pousse-pousse ride, we had encouraged this idea, by overpaying our rikisha men with thirty cents an hour. The Annamite waiters at the hotel, appealed to for information regarding the rates, had been greatly embarrassed; they did not like to earn our ill-will by naming too high a price, nor did they like to offend the pousse-pousse coolies by naming too low a price; forced to use our own judgment, we had tried to be stingy and had been extravagant. Wherefore our table became a Mecca for all the peddlers and beggars of Saigon, who look upon visiting tourists as persons specially appointed by the gods to distribute wealth among the deserving.

Cripples gathered in swarms, displaying their injuries to excite our sympathy; children came with trifles to sell—postage stamps, curios, vile French postcards of ladies and gentlemen in compromising situations; even the Chinese bank cashier who had cashed my last and only check came around to inform me that he had paid me twenty-seven centimes too much and would have to assume the responsibility if I did not make good his deficit. The curb beside our table became a rendezvous for all the unemployed pousse-pousse coolies in town, who squatted there upon their bare feet all day long, clad in a straw hat and ragged pair of drawers, ready at our slightest movement to rush toward us with their carriages.

These Annamites are related racially to the Chinese, but their faces are not quite so long, and lack the keenness of the Chinese faces. The nose is flatter, the complexion darker, and they are more apt to have a sodden expression, as though they had indulged too freely the night before in rice wine and opium. As a rule, they lack the mental alertness of the neighboring orientals; in Japan or China, for instance, the rikisha runner frequently speaks enough pigeon-English to guide the foreigner about town, while the hotel boys almost invariably speak it; in Indo-China the runner seldom, if ever, speaks a word of French, while the hotel boy, if he speaks it at all, finds the grammar so difficult that he butchers his pigeon-French ten times worse than the pigeon-English was ever butchered. There is little dignity about the Annamites; they are rather inclined to slink past a white man like whipped dogs—for the French, although the fact seems out of keeping with our usual idea of the French character, have been severe in the East in their rôle of white conquerors, and have instilled a genuine respect and fear into the natives. Even the rikisha men accept whatever the passenger chooses to give them, always holding the hand out for more and affecting an expression of disappointment even when they know the pay to be ample, yet never voicing a protest when they know it to be too little.

Sitting at our table, with all Saigon fawning upon us, the poet and I felt like millionaires. And then, after two weeks of it, we made a discovery. It seems strange that in these lands of cheap labor a visitor's money can dwindle so rapidly, but it's a fact; you never know where it goes, but it goes, and it goes just about as rapidly in an Oriental city as in any other big city, and ours was no exception. In spite of our economy, we began to wonder whether we had enough left to keep us in our accustomed style for another week.

We could go out into the suburbs, and rent a straw sleeping mat, in some thatched hut, or—but perhaps, after all, the sailing date had been advanced. Hoping and praying, we hurried around once more to the steamship agency, only to learn that the date had been postponed. And that was not the worst. The agent had received an answer to his cable. He was sorry, very sorry, but I would have to pay my passage. Perhaps, when I regained my baggage in Singapore, and found the stub of my ticket, I could have the money refunded. He ended with a shrug of his shoulders such as that with which shopkeepers used to accompany "*C'est la guerre,*" when charging a doughboy double the usual price.

"Surely *monsieur* does not mind such a small matter."

The poet waved his hand in a graceful gesture.

"Surely not. What are a few score dollars to a man like *monsieur?*"

But the time for pretense was past.

"When does the nest river boat start upstream?" I demanded.

It was in miserable French, but the agent understood. He pointed to a small vessel at the wharf. Smoke was already pouring from its funnel. Several Annamite deck hands were already fussing with the gangplank. A French captain, a nervous, excitable chap with a whiskey-colored mustache and a complexion reddened by the tropical sun, was blustering at the coolies who carried aboard the last of the cargo.

"In ten minutes," said the agent.

There was no time to lose. I handed the poet some money.

"Get me a steerage passage on that boat," I directed.

"But where you go?"

"To Battambang—to the beginning of that dotted line. You've got your ticket; you can go to Singapore, get your own baggage and mine, and meet me in Siam—meet me in Bangkok. I'm going to walk!"

I raced to the hotel, found the clerk, fretted while he wasted the precious moments in figuring my account, wasted a few more precious moments myself in trying to prove to him that he was a swindler and a thief, and raced back to the steamer.

It was still there—a slender little craft with a tiny cabin perched away up forward in the bow and several tiny staterooms perched away back aft in the stern, so that its general form suggested the discarded rind of a melon, an illusion made realistic by the stale odor from two hundred Asiatic steerage passengers of every size, sort, sect, sex, and species, who huddled in a mass of humanity upon the deck.

The poet thrust a ticket into my hand, and rushed on board with me to bid me farewell. I divided the remaining cash equally between us, and he embraced me in true Italian fashion.

"Kiss me upon the cheek, Foster!" he cried. "You are nice fellow, but you will meet one tiger or one rhinoceros, and good-bye Foster! Kiss me upon the cheek!"

The excitable captain was frothing at the delay.

"*Sacre bleu!* Visitors ashore! Cast off!"

"Kiss me, Foster! Kiss me upon the cheek! You will meet the tiger, and what will you do?"

"I'll choke him with my hands. And I'll choke you in a minute. I don't kiss men."

I seized his hand and shook it.

"Good-bye, foster!"

"Good-bye, old man. Good luck. Meet me in Bangkok!"

He turned to dash down the gangway. Then he paused. The gangway had been withdrawn. We were already clear of the dock, and surging through the murky water of the tropical river. We shouted to the captain to put back.

"*Sacre bleu!* I do not put back for steerage passengers!"

Wherefore, still comrades, we crawled into the center of that odorous horde of Asiatic bedfellows, found a small, unoccupied portion of hard deck between a couple of pajama-clad Annamite ladies, and adequately chaperoned by the rest of the steerage passengers, who crowded about to discuss our advent in all the guttural languages of the Far East, we proceeded somehow to fall asleep.

The Fool-Killer's work was beginning to bear fruit.

CHAPTER THREE

UP THE MEKONG TO PNOM PENH

I

The steamer during the night descended from Saigon to the sea, crossed a short strip of ocean to the mouth of the Mekong, and at daybreak was crawling slowly up a wide, turbid river.

The poet and I sat in the midst of our fellow steerage passengers and scratched mosquito bites—or some kind of bites.

The Asiatics were already awake, drinking their morning tea with an excess of gurgling enjoyment, or squatting upon their bare heels about the family rice bowls, into which a dozen of them would dig their chopsticks or their fingers, all at the same time, in perfect amity.

For nearly an hour we watched them with disdain and disgust. Then, becoming hungry ourselves, and realizing that in the excitement of embarking we had neglected to supply ourselves with provisions, we hailed a steward from the first-class cabin, offered him several brass pennies, and requested him to bring us a sandwich. He replied in pigeon-French—or *petit negre*, as the French call it—that his pantry contained no sandwiches. Well, then, was there any bread? Yes, there was bread. And was there any meat? Yes, there was meat. Then, we explained, if he would put a slice of meat between two slices of bread, it would serve just as well as a sandwich. Having made this idea clear to his Far-Eastern mind, which, despite its shrewdness, was neither original nor inventive, we finally sat down upon the deck and ate our sandwiches, while several Annamite infants romped across our laps, and the adult population of the steerage crowded about to inspect our operations with the usual ill-mannered curiosity of orientals.

The sight of two prosperous-looking white men in immaculate clothing, but sitting upon the deck like natives, was one that called for much speculation. The Asiatic was familiar with only two types of white men—the dressed-up individuals who rode in rikishas, lived at the best hotels, traveled first class, and strutted about like the lords of the universe, and the unmistakable bums, who dressed shabbily, and hung about the seaports to beg alms from their more fortunate fellows—and we, who dressed like the lords and traveled like the bums, defied classification.

They gathered about us in a swarm, the whole two hundred of them, while several amateur humorists among them made comments and suggestions in a chorus of grunts and whining noises which seemed to provoke much shrill laughter. One fellow in particular appeared to be especially witty. He was a fat, round-faced Chinaman, evidently a professional storyteller or a comedian from some local opera company, dressed in a flowing robe that hung to his feet like a skirt. He stood beside me, pointing to me and reciting something in a sing-song chant in so ludicrous a manner that I might have enjoyed it myself had I not been the object of his ridicule.

But, like any other white man, however lowly his temporary station in life, I resented being laughed at by a yellow man. For some moments I checked my rising anger, trying to eat my sandwich with dignity, but when at length, at the climax of his recital the comedian lifted my sun helmet from my head, my resentment boiled over. Leaping too my feet, I seized him by the folds of fat skin that bulged from his neck, and started toward the rail, with some vague intention of feeding him to the alligators or whatever creatures happened to inhabit the brown tropical river.

A vast commotion arose. A dozen other Chinamen or Annamites rushed to the comedian's assistance and tore him from my grasp. The poet shouted in French for help, while I seized the first available weapon, which happened to be somebody's rice bowl, and backed up against the mast in self-defense. But a firm hand seized me by the shoulder, a white hand, and I turned to look into the face of the French captain, who had spoken so abruptly to us the night before. Here, I thought, was the end of my ridiculous cross-country journey; I saw myself returned under arrest to Saigon, to be handed over to the American consul and shipped ignominiously homeward upon the first shipping-board vessel to touch at the Indo-Chinese capital.

The captain's voice, however, was this time friendly:

"*Monsieur*," he said, "should not remain here. It is not good for white prestige. I shall put *Monsieur* and his companion in a first-class stateroom."

II

Accepting the social promotion, we seated ourselves in deck chairs upon the forward deck, again beginning to feel like a pair of wealthy tourists.

There was a French army officer on board, going up-river to some village of the interior, accompanied by his wife, a slender young woman with roguish eyes. The poet, seeing her, brightened immediately, and camped beside her with the air of a man who intends to stay there indefinitely, to the evident annoyance of her husband, who sat on the other side of her, his military mustachios bristling aggressively.

"She say she is seasick from last night on the ocean," the poet explained in a side whisper, "but I think if her husban' go ten minutes downstairs, she will not be so sick."

But the husband was not obliging.

The sun rose higher in the heavens, shining with such force that the shadows of the clouds stood out in clearly defined patches upon the placid surface of the stream. On either shore the banks were low and marshy, and from the purplish muck arose a tangle of vegetation so brilliantly green that it almost pained the eye. Sometimes rice fields bordered the river; sometimes groves of palms, areca palms, with very tall and slender trunks of grayish white surmounted by a tuft of plumes, standing in rows like soldiers on parade; sometimes just a rank, undisciplined riot of jungle, wet with the morning dew and glistening in the sun, always of that vivid, painfully brilliant green.

Occasionally we passed a cluster of thatched huts perched high upon stilts, with a dugout canoe moored among the lily pads before it and naked brown children splashing about in the water; occasionally we sighted a herd of domesticated water buffaloes, sometimes wallowing in the mud of the bank where their purplish-brown hides blended with the purplish-brown of the mud, sometimes standing all but submerged in the stream with their flat, cow-like snouts and their massive horns rising above the surface; then, very slowly, the village and the children and the animals drifted past and again there was the limitless expanse of low green jungle on either side, and the unending ribbon of turbid water before us.

Now and then we met a fishing boat, with brown sails flapping idly in the calm; if the Annamite crews failed to give us leeway, our excitable captain would rush from the cabin and hurl anathema upon them in French, interjecting in cockney-English his one Anglo-Saxon phrase of "Bloody fools!" which he had evidently learned from some British seaman in Saigon. He would jump up and down, cursing and tearing his hair, while our two native pilots—two brown-bodied Annamites with handkerchiefs twisted about their heads and the ends sticking up like horns—would regard him without emotion visible upon their mask-like faces, marveling perhaps at the inexplicable excitability of white men.

Of the scenery or the incidents of the voyage, the poet took little note, nor had he ever jotted down his impression of Saigon. Notes, he maintained, served only to restrict the free play of an author's imagination. Moreover, he had discovered, so he said, that it was easier to buy books or magazines articles in English or French, translate them into Italian, and sign his own name at the top. His graceful literary style, he explained, would make up for whatever his writings lacked in originality.

We stopped finally at a river port where several other first class passengers joined us; those who prefer to do so may remain overnight in the capital and pursue the steamer by automobile upon the following morning, to overtake it at this port.

Among them was an American woman—a big Amazonian person with a masculine stride. Her face was red from a scornful defiance to the tropical sun and a wholesome contempt for powder or cold cream, yet her dress was girlish and summery, and in her arms nestled the fuzziest of little white poodles. Her voice, too, and it sounded strangely out of place when coming from such a huge powerful body, was sweet and honeyed as that of a sixteen-year-old flapper.

She was Mrs. Rooney, she said, and she came from nowhere in particular. Ever since Rooney died—it seems he had an athletic heart from wrestling and boxing and putting the shot and throwing the discus and one thing or another—she had simply wandered about the world, spending Rooney's money, seeking new experiences and new sensations.

She herself, she explained, was athletic. She might look fat, but she was all solid flesh, and to prove it she slapped her ample thigh with a resounding whack as of metal striking metal. She did not believe in corsets, but wore an elastic band, and to prove this, she seized it through her dainty shirt-waist and snapped it. She slept always in the open air, walked five miles every morning before breakfast, and just doted upon calisthenics; to prove the latter statement, she began to stride up and down the deck, exercising her ham-like arms to the count of "One, two; one, two."

"But you should have seen Rooney," she told me. "My, but there was a man for you! Six feet three in his socks and strong as an ox! Rooney could pick me up in one hand and shake me 'til I begged for mercy! I couldn't have loved any man that couldn't do that."

Even Sniffles, her poodle was athletic. Not now, of course, for Sniffles was growing old. But in his prime, that was a dog! My what a dog! He could chase cats and kill mice and bark at burglars just like any other dog. Sniffles was no mollycoddle, no, sir-ree! Whereupon she gave Sniffles a bath, and crooned over him in her honeyed little voice, and blessed his poor dear heart, and talked sentimental baby talk to him.

Somehow, Mrs. Rooney made me feel insignificant, probably because I am only five feet six in my shoes, and even less in my socks. But the poet admired her vastly.

"Fine big woman!" he said. "Fine big woman!"

The Captain's invitation to occupy a first-class cabin did not include first-class meals, but we purchased coconuts and bananas at ports along the river, and finally, at the end of a long hot day, the poet and I retired to our berths prepared to enjoy a really comfortable night's rest.

My berth, I found, was not only extremely narrow, but almost as hard as the deck. Also, although I had arranged the mosquito net with extreme care, I was no sooner undressed and inside it, than I heard a strangely familiar hum. Perhaps, I hoped, it was outside the net.

"There are no mosquitoes in this berth," I repeated aloud to myself with forced confidence. "If I seem to itch, I must have the hives."

But the hives began to grow worse. First I itched in one spot, then in another; then simultaneously from head to foot. It became unbearable. At length, with much reluctance, I crawled out and rummaged through my pockets for matches and cigarettes. I lighted one of the matches. My berth was swarming with mosquitoes. Swearing vengeance upon them, I rearranged the net to prevent their escape, and set forth upon a systematic campaign of extermination.

It had to be done systematically. There was only one spot in which they could be efficiently slaughtered. This was at the head of the bunk, against the wooden partition. Elsewhere my blows would merely disarrange the net and admit still more. So, lighting a cigarette, I would crawl to the foot of the narrow berth, and blow smoke at the insects until I had driven them to the head; then, lighting a match, I would crawl after them, and pound as many as possible against the partition before the survivors, eluding me, had returned to the foot.

It was a hectic night. The sight of the poet, sleeping contentedly in his own bunk and snoring the snores of the just, added to my annoyance. Again and again I repeated my tactics, crawling back and forth along the narrow berth, alternately smoking and pounding, but as fast as I killed the pests, others found their way through that supposedly impenetrable net to take their places.

I began to wonder whether I might go insane. It would not be the first time that a white man, in the heat of Indo-China, had become mentally unbalanced. But there was one thing that saved me. It was a beetle—a large black beetle with long horns—who had somehow found his way into the berth, and who seemed intensely interested in my strange maneuvers. Possibly he was fascinated by the flare of my matches, for he followed me back and forth from head to foot and back again, staring at me and wiggling his long horns. My first impulse was to kill him; then it occurred to me that he also might be after the mosquitoes; as this idea took hold in my fevered brain, I began to develop an affection for him such as I had never before entertained toward any living bug. In my various travels I have met caterpillars and scorpions and spiders and centipedes, but never a companionable, sympathetic, encouraging insect like that beetle. The idea of our crawling up and down a narrow bed together was so ludicrous that I began to enjoy it.

And finally, at the end of several hours, we had slain every mosquito under the net. Then, for nearly another hour, I lay still burning match after match, watching for the return of any that might have hidden themselves among the folds of the sheets, daring them to come out and continue the fight. None of them dared. I extinguished the last match. The beetle crawled upon the pillow beside me. I sighed contentedly. Now for a comfortable sleep.

Just then, from the deck outside, there sounded a scream—a shrill, blood-curdling feminine scream.

"Help!"

I leaped out of bed and into my trousers and out of the stateroom, all in one movement.

There stood Mrs. Rooney, struggling in the arms of the captain and three French passengers! Were they attacking her? Or had she also fought mosquitoes, without a beetle to save her from insanity? She was dragging the four men toward the rail, it seemed with the intention of leaping overboard. They threw her flat upon the deck, and she rose again, breaking free from them only to be tackled and thrown once more.

But both my suppositions were wrong.

For as I rushed to join the struggle, she suddenly ceased her efforts, and collapsing upon my shoulder, commenced to sob.

"Oh," she cried, "the fish will eat him! The fish will eat him! What shall I ever do without my little pet?"

Sniffles, it appears, had waddled to the rail and fallen overboard.

III

The steam was bound for Pnom Penh, the capital of the kingdom of Cambodia.

Indo-China is divided into five administrative divisions—Cochin China, Tongking, Annam, Laos, and Cambodia. Theoretically, Annam and Cambodia are native kingdoms under a French protectorate, and the native kings exercise unlimited authority over their subjects—provided they exercise it as the French government directs.

We anchored off Pnom Penh at noon of the succeeding day.

The jungle upon the shore gave way to a strange jumble of nipa-thatched huts and stucco shops, and above them rose a cluster of golden-roofed pagodas and gilded spires that gleamed in the sunlight as though inlaid with pearls, the temples and palaces of the King, magnificently barbaric, delightedly heathenish—the sort of temples and palaces which one vaguely recalls having seen in the illustrations of fairy tales. At last we had reached the interesting part of Indo-China.

A sampan carried us ashore.

Squarely before the wharf loomed a big hotel, the Gran Hotel de Madame Duguet, a surprisingly large structure of yellow stucco, built like the big hotels of Saigon, with tables everywhere, tables on the porch, tables in the dining room, tables in the office—tables with marble tops, which fairly screamed an invitation to sit down and order a brandy-and-soda. But on each of the stucco pillars which supported the high roof, a placard stated in French:

"Madame Duguet has the honor to announce to her distinguished clientele that owning to the expense of transportation, the price of brandy and soda has been advanced to one piastre and fifty centimes."

Madame herself was seated upon a high, throne-like chair, behind a high, pulpit-like desk, squarely in the center of the principal salon, from which point of vantage she could watch her entire establishment. She was a middle-aged French lady with a stout figure and a thin face, with a pleasing smile, but a rather sharp chin and an uncompromising mouth. There was something about her which warned me that her rooms would cost at least seven piastres each, payable perhaps in advance, and that guests who failed to vacate before noon would be charged an extra day.

When a French official approached us to secure the long list of information, which we had already given to a dozen similar officials in Saigon, we promptly asked where we might find another hotel.

"This is the only hotel, messieurs. But you will find it very comfortable."

That was our main objection. It was too comfortable, and too expensive. But the poet was an excellent bluffer.

"Ah, yes," he said in his perfect French, which was far better than his English. "We are in the interior now, and we must make the best of things. But it is not what we are accustomed to."

And having to spend the night somewhere, we registered with Madame Duguet.

We had but one day in town, since the poet was to return down river to Saigon upon the following morning, while I was to continue upstream into the interior. We made the best use of it by calling upon the French Resident—the official who tells the king how to use his unlimited authority—and requesting permission to interview his majesty.

The Resident smiled. King Prea Bat Samdach Prea Sisowath, it seems, was not giving out any interviews. He was ninety years of age, and he was aware that all visitors to Pnom Penh considered him a funny old curiosity of a monarch, wherefore he refused all audiences with strangers, remaining in his gilded palace, spending the $20,000 a month which the French government pays him for being king—a figure which I could not verify, but which seems more than he is worth. He is said to be a hale and hearty old gentleman, maintaining a harem of two hundred and forty dancing girls and concubines, two sacred white elephants, a complete cabinet which includes a Minister of War, a navy which consists of the royal yacht and a dilapidated gunboat, and all the other accessories of regal pomp and splendor. But while we could not see the King himself, we might inspect the royal palace.

That permission delighted the poet.

"*Bien!*" he whispered. "We see the dancing girls. To —— with the King!"

The Resident assigned one of his aides to escort us, an Annamite soldier in a neat white uniform and bare feet.

He felt that we should hire a barouche in which to ride to the palace, but we compromised on rikishas. Away we went through the city, which consisted of block after block of little stall-like shops, kept usually by Chinamen—for while the French government in Indo-China taxes the Chinese upon their entry into the country and at various other occasions during their sojourn, they have poured into these provinces as into all other lands where their entrance is not absolutely prohibited, and by their superior industry and frugality, have gradually displaced the natives as tradesmen and merchants.

The aide's first stop was at a museum. The French have brought their culture with them to Asia, and while Saigon had its opera house and libraries and botanical garden, Pnom Penh had its museum, and a very excellent establishment, whose director, another bemustached Frenchman, showed us about in person, exhibiting golden Buddhas and richly embroidered brocades of cloth-of-gold worn by all the ancient Kings of Cambodia, much to the annoyance of the poet, who fidgeted nervously, anxious to get to the palace to see the royal ballet.

Then the aide took us to the Pnom, a ninety-foot hill in the center of the city, surmounted by a huge prachadee, or spire, dedicated to Penh, a celebrated Cambodian queen of the past. Again the poet fidgeted; he was not interested in queens of the past.

But at length we reached the palace. It was surrounded by a high wall, and guarded by several Cambodian soldiers in French khaki uniforms, with sun helmets topped by brass spikes. A dozen brown courtiers, clad in pantaloons of red, purple, or green silk, came paddling out upon their bare feet, and welcomed us with many bows, escorting us through the gateway into a barbaric courtyard that contained all sorts of strange buildings—pavilions, pagodas, harems, temples, with the palace itself rising in the center, a large structure of marble, roofed with tiles of turquoise, crimson, peacock blue, its gables curved, its ridges lined with horn-like ornaments designed presumably to keep evil spirits from sliding upon the roof.

"Now we see the dancing girls!" exclaimed the poet.

The attendants, not understanding the poet's chief interest in life, led us first into a small building to show us the Sacred Sword. They brought it out with an air of great reverence, speaking in whispers in its presence. It was an immense weapon, at least five feet long, weighing about eighty pounds, its scabbard of beautifully carved bronze, its blade of beautifully carved silver, its hilt of beautifully carved gold, every inch and fraction of an inch intricately and artistically worked in the most minute designs—a magnificent work of art.

"Wonderful! Marvelous! Now show us the girls."

But next came the throne room in the main palace, a lofty salon in gold and green, in the center of which was a gorgeous golden dais, covered by canopies. Then came other royal rooms, and finally the royal elephants. The so-called white elephants are in reality animals that suffer from a skin disease which gives them a blotchy, yellow-gray appearance, but in the ancient superstition of Siam and Cambodia, they contain the souls of great Buddhists, and are worshiped accordingly.

The King owned two of them, and the attendants exhibited them with the same air of reverence with which they had exhibited the sword. At a command from the keeper, the larger elephant bent one knee and bowed to us. Wishing to reward him, the poet fished through his pockets and found a cigarette, which the big beast accepted with an air of condescension, and proceeded to eat. But it happened to be a French cigarette, and the elephant's taste seemed to agree with my own, for having swallowed it, he trumpeted loudly, galloped to a water trough, sucked up about twelve gallons of water, and as though to wreak vengeance upon humanity in general, squirted it through his trunk upon the nearest human beings, which happened to be the pantaloon-clad courtiers.

They were jabbering their sentiments in what sounded suspiciously like very uncourtly language, when out of the adjacent women's quarters came a stream of young girls, also in pantaloons.

"The harem!" exclaimed the poet.

Seizing my hand, he started to run with me in a most undignified manner across the royal courtyard.

The girls, rather pretty little things, wearing their hair not clipped as did most of the Cambodian girls in town, but flowing in black masses about their golden-brown necks, were climbing into a long line of automobiles—Fords—which clashed ridiculously with the barbaric structures of the palace.

"Are these the dancing girl?" demanded the poet, in French.

"No," said an attendant. "Strangers are not allowed to see the dancing girls. These are the servant girls. They're going to town to see the moving pictures of the Dempsey-Carpentier fight."

And it might be added, just for a further suggestion of incongruity, that King Prea Bat Samdach Prea Sisowath does not live in any of the barbaric structures of his palace yard, but in a European building, with all European comforts, which French architects have built for him behind the old barbaric structure.

Disappointed, we bade adieu to our escort, and strolled across the street to the royal temple.

It was enclosed by another high wall, of the same identical pattern as that which enclosed the palace. The inner side of it was covered with mural paintings depicting the legendary history of Cambodia, the most amusing and bizarre paintings imaginable. Grotesque warriors with the bodies of human beings and the faces of dogs fought battles with other grotesque warriors mounted on dragons; princes and potentates rode in strange processions upon the backs of giant roosters; funny little slaves brought funny little offerings to funny little kings; other slaves marched in long columns with ropes tied to their necks—all in a blaze of color and nightmarish imagery. The enclosure was the size of a city block, and the legend ran all the way around it, yet it never ceased to be fascinating in its weirdness.

Within the enclosure were many shaven-headed priests of the Buddhist religion, dressed in yellow robes which they wrapped around the body, enfolding the left arm, but leaving the right arm and shoulder bare. The Cambodian is almost as dark as a negro; against the light yellow of the robe, these naked limbs stood out almost as black as the umbrella which each monk carried to shelter himself from the glaring sun.

The temple, a magnificent edifice of white marble with another glittering roof like that of the palace, stood in the center. Its floor was of silver, genuine silver, set in little square plates. At one end was a golden Buddha, larger than a man, and inset with diamonds. Behind it, upon a golden pedestal, sat another Buddha of translucent jade. Upon the many steps of the pedestal sat other Buddhas—Buddhas of bronze, Buddhas of silver, Buddhas of gold. Everywhere was gold, real gold, gold inset with jewels! Here, in the center of a city of poverty-stricken thatched huts, lost in the swamps of Cambodia, was a temple filled with treasure the sight of which would have made Tiffany dizzy! A temple filled with gold, gold, gold!

I never knew there was so much precious metal in the entire world. I was seized with a strange desire to grab a golden Buddha and run. The poet beside me was breathing heavily; his fingers clasped and unclasped; his hand groped toward one of the images.

"*Mon dieu!*" he muttered. "And we are almost penniless!"

Several attendants, or guards, with big curved swords in their silken sashes, drew closer to us, as though they suspected our temptation.

"Come away from here!" I breathed.

We hastened from the place, and walked back, silent and thoughtful, to Madame Duguet's hotel. Wine was served free with the dinner, and we imbibed freely. It stimulated the poet's romantic soul, and his mind returned again to the dancing girls. We could not leave Pnom Penh without seeing the harem. Think what a story it would make! Personal experiences in a harem!

We had to see it, but how? We were still debating the question as we strolled through the Chinese bazaars after dinner, and we continued debating as we strolled farther out through thatched suburbs. And suddenly, as though our aspirations had unconsciously guided our feet, we came down a side alley, and there before us was a high wall, with a barbaric roof gleaming beyond it in the moonlight.

"Quick!" gasped the poet.

We were somewhere at the rear. There was not a guard in sight. I stood against the wall, and he climbed upon my shoulders. From the top he reached down a helping hand. We lowered ourselves on the other side, dropping softly to the ground.

And then—

"*Mon dieu!* It is not the palace! It is the temple!"

We had scaled the wrong wall. We were inside the wall which surrounded those millions of dollars worth of precious Buddhas—those Buddhas which had tempted us not four hours before. Not a guard was in sight, for these priceless ornaments, sacred to all Cambodians, are guarded as a rule only during the visits of strangers. They were ours for the taking—these things of gold and silver!

And with the realization of this, we were both struck with terror. Instead of taking them, we wanted to run. We weren't used to being left alone and penniless with millions within our grasp. And scrambling back over the wall, we never ceased running until we reached the hotel.

IV

On the morrow we parted company.

Two river steamers lay at the wharf, one bound upstream, the other down.

Mrs. Rooney was also present, about to return to Saigon. When she heard of my wild plan to walk overland to Siam, she crooned over me as she had crooned over Sniffles. She called me her poor, dear little adventurer, and almost wept, and presented me with a tin of gold-tipped cigarettes.

The poet embraced me again and again. Tigers would eat me, he said. I must come back to Saigon with him, and trust to luck to find the price of a passage to Singapore. He himself had little money left, for this trip to Pnom Penh had further reduced his half of our finances. He had just enough, he figured, to send that cablegram to the chorus girl in Shanghai:

"Come to Singapore. All is forgive."

Had I known then how much trouble his love affairs were destined to cause me before I left the Orient, I should have completed the Fool-Killer's work by drowning him in the Mekong. But not knowing it, I shook his hand. He climbed on board the down-bound steamer, with Mrs. Rooney, the whistles shrieked an echoing farewell, and I was left alone.

My own long journey was begun at last.

CHAPTER FOUR

THROUGH CAMBODIA BY SAMPAN

I

There was nothing to do but hit the trail—provided there was a trail to hit.

Another river steamer—smaller and dirtier than the first—carried me up a swamp-lined stream which was narrower than the Mekong, and across the Great Lake of Cambodia, an immense shallow pool in the heart of Indo-Chinese swamps, where no dry land could be seen on any side, and where palms grew up out of the water and whole villages of thatched houses floated upon rafts.

So far as I had been able to ascertain in Pnom Penh, this vessel was to carry me to a town called Battambang, where the trail—if trail there was—began. But at daybreak of the second day, having crossed the lake, we anchored beside a mud bank topped by a dozen nipa-thatched huts, and an Annamite steward bundled me into a dilapidated launch.

"*Schloop partir!*" he exclaimed in execrable pigeon-French.

"But where does it *partir* to?"

He waved his hand in the direction of a small brook that led into the jungle, as though this was all I needed to know. Another Annamite turned the flywheel, the engine commenced to chug, and away I went, wondering where I was going.

The brook twisted about through an inundated forest of scraggly brush so thickly covered with climbing vines that the brush itself was frequently hidden. It was a snaky-looking region. The stream wound here and there in serpentine figures; the brush was gnarled and twisted; even the occasional trees which towered above the lower vegetation sent out long shiny roots that coiled through the muck like reptiles. Cranes stood in the shallow water with one long leg poked out behind them. Pelicans rose in flocks at our noisy approach, to flee before us with a prodigious flapping of wings that seemed scarcely strong enough to propel their big, lumbering bodies.

We did not go far. Lily pads clogged the propeller, and we came to a stop. A waiting sampan slid alongside, and I was bundled into it.

"Now where in thunder is this thing going to take me?" I demanded.

My fellow passengers, a Chinese family and several Cambodian soldiers in khaki coats and plaid skirts, listened to the words without understanding, chattered among themselves about me, and giggled shrilly. A native boatman leaned upon his pole, and away I went again, still wondering.

II

The sampan was a long, slender affair, with a barrel-shaped roof of nipa-thatch forming a cabin amidships.

Its progress was painfully slow.

Also, having been dumped of the steamer before breakfast, I was painfully thirsty and painfully hungry. My fellow passengers drank the filthy brown water of the stream, and breakfasted upon scaly little raw fish which they carried, but the stream served both as a reservoir and sewer while the fish were far from appetizing, and I refrained from following the example.

Instead, I crawled into the low den of a cabin, bumping my head frequently upon its hardwood framework, and sought to forget my thirst and hunger by studying French from a paper-covered pamphlet which I had purchased during my days of comparative affluence in Saigon. The first page to which I opened contained the following:

> "Voulez-vous boire quelque chose?"
> "Will you have something to drink?"
> "Je prendrai une bouteille de bierre."
> "I'll have a bottle of beer."

Hastily I turned over the page:

"A quelle heure dinez-vous?"
"At what hour do you dine?"
"Voulez-vous de bœuf roti?"
"Would you like some roast beef?"

That was sufficient.

I closed the pamphlet, and crawled out of the cabin again. Another sampan was approaching us, filled to the water's edge with coconuts and bananas. It was propelled by an aged brown gentleman whose whitish-gray hair above a sepia skin gave him the appearance of some silver-haired monkey. I jumped up and down, shouting to him in French to draw alongside, but he merely stared at me with a blank expression, bowed in response to what he mistook for a friendly greeting, and drifted past.

Behind him came a second craft, a canoe laden with other tropical fruits. It was rowed by a Cambodian girl dressed in only a brief skirt that covered but a third of her stocky bare legs. Again I jumped up and down, clarifying my French by waving a five-centime piece at her. But she merely surveyed the coin with scornful disdain, turned up her nose at what she mistook to be my amorous advances, and bent to her oar with redoubled energy.

III

Hour after hour we crawled slowly along. Sometimes the boatmen poled, sometimes they rowed, sometimes when a path bordered the stream they walked along the shore and towed us with a rope.

The brook had widened, and was now clearly defined by high banks, sometimes dry, sometimes trampled into muck by the big water buffalo, animals twice the size of a domestic cow, which stood in the water, trying to find solace from the raging heat of tropical mid-day. The country, in contrast to the fertile green lake region, was now brown and parched. Cane-walled dwellings, built upon stilts for the long-past rainy season, stood high and dry above the sun-cracked banks. Behind them a jungle of brown grass, higher than a man's head, crackled like tinder in the faint breeze which came down the river at infrequent intervals—a faint, hot breeze which brought no relief from the heat.

The natives here were Cambodians, a people distinct from the people of Saigon. The Annamites had been slender and wiry; these Cambodians were short and stocky. Both men and women dressed not in pajamas but in a sort of skirt made by wrapping a piece of cloth about the waist and bringing the ends of it up between the legs to convert it into an imitation of pantaloons. The women wore their hair clipped short—bobbed, so to speak—but made no further effort to disguise their sex, for over their solid little breasts they wore only a thin drapery which merely accentuated the figure, and as the day grew warmer, they frequently discarded even this garment. They were husky little creatures, plump but never fat, with too heavy ankles, perhaps, but with beautifully rounded throat and shoulders. Like the Annamites, however, they had lacquered their teeth—usually all the teeth being black, but sometimes every other tooth—and their mouths were stained with betel nut.

Their children, particularly the boys, ran about naked, and like most children neglected by their parents seemed to thrive upon the neglect. Tiny mites who in America or Europe would still be in the nursery were splashing about in the water, or climbing trees, or tending the family herd of buffalo, riding fearlessly upon the backs of the huge beasts, or leading them about by a rope tied to a ring in the nose.

Cane dwellings became more frequent, until they bordered upon the river like houses upon a street. Tiny spirals of smoke were rising above their thatched roofs; the wood had a deliciously sweet odor as of joss in a Chinese temple. Each wisp of smoke suggested cooking, and cooking suggested food. My Chinese fellow-passenger, who evidently was a merchant of wealth as indicated by the fact that his wife wore socks, owned a watch, and by first pointing upstream and then at the chronometer, I managed to inquire when we might reach our destination. He pointed to two o'clock. But two o'clock passed, and each turning of another river bend showed only another stretch of river ahead. When I asked him again, he pointed to four o'clock, very calmly, with the patient disregard of time or accuracy which is typical of the Celestial. At four o'clock, he pointed to six.

But at length, coconut palms and banana trees began to replace the jungle grass, the tow-path widened into a road, and the thatched huts became more numerous. And finally—unmistakable sign of our approach to civilization—there appeared upon the road a dilapidated hack with a native coachman on the box and two diminutive ponies between the shafts.

The Chinaman hailed it, packed his wife into one seat, and motioned me into the other. In pursuance of my increasingly rigid program of economy, I should have declined it, but just then I spied a native shop beside the road with bananas for sale; I offered the shopkeeper a ten centime piece, wondering whether he would cry for help if I took a whole bunch in exchange, and instead of creating a scene he calmly handed me two additional bunches; elated with the discovery that I was beyond the trail of the tourist and that the brown men here had not learned to overcharge the white, I leaped into the coach.

The Chinaman bowed, and away I went again—with his wife.

I was somewhat puzzled. Had he made me a present of her? On the sampan she had appeared middle-aged; now she began to look suspiciously young. Furthermore, she was laden with cooking utensils, a bag of flour, and blankets, and the whole ensemble resembled a family camping outfit. We looked as though we were just coming in from a prolonged picnic in the woods somewhere, and I had a moment of misgiving as I pictured myself riding into a town in this fashion. But the bananas cheered me considerably, and strewing the peelings behind me, I went galloping along in the rickety coach beneath the palm trees toward what I hoped was Battambang.

IV

My usual luck prevailed. The lady left me upon the edge of town. The driver carried me into town. The town proved to be Battambang. And from Battambang there was a trail—at least as far as the Siamese border.

All that I needed now, it seemed, was permission from the French Resident to proceed upon my journey. The only trouble was that today happened to be the day before Christmas, and the Resident would be celebrating Christmas Eve.

"Then I can see him tomorrow?" I asked another Frenchman.

"Tomorrow he will be celebrating Christmas."

"Then the day after tomorrow?"

"The day after tomorrow he will be recovering from the celebration."

I settled down to wait.

As in Pnom Penh, there was only one hotel, but it was a government rest house with prescribed prices in keeping with my rapidly thinning purse. It was a modern building of yellow stucco, as cool and comfortable as a hotel could possibly be in such a climate. The Number One Boy, a thin-chested Annamite gentleman with his long hair tied back into a knot at the back of his head in the style which the average mind associates with New England maiden ladies, led me upstairs to a large, airy room with bath attached, all for about fifty cents a day.

There were no other guests in the establishment, but all the French officials in town—totaling about six—took their meals here, with the exception of the First Resident, who held aloof. There were also two French civilians. One was the manager of the bank which paid the officials their salaries, and the other was the manager of the ice plant which supplied ice for their cognac-and-soda which, with quinine, appeared to be the principal diet of the colony. As elsewhere in Indo-China, where officials are content to be officials and where the government makes little intelligent effort to encourage commerce and industry, there seemed to be little economic reason for Battambang's existence. It consisted only of a few blocks of Chinese shops surrounded by the thatched huts of the Cambodians. As elsewhere, the invading Chinese merchants had practically a monopoly of the business. But as elsewhere, the French government had built several of the yellow stucco offices and residences, and had provided its own officials with all the comforts of home.

My own room fronted upon the river, and I could look out through the palms to the winding stream with its traffic of thatched-roofed sampans, its wallowing buffaloes, and its bathing maidens of dusky skin and brief skirts; or across the stream to a Buddhist temple with its gilded roof of barbaric design and its yellow-robed monks; or farther beyond to a forest of coconut palms outlined against a gloriously blue sky.

That temple in particular fascinated me.

Its bells lulled me to sleep. They were not rung, but beaten with a rod, beginning with a few gentle strokes that increased in strength and rapidity until they beat a tattoo like the roll of a drum, yet they were sweet in tone, far sweeter than the church bells of an y Christian land. And after the temple bells had lulled me to sleep, the temple dogs would set up an unearthly howling, as though performing some heathen rite connected with their residence in the monastery, and would wake me again.

In the morning the priests came out in their yellow robes, and perched upon the river bank in meditation, looking like a flock of canaries. While the title of "The Kingdom of the Yellow Robe" is usually applied to Siam, Cambodia before its occupation by the French in 1862 was a part of Siam, and is still Siamese in dress, customs, and religion, and Battambang was full of temples and full of yellow robes.

Buddha adopted this beggar's robe in order to make himself odious in the eyes of the world, that the world might be less likely to offer him temptation. A Buddhist monk today is allowed by few possessions besides this robe: needles for repairing it, a girdle and a filtering cloth, an alms bowl, and a razor wherewith to shave his hair and eyebrows. He lives entirely upon the offerings of the people. Each morning he makes his rounds, walking very solemnly from hut to hut, preceded usually by a boy who carries his bowl and announces his coming by tapping upon a gong. Before each dwelling he stops and waits in silence, accepting whatever food the occupants choose to give him, and walking away without a word of thanks, the idea being that the practice shall call forth the spirit of generosity from the giver, who shall expect no thanks. Sometimes on his rounds, the priest carries a fan wherewith not only to guard his shaven head from the sun but also to shield his eyes from too worldly sights; usually, however, he carries an umbrella, or allows a boy to carry it for him.

Buddhism, of course, is subject to variation in all of the many countries in which it has gained followers, but in general it consists of a moral code not unlike that of Christianity, save that—like all other oriental religions—it is a male code with little consideration for the female of the species—and upon entering the priesthood, a Buddhist takes vows to refrain from killing, stealing, impurity, falsehood, liquor, over-eating, singing or dancing, using perfume, sleeping in too comfortable a bed, and accepting gold or silver, so that his life is one of greater abstinence, if he observes his vows, than is the life of a Christian clergyman or priest. He has few ceremonies to perform, however, except in countries like Siam, where life is one long succession of ceremonies (half of which are not really Buddhist at all), and when not engaged in teaching the boys of the monastery from Buddhist scriptures written on palm-leaf scrolls, he devotes most of his time, or is supposed to devote it, to meditating upon the wickedness of the world. If he eats at all, he must eat before noon, although after this hour he may smoke, drink tea, and chew betel nut.

In Pnom Penh I had visited a temple, but it had been more of a combined treasury and museum for the treasures of the king. Wishing to see a real place of worship, I set out to visit the pagoda across the river. To reach it, however, I had to ascend some distance to a bridge. But the dogs—mongrel curs which take advantage of the Buddhist prohibition against the killing of animals, and which hang about the temples in great numbers—gave the alarm at my approach, and by the time I reached the place, the monks had vanished, and the doors were locked.

Thinking that I might have arrived by chance at a moment when the priests were going elsewhere, I returned to my hotel, glanced back again, and there sat the flock of human canaries upon the river bank as though nothing had happened. Back I went again, and again they vanished. It was vastly amusing. Never in my life had I put so many clergymen to flight. It was as though I were the devil himself. I stalked them, back past the temple to the thatched huts in which they dwelt, but all I could see was an occasional flash of yellow as they sneaked away among the banana trees. They were not afraid of me personally, for when I met them upon the road away from their temple, they surveyed me rather contemptuously; they merely did not wish to open their sacred places to an unbeliever, and took this means of denying me admittance.

I wandered throughout the town and into the suburbs, trying to find other temples; I found them, but all were deserted, even the leading monastery, the Pagoda of the White Elephant, a big stone building with a glittering porcelain roof, guarded by statues of white elephants, and its outer wall covered with carvings or paintings representing the various Buddhist hells, where men were reincarnated in the bodies of animals, or tortured by fiends, hacked to pieces with swords, drowned in molten iron, flung upon spikes, pounded with sledge hammers, and if that didn't fix them, were eaten by giant dogs with iron teeth—all in horrible drawing and sculpture, with oriental crudeness and lack of perspective, but understandable and terrifying. Perhaps they represented what would happen in the hereafter to the monk who desecrated his temple by admitting me.

But at length I found one who would take a chance. I had wandered far off into the outskirts to stumble upon a weather-beaten pagoda whose shabby interior was offset by a gilded spire that looked like a series of bird cages piled one on top of another. I knocked on the door, a window opened, and a shaven head was poked out.

"May I come in?" I inquired, or tried to inquire, in French.

His brow-less eyes examined me without comprehension.

"I do not understand French," he said. "Do you not speak English?"

"Yes, but how is it that you speak it?"

"I am Burmese. I have pursued my studies for many years in the university at Rangoon. But who are you? And why do you wish to come in? And what is your religion? This is the house of Buddha."

It sounded like the questionnaire with which French officialdom had already so often presented me. But finally, upon my promise to remove my shoes, he admitted me. The interior was dark, and there was little of interest; along either wall a row of china or porcelain Buddhas, clad like the priest himself in the yellow robe; before them were vases of flowers and plants preserved in rows of jars which somehow suggested the appendices and tapeworms sometimes displayed in the windows of small town drugstores. But they were very neatly arranged and the temple was spotless.

Upon leaving the place, I offered the monk a coin, but he motioned to me to give it to the doorkeeper, who was not of the cloth. He bade me good-day, but did not invite me to call again.

And failing once more to gain admittance to the temple across the river, I adjourned, only partially satisfied, to the Christmas dinner. The Frenchmen, already assembled, were partaking of "appetizers." One of them attempted to welcome me in English, but was terribly embarrassed; evidently, in his confidence that no English-speaking person would ever visit Battambang, he had been posing before his fellows as a linguist, for now, after many stammerings, he explained to them that the Anglo-Saxons had two different languages; he spoke Saxon, he said, and I spoke Angle. Whether because of ignorance or appetizers, the others accepted his explanation. I made the best of my miserable French, and was welcomed with that heartwarming courtesy and kindliness for which the French people are noted.

It was a gloomy party. Like the officials in Saigon, they were bored to death with their exile in the Asiatic provinces; life in Battambang furnished little matter for conversation, and even this conversation, in spite of the wine which accompanied the dinner, was devoid of merriment. Several Annamite girls sat upon the lawn outside, with half-white babies in their arms. No one seemed to notice them. We lingered after the dinner was over, while the Number One Boy, who had spent the morning with a piece of tablecloth wrapped about his middle but now appeared in pajamas and bare feet, paddled silently into the room from time too time with glasses of champagne. No one became gay, however; instead, every one sat with his head in his hands, dreaming of home, and studying the glass before him as a high jumper studies the bar over which he is about to jump.

Finally, after I told them my experience with the monks across the river, they all volunteered to accompany me on another attempt. We set out unsteadily, each assisting the other. Native soldiers and policemen snapped to attention and saluted us, as they are trained here to salute all white men, and the other natives doffed their hats in cringing humility. We strutted past them. We were the representatives of the dominant race. But we never reached the temple. We happened to pass the post office, and the postmaster, pausing and cocking his head on one side and gazing at it as a mariner might gaze at an unexpected but welcome haven, headed rapidly toward it with the air of a man about to go to bed. We passed the ice plant, and its manager did the same. We passed the police barracks, and the Chief of Police dropped out.

And at last, left alone, I returned to the hotel. It was late afternoon, and the entire native population was seeking relief in the river, where all Battambang sat submerged to the neck. I would have joined them, but I knew my white skin would arouse an excess of curiosity. And so, like the Frenchmen, I headed rapidly towards my fifty-cent boudoir and went to bed.

Through the open window I could see the monks sitting upon the opposite bank like a flock of yellow canaries.

CHAPTER FIVE

HITTING THE TRAIL WITH HENRI

In Battambang I met Henri.

Henri was otherwise known as Henri Lesseur, Surveillant et Inspecteur des Postes et des Telegraphes de Cambodge.

Once each year, or every other year, or every year after that, or whenever he got ready, it was his duty to inspect a telegraph line which ran through the jungle to a French garrison on the Siamese frontier. By sheer, blind good fortune, I landed in Battambang just as Henri was preparing to start, and was invited to join him.

"Of course," he explained, "monsieur must be prepared to rough it."

As I was very nearly broke by this time, I was quite expecting to do something of that sort.

Henri himself, after the manner of a Frenchman, had prepared by donning a neat little khaki suit, with trousers creased like razor blades, and with a hunting coat tastily cut to a form-fitting waist and a skirt-like flair beneath. Having manicured his nails and had his boots polished, he was now waiting only for the French Resident to finish celebrating Christmas and supply him with eight or nine ox carts to carry his personal baggage, and thirty or forty native servants to minister to his comfort on the road.

We waited together.

Henri, a quiet, stocky little chap in his khaki regalia, sat at the hotel table and sipped cognac, and voiced an occasional impatient French equivalent of "Darn!" On the day after Christmas, the French Resident summoned the Cambodian governor, who (while the nominal chief authority of the region) lived in a cane shack across from the Resident's stucco Residence, and whose principal duty was to use his authority as the French official directed. On the second day the governor began to follow the directions by hunting about town for the ox carts. On the third day they began to arrive at the hotel, one by one, at twelve-hour intervals.

But at length, early one morning, Henri's caravan lined up in the road.

It looked like a circus parade.

The corps of servants included Tonkingese, Annamites, Cambodians, Laos and what not—natives in blue pajamas, or pink pajamas, or no pajamas at all—natives in topees, others with towels wrapped around their heads, others carrying paper umbrellas—lady cooks and bottle washers with blackened teeth and betel-stained lips—yellow men, brown men, black men—men with pants and no coats; men with coats and no pants—all barefoot except the chief cook, who rode like a queen in the leading ox cart and carried her shoes in her hand, partly to avoid the discomfort of wearing them, and partly to display her pink heels, which are considered a special mark of beauty among the Cambodians.

It was an astounding crew of ox-drivers and assistant ox-drivers, gun-bearers and assistant gun-bearers, custodians of the folding bathtub and assistant custodians, and behind them were the ox carts, a long train of them drawn by lumbering oxen and water buffaloes, bringing crate after crate of vin rouge and vin blanc, cognac and champagne, with big slabs of ice packed in sawdust, folding cots, folding chairs, folding tables, and a library full of Henri's books. The only reason that the equipment did not include a piano was that Henri was not a musician.

So this was roughing it!

Henri and I took our positions at the head of the column.

"*Marchon!*" commanded Henri.

Two semi-naked brown boys came to hold umbrellas over our heads to shelter us from the sun; a third fell into line with a thermos bottle full of soda water; and off we marched.

II

The road led out from the town across a brown plain covered with the parched stubble of dried rice-fields, where the water buffaloes stared at us curiously and the native toilers looked up from their work to doff their conical straw hats in respectful salute.

It was a wide road—wide and long and extremely dusty. The sand upon it was two inches thick. Even the holes that once had been buffalo-wallows were now dried, still showing the fantastic tramplings of the huge beasts, but dried and cracked by the merciless sun. The dust rose behind us and concealed the caravan from our view. The only evidence that the countryside had ever witnessed a rainy season consisted in an occasional pool in the roadside ditches, a muddy pool where tiny fish would leap in silver showers as a water snake wriggled across the muddy surface to disappear in a shining black streak among the bushes beyond.

The sun poured down upon us. Perspiration oozed from our foreheads and trickled into our eyes and left a salty taste about the lips. Henri's shoes lost their polish. He began to plod determinedly, with a set expression upon his face. I was just beginning to feel that we *were* roughing it, after all.

Then we stopped at a native village for lunch. Out of the wagons came tables and chairs, ice and wine, and Henri, seating himself like a king beneath an awning which his servants erected above us, invited me to a cooling drink. I looked at him, and could not help feeling as I had felt in France when first I looked at a French officer all dressed up behind the lines in skin-tight scarlet breeches.

We dined in state, with several courses served by several servants. Even Henri's dogs, two big white animals known respectively as "Pa" and "Ma," seemed to think that they belonged to a king, for they sat beside us in proud disdain of the village curs which snarled at them from a safe distance. I felt like a royal guest myself, sitting there in the jungle beneath a canopy, and sipping iced wine. The villagers came to us to pay court, telling Henri through his Annamite interpreter of a man-eating tiger which had been prowling about the vicinity, and which, not ten days before, had snatched an infant from one of the thatched homes.

Henri listened to the tale, shrugged his shoulders, drank another pint of *vin rouge*, and asked quietly:

"Where does that tiger live?"

I repressed a chuckle. He reminded me somehow of the mouse that fell into a rum barrel, and climbed out to inquire, "Where's that cat that's been lookin' for me?"

But Henri meant business. He called for his tiger gun. It seems that he carried a regular arsenal, one gun for elephants, one gun for rhinoceros, one gun for tigers, one gun for birds, as many as a dozen. Repressing my impulse to ask him what he'd do if an elephant chased him while he had the rhinoceros gun, I followed him into the jungle, as did the rest of the villagers and servants to witness the thrilling encounter.

The natives led us through a thicket of wild cane, and indicated a cave halfway up a hundred-foot cliff. How any tiger ever reached it without wings was more than I could imagine, but Henri asked no questions. Straight up the cliff he went. The cliff itself went straight up, with only a few spongy-looking holes where the limestone had crumbled, and which afforded but a poor foothold. Henri climbed with toes and fingers, but he went.

It was a ridiculous thing to do, but I couldn't stand below and watch a little dude like Henri fight the tiger alone. So up I started after him. It was not an easy climb. We would get halfway up to the cave, only to discover that we must retrace our steps and ascend by another route. I slipped and fell, dug my nails into another crevice, and kept on climbing. It was America versus France, and the little Frenchman kept on going, and I was forced to follow him. He found his rifle an impediment, and left it behind, trying again with only a small revolver. Personally I was not enthusiastic about facing the tiger with only that small weapon, but Henri was digging his toes into the cliff, and pulling himself from ledge to ledge above me, and up I went again. And finally, when I could get no farther, Henri reached the top—not only reached it, but offered me his hand and pulled me after him—and when I struggled over the edge, disheveled and covered with dirt, there he stood, as neat and dude-like as ever, calmly manicuring his nails with a manicure set which he always carried in his pocket.

And much to my relief, the tiger was not at home.

Henri led the way back to town, seated himself beneath his awning, and opened a bottle of champagne. But I looked at him now as I had looked at those scarlet-trousered French officers after seeing them march debonairly into Verdun. Henri was a He-Man.

III

And in spite of the luxuries which Henri provided, the journey was by no means a picnic.

We ascended steadily from the swampy lake region of Cambodia, into a country that grew drier and dustier. The parched jungle-growth became wilder, the thatched villages less frequent. It was a hot, fatiguing hike for everyone concerned. Even the dogs, at the end of a day's march, would stretch out flat upon their backs in a most un-doglike posture, their feet pointing skyward, their tongues hanging from their panting mouths. Once a buffalo fell in its tracks in an epileptic fit, frothing at the mouth. For two hours after the drivers had urged it to its feet, it stood trembling and frothing, its bovine eyes gazing reproachfully at the circle of natives surrounding it.

Only the first afternoon was easy, for just beyo0nd our first lunching place we came upon a narrow gauge railway like those laid for pushcarts in a construction camp, built evidently for the transportation of rock to Battambang from the distant mountains that we could see rising from the plain several miles ahead. A gang of naked brown coolies navigated it upon a small flat car, sitting upon its edge and poling it along with bamboo rods as though pushing a sampan upstream. Henri promptly commandeered it, and we traveled in style, but not in comfort, for there was no road bed, and where the track crossed a hollow, we bumped up and down until our teeth rattled, but we arrived long before nightfall at a government shelter, where our caravan eventually caught up with us, its approach heralded by a protesting shriek of ungreased wheels.

The shelter was an unfurnished nipa-shack perched upon high stilts to protect its occupants from tigers. A small village surrounded it, and beside it lay the crumpled ruins of what had once been a Buddhist temple but now appeared to be inhabited only by reptiles that crawled out of sight among the tumbled bricks at our arrival. The native servants, shining with sweat from their walk, quickly built fires of dried coconut husks, Henri's iced drinks made their appearance, lamps and cots and bedding came out of the wagons, and the bare shack soon became a home.

From a thatched hut across the road there came the sound of music—a squeaking Chinese fiddle, a clacking homemade xylophone, and a barbaric tomtom. The villagers, it seemed, were entertaining Henri's servants with a booze party of their own. After our supper, we strolled over to see it. The tropic night had fallen swiftly, but two or three tallow candles illumined the interior of the hut, shedding a weird, faint light upon a wild-looking mass of half-naked humanity, crowded from wall to wall, squatting upon bare heels as a *tchoum-tchoum*, or native rice brandy, passed from hand to hand.

In the center was a man dancing. He danced entirely with his arms. His body did not move save when he arose from his knees to his feet, yet it was a dance, a strange heathenish dance, comprehensible even to one who had never seen such an exhibition before. His arms represented serpents. He twined them slowly about himself to the rhythmic beat of the tomtom, while the hands twisted and turned upon the wrists as serpents might twist their heads. It was fascinating. The spectators, watching him, did not notice our advent. The man himself was so carried away with his own pantomime that he gazed with genuine horror at his serpentine hands. He was the charmed victim of two poisonous reptiles, foreseeing his fate, yet powerless to escape. Slowly the arms crept closer, the hands twisting and twining more rapidly, circling about his neck, drawing back as though about to strike. The tomtom changed its rhythm. Its note became ominous. The serpents struck. The man, trembling with pain, made a last effort to escape. They struck again. The man's face became contorted with agony. He fell to the ground, writhed and struggled, and finally—to the ruination of the whole artistic effect—flopped up and down like a newly beheaded chicken.

The music stopped. The spectators applauded with loud shouts. Someone saw Henri and myself in the doorway, and the festivities stopped. The Chief of the Village, an aged brown man with gray, goatlike tufts of sparse beard upon his chin, lowered himself upon his knees, and bumped his head three times upon the cane floor in salute. In pigeon-French he bade us welcome, but it was evident that our presence embarrassed the natives, and Henri, giving the Chief a piastre wherewith to treat the crowd, led the way back to our shelter.

Behind us the sound of merriment increased again, swelling in volume as the party became an orgy. Henri summoned his head man, and had his rifles and ammunition placed in his own room beside his cot.

Beneath the humility of these cringing people of Indo-China, who kowtow to their French conquerors, I had perceived something in the slanting oriental eyes that strangely resembled a long-suppressed hatred, and I understood the care with which he bolted our doors, and tied the two dogs just outside.

But when Henri called me at four o'clock in the morning, the natives showed no sign of their carousal. Quietly and efficiently they were rebuilding their fires of coconut husk, heating the morning coffee, and repacking the ox-carts. They had been up all night, but being Orientals, they gave no indication of fatigue.

IV

Day after day we hiked through the brown wilderness, setting out before sunrise, halting for two or three hours in the middle of the hot day, and arriving at nightfall at another thatched shelter.

Henri and I both took pride in concealing our fatigue. At lunch or dinner, we were friends; on the road we were rivals.

The path narrowed until it became barely wide enough for the carts, with a tangle of vines or brush on either side. Where it crossed the bed of a river, now dry save for an occasional mud puddle, the vegetation became green, great masses of tiny purple flowers blossomed and filled the air with a nauseously sweet odor, and clumps of giant bamboo arose to a height of forty feet, tapering like thin skeletons, many shoots rising from a cluster at the ground and bending gracefully outward at the top like jets of water from a fountain.

As we hiked along we could hear things creeping out of sight before us. Once I barely avoided stepping upon a slender snake which shot across beneath my feet like an animated thread. Twice we saw animals across the trail ahead, reddish-gray animals that disappeared too quickly to be identified—panthers, perhaps. Sometimes, as we lunched upon the road, the dogs would bristle and snarl, and Henri, calling again for his tiger gun, would lead the way through the bamboo thickets on the high grass in search of big game, but we never encountered anything. One night we built a platform in a tree-top, and set out bait in the form of a dead pig, a pig which had been dead for so long that any tiger within a hundred miles should have detected it, but although we sat on the platform above it all night, holding our noses, we attracted nothing but mosquitoes.

The tiger, like any other wild animal, is born with a fear of man, and becomes a man-eater by accident rather than by design. Beginning by stumbling upon domestic cattle in the neighborhood of a village, he discovers that they are much easier to catch than the wild animals; he beings to frequent the outskirts of the village, and some day when domestic cattle do not seem plentiful, and hunger makes him desperate, he pounces upon some unsuspecting native. Discovering that the dreaded humans are not only tender and delicious, but an extremely easy prey, the tiger becomes a source of terror to the entire neighborhood. In India, according to William T. Hornaday's "Two Years in the Jungle," a single man-eating tigress caused the desertion of thirteen villages, and the same fear of the beast prevailed, I discovered, among the natives of Indo-China.

A tiger has been known to steal a child from one town in the early evening, and then to pounce upon another infant in a town five or six miles distant just a few hours later. The beast travels so quickly, and roams so extensively, that the villagers everywhere must always be on guard. All of the huts along the trail, like the government shelter in which we slept, were perched for protection upon high stilts. Partly because of the strength and ferocity of the tiger, and partly because of his miraculous habit of appearing where he is least expected, the natives regard him with a superstitious awe, and will never mention the word "tiger," believing that in some supernatural way the beast will hear his name and will slay the man who pronounces it. The Cambodians, forbidden by the French government to own or purchase firearms, are quite unable to hunt their enemy, and while they sometimes dig pits or leave poisoned bait for their persecutor, even these measures are seldom practiced because of the superstitious belief in the tiger's supernatural power, the natives fearing he will see through their devices and punish them. When Henri's interpreter spoke of the beast, he would always refer to him in some roundabout way, using a pronoun, or speaking of "The Mighty One."

But since "The Mighty One" seldom appears where he is sought, our efforts at hunting were fruitless. The only game we shot consisted of birds, which usually perched upon the tops of the bamboo and when shot, fell among the thorns where they could not be recovered, necessitating an unmerciful and inhuman slaughter before we could finally obtain enough to make a meal.

Henri was a most considerate host. Although I had started out as a vagabond, I found myself treated as an honored guest. With the hospitality and courtesy of the true French gentleman, he was constantly anticipating my wants. "Monsieur would prefer the chicken well done? Here, madame, fry Monsieur Fostair's chicken again." And after dinner, "Monsieur would write his impressions? Here, boi-ee, bring Monsieur Fostair's note book."

In the evenings I would sit at his folding table, writing by the light of an oil lamp, while Henri sat across from me, wondering as old-timers in these countries always wonder how the newcomer can see anything interesting in the place to write about. Ever since the end of the war, in which Henri had been a poilu and from which he still carried the scars of a dozen wounds, he had been inspecting telegraph lines in the jungles of Indo-China, and these scenes and experiences were commonplace to him.

At first, because of my bad French, conversation was limited, yet we both felt a sense of companionship as we sat silently together beneath a thatched roof, sipping Henri's wine, and watching the moon rise through the palms. Slowly my French improved, and Henri brought out a dictionary with pictures of animals; he would hunt through its pages for pictures of llamas or condors or other creatures from South America where I had done most of my world-wandering, and would ask questions about them until late into the night, while bugs and beetles and moths of all sorts climbed across the table before us or flitted about the lamp.

Madame, the Chief Cook, objected to our long sessions. She would sit upon the cot beside us, yawning, and watching us with an expression of annoyance, as though she would like me to retire and let Henri do the same. Madame, unlike most Oriental women, had a mind of her own. She was Tonkingese, about twenty in age, with nice, clear-cut features, and eyes surprisingly large and brown. She never dared to voice her displeasure directly to us, but would chatter away to the world in general whenever she was aroused.

It was the typical Asiatic custom. If a woman in China or Annam or Cambodia or any of these countries is incensed about anything, she goes to a corner of the market or some other public place, and tells the world about it, shouting in her high-pitched unmusical voice so that all the neighborhood may hear it. Once, when her ox-cart stopped so abruptly that Madame was thrown from her seat into the dusty road, she sat where she landed for twenty-six minutes—by Henri's watch—and chattered at the top of her lungs. And when, during our evening sessions with the dictionary, I could hear Madame beginning to mumble to herself, I would bid Henri good-night and retire to my cot, knowing that presently she would begin to shout her sentiments at the top of her healthy young lungs, and might continue to shout until dawn.

I like and admired Henri, but as we hiked day after day, our athletic rivalry increased; I began to watch him from the corner of my eye for signs of weakening, and sometimes caught him watching me in the same way. Our halts to rest became farther and farther between; neither of us would allow the other any satisfaction by suggesting a halt. And one evening, the last evening before we expected to reach Pailin, our destination, we came to a village beside a river, a real river with water in it instead of the usual mud puddles. We stripped and took a bath in fine disregard of the native girls who gathered upon the bank to comment upon the whiteness of our skin, and during the bath I not only outswam him, but could throw stones across and hit a tree on the opposite bank when he could throw but half-way across. That evened up his lead as a cliff-scaler, and when we hit the trail upon the following morning, we were both out for blood.

A tropical shower fell during the night, the first in many weeks, and the road that morning was a bed of muck. Travel in this region, unpleasant enough in the dry season, was almost impossible after a rain. The ox-carts became lodged in the mire, and we left them behind. The mud clung in round balls upon the heels of our shoes, and our feet were as heavy as lead, but we kept on and on, each slowly increasing the pace.

The sun came out, hotter than ever before, blazing like an inferno. It seemed to pierce straight through our clothing and left blisters upon the skin. It heated the faint breeze and made it a blast from the door of Hades. It dried the muck, but left it crumbly, so that the uneven ruts upon which we trod would fall beneath our feet and send us sprawling upon the ground.

The dogs, which had started out with us, dropped behind. The umbrella-bearers and the canteen-bearer lagged, and disappeared.

A bird hidden in the forest commenced to whistle at us. Its whistle sounded like a human whistle. It came with a regular cadence, in a sort of toot-ta-toot, toot-ta-toot—a refrain which corner loafers might whistle at a passing girl—toot-ta-toot, toot-ta-toot, toot-ta-toot-ta-ta-toot-ta-toot! We began to keep step to it. It was cheering, at first, as when a band strikes up during a long tiresome march, but it grew monotonous. Other birds of the same species took up the refrain. Were they keeping time to us, or were we keeping time to them?

I suddenly discovered that I was whistling with the birds. That confounded tune was running through my head. Hour after hour passed. I became footsore. I could feel a throbbing in my temples. I glanced at Henri. His little black moustache was drooping, and his mouth was set in a firm line. The veins stood out upon his forehead. Sweat poured from his face and neck, and trickled over his once spotless clothing, leaving stains. The sun mounted higher until it was straight above us. We had already been tramping for six hours without a break, but Henri showed no sign of stopping. I increased the pace, and he lengthened his own stride.

And then we turned a bend.

Before us stood an isolated thatched hut with a shady porch.

In mutual surrender we staggered toward it, dropped upon its bamboo floor, and collapsed. Honors were even.

A native woman found us there. She was an aged hag, with white hair and wrinkled face. She was small and extremely thin; her bare legs beneath a short skirt were pipe-stems; her breasts hung naked like strips of parchment; the skin clung tightly to her skull-like cheeks; her teeth, protruding beyond her withered brown lips, were black.

Ugly? Never had I seen such an apparition. It was as though a messenger of death had come upon us.

But she brought us coconuts. Squatting upon her skinny heels, she split them open with a knife. She raised our dizzy heads, and poured the cooling beverage down our parched throats. And as she ministered to our needs, there came into her slanting eyes a kindliness that transformed her into a thing of beauty. It was the spirit of the eternal mother, which recognized no distinctions of creed or color. She smiled upon us with sympathy, and talked to us in a language which neither of us could understand, yet which was strangely comforting. She ran on her weak little pipe-stem legs to fetch pillows of rice-stubble; she propped us up and placed them beneath our shoulders. She gave us more coconuts to drink, removed our helmets and fanned us, and when we had recovered sufficiently, she brought us rice to eat, smiling at us with a smile that had once seemed loathsome but which her kindliness had changed into something sweet and holy, chattering those unfamiliar heathen words that were more solacing than any sermon that man can preach.

And Henri and I, who despised and scorned the yellow race, accepted her offerings, and blessed that little mother, and having blessed her, slept upon her bamboo floor until Henri's dogs announced the coming of the caravan by licking us frantically in the face.

V

We remained there overnight, and in the morning, from a hill, we caught a glimpse of our destination, the village of Pailin.

It was a beautiful sight.

We stood upon a crest beside an ancient temple. Above its whitened walls was a roof that sparkled with inset pieces of glass, and from its gilded spires a myriad of little bells were tinkling in the breeze. Before us the sandy road curled downward like a silver-gray ribbon through a forest of waving coconut palms. Thatched roofs bordered it, some standing boldly above the green, some half-hidden beneath it. Upon all side of the village the palms stretched away in a vast rolling panorama to a circle of mountains, jungle-covered mountains, that towered one above another, growing blue in the distance, and losing their peaks among the fleecy white clouds. And above it all was the bluest of skies.

We swung down the road through the lazy, sun-basking village, to the home of the French Resident—a big wooden house with wide verandas.

The Resident himself came out to meet us. Although he was the only white man in a tract of several hundred square miles of jungle, he was as neatly dressed in his linen clothing as though about to attend a social function. A plump, nice-looking man, he lived alone here, seeing another of his own race on the average of once every six months. I had expected to sleep on the floors of thatched huts during my travels, but I found myself presently in one of his guest rooms, a large airy room with screened porch and shower-bath attached, and later at luncheon upon his wide veranda, where he and Henri, with French politeness, included me in the conversation, and leaned forward with knitted brows in their efforts to understand the French with which I answered their questions regarding events in the outside world and particularly regarding the success of prohibition in the United States.

Afterwards, the Resident excused himself. It was payday in Pailin, and he seated himself at a table beneath the palm trees on his front lawn, with an armed guard of Cambodian soldiers behind him, while he paid off the government's hundred or more native employees. The soldiers saluted him as they approached the table; the civilians held their hands together before the chest and moved them up and down three times, sometimes kneeling as they performed this obeisance. Across the road the nominal governor lived in a thatched hut.

Pailin, with a population of about two thousand, owed its existence to a few ruby and sapphire mines in its vicinity. I visited them, but the mining operations were not spectacular. In one or two brooks that flowed through the village, a few natives were digging lazily in the purplish muck. In the shops I found many of the jewels, but always of low grade, and the villagers themselves, all of whom owned several handfuls, seemed to consider them of little value.

The village itself was a gem in its setting of coco-palms. The houses were built of teakwood from Siam. The entire front consisted of a folding door, or series of doors, which were thrown wide open in the daytime, so that one could look into the interior as into a house upon the stage. The floors were covered with clean yellow matting; the bedding and other furnishings were neatly piled about the walls; in the rear stood an image of Buddha surrounded by vases of flowers or joss sticks; and upon the floor of this toy-like stage setting the people squatted cross-legged after the manner of the Japanese.

The people, as is usually the case among dwellers in the tropics, seemed to do nothing but sit about and enjoy their idyllic existence. They were a mixture of many races, mostly Cambodian and Siamese, but with a sprinkling of Annamites from Cochin-China and Burmen from British Burma, for Pailin stood midway between all these countries. On the whole, they were lighter in color than the people of Saigon or Pnom Penh, the women in particular being of a light golden-brown tint. They dressed in all colors of the rainbow, usually wearing the *panungs*, or pantaloons of Cambodia and Siam, and when they ventured into the sunlight, they carried paper umbrellas of many vivid hues, until the winding street was a blaze of color.

With the joy of a world-wanderer who has at last discovered something picturesque, I unslung the battered relic of a camera which I had purchased in Saigon. Immediately, as though I had unslung a machine gun, every man, woman, and child in Pailin fled for cover.

In many lands I had met with the same experience, usually because of native ignorance or superstition. Pailin was not unfamiliar with photography, for a Burmese photographer had already established himself here, but the Oriental is by nature conservative and does not like to do what he has not done before. No one had ever posed for a white man, and no one was going to risk the chaffing from his neighbors by breaking the tradition.

I tried diplomacy. I seated myself upon a stool in a Chinese shop—even in Pailin the Chinese merchants had come and now owned most of the shops—and through the proprietor offered five centimes to any one who would pose. The rest of the village, gathering in the houses across the way, peered curiously at me from the protecting shadows, and kidded me in a mixture of dialects.

I particularly wanted a picture of two little twelve-year-old girls in the house next door. They were exceptionally pretty little slant-eyed creatures, and their piquant oval faces beneath long black hair would peer cautiously at me from the doorway, but at my approach they would disappear with shrill giggles. I even raised my offer to ten centimes—a high payment in these parts—but when their mother tried to catch them for me, they fled back into the palm forest and hid themselves.

I then tried strategy. I threw my ten-centime piece into the center of the sunny road, and focussing my camera upon the spot, waited for some pedestrian to pick it up. But the whole village conspired against me. If a stranger approached down the road, a hundred shouts of warning in half a dozen languages came from every doorway, and my vicinity was shunned as though I had the plague.

I became a marked man. I walked the meandering street from end to end, and its traffic of colored parasols and colored pantaloons vanished at my advance. Finally the male population overcame its timidity, and crowded about me, looking into the lens of the camera and trying to finger the instrument, but the female population made it a special point of honor not to pose, either for love or for money. I had very little money and was not adept at blandishment in any of their languages.

At length, having given up the attempts, I had climbed the hill to the old temple, and was enjoying the view, when a man in a plaid skirt—evidently Burmese—approached me with many bows.

"Yes," he said in English. "All right."

This was all he could say, but he led me down the hill, and I followed him along a side street to a thatched house, where he pointed to a Siamese girl in red pantaloons and thin white chemise. She was very cute, with shapely little figure, and a face that was extremely pretty according to Oriental standards of comeliness.

"Yes," said the Burman. "All right."

"Fine," said I. "Tell her to step out here in the sunlight."

But as I unslung the camera she leaped to her feet and fled, for photography had not been her aim. Ladies really must draw the line somewhere, and the ladies of Pailin drew it at photography.

CHAPTER SIX

OVERLAND THROUGH SIAM

I

In Pailin I learned that there *was* a trail to Siam.

It zigzagged through the mountains to the Siamese port of Chantaboun, not far from Bangkok. There were occasional native dwellings along the way, and I could live cheaply upon rice, but I must have a guide of some sort.

The French Resident summoned Moung Ba, a young Burmese manager of the gem mines, who frequently sent his caravans over the road. Moung Ba was very tall and thin, and wore a flowing robe that enhanced his natural dignity. He had been educated in a British school at Rangoon, and spoke good English.

None of his men were making the trip at present, he explained, but he would be only too glad to accommodate a friend of the Resident and he forthwith provided me with an aged, decrepit-looking pack-horse, and a still more aged, decrepit-looking guide—a Burmese coolie in a long coat and a breechcloth, with so much tattooing upon his matchsticks of legs that trousers would have been superfluous.

I found myself wondering what disposition should be made of his remains in case he died en route, but hesitating to question such a kindly proffered gift, I hastened to a Chinese shop, purchased a moth-eaten blanket and two cans of preserves to supplement the rice upon which I must live for days, and with only a few small coins still jingling in my pocket, I took my final leave of my kindly French hosts. Henri pressed upon me a thermos bottle, a packet of quinine, a few bars of chocolate, and a flask of *vin rouge*, and accompanying me to the edge of the village, where a tiny trail led away through the jungle, left me alone with old Gungha Dhin.

II

I did not remain alone.

I had not plodded for more than half a mile through the woods, when I came across an Annamite girl.

She sat beside the trail, a dainty little brown maiden in black pajamas, evidently waiting for some one, and as we reached her, she arose, held a conference with the guide, calmly placed her bundle of possessions upon his pack-horse, raised her parasol and fell into line. I wondered what her intentions might be, but neither she nor Gungha Dhin spoke French or English, and it seemed ungentlemanly to kick her out of the party.

Off we went, a strange procession. I led the way in a white linen suit, looking rather dignified in a pair of brown goggles which I had purchased in Saigon during my affluence. She followed in her bare feet with the parasol over her head. The aged, spindle-legged guide brought up the rear with Moung Ba's equally aged and spindle-legged horse. We arrived in that order at nightfall at a thatched cottage in the jungle, supped upon rice, and slept in a row upon the teakwood floor with the half dozen other natives who lived there.

It was an isolated cottage upon the bank of a forest-bordered stream, surrounded by the wildest tangle of cane and bamboo, but the people were kindly and hospitable. Seldom seeing such a thing as a white man, they still respected my race. They brought me rice to eat, and gathered about to watch me eat it, while that brown Annamite maiden exhibited me with what seemed suspiciously like the air of ownership peculiar to young brides, although, when the whole crew of us stretched ourselves for the night upon the hard boards, she retired discreetly enough to the far side of old Gungha Dhin.

The others slept in the clothes which they wore by day, and when, under cover of my blanket, I proceeded to disrobe, they watched me with much curiosity, speculating no doubt as to whether the whiteness of my shoulders extended all the way to my feet. But their bad manners were due merely to ignorance; they were generous and kindly, bringing me a piece of straw matting to soften the boards, and in the morning refusing the coin which I offered in payment for their hospitality.

It was an experience which one encounters only in the far interior of Asia. Where the tourist is a familiar sight, every native from baby to grandpa recognizes him as an "easy mark," and treats him accordingly. But here upon this lonely trail through the wilderness, where the people kept open house for all travelers who cared to stop, even a white man found kindness and courtesy. They discussed me and laughed at me, yet their attitude was friendly, and I thanked the Lord that I had at last discovered some likeable Asiatics.

And just then I met the Christian.

Whence he came, and how he reached this remote hole in the mountains at five o'clock in the morning, I could not ascertain, but there he was—a life-sized specimen of John Chinaman, a barefooted youth in European clothing, with his hair not clipped short as the Chinese usually clip it but long and parted in the middle in college boy fashion.

Instead of approaching me with the humility of the Cambodians or Annamites, he swaggered up to me as man approaches man, and delivered himself of the following:

"Me good Chlistian. Me spik English allee-same you, oh yes, oh yes, oh yes. You go Chantaboun, me go Chantaboun, oh yes, oh yes, oh yes."

In consummation of this proposal, he presented me with a cigarette, a box of matches, and a hard-boiled egg, and then tried to borrow five dollars. There was something about him which I did not quite like, but I couldn't figure out just what it was. I was tempted to bid him go to some place even warmer than Chantaboun, yet hoping that he might prove an interesting and helpful member of the party, I gave him permission to join, but without the five dollars.

He promptly drew a harmonica from his pocket.

"Me savvy Tipperary," he announced.

And blowing lustily at the old war song, with no sense of rhythm and hitting a false note at the end of each measure, that Chinaman took his place at the head of the column, as though he were the leader of it, and away we went again—an increasingly strange procession—through the jungles toward Siam.

III

The trail led through dense woods, ascending gradually toward the ridge of mountains which forms the Indo-Chinese border. The vegetation became less tropical; save for climbing vines that crawled snake-like over the ground and twined upward about the tree trunks, there was little to distinguish the forest from a forest of the temperate zone.

From time to time the winding path took a sharp dip and crossed a mountain stream. Here my companions were at an advantage. Gungha Dhin strode nonchalantly across on his thin bare legs, while the girl and the Chinaman rolled their pajamas or trousers up above the knees and followed him, to laugh at me from the opposite bank as I laboriously untied my shoes and stumbled upon my unaccustomed and tender feet.

The girl was an amusing little creature, scarcely more than a child. She would walk behind me, taking ridiculously long steps in an effort to plant her feet where I planted mine, giggling merrily at her failures. If the trail divided into two parallel paths, she would take the opposite one and try to outwalk me.

The Chinaman, however, was a nuisance. When not blowing furiously upon his harmonica, he insisted either upon singing in a shrill falsetto voice or talking to me in his abominable English, following each phrase with his thrice-repeated "Oh yes, oh yes, oh yes." His people in Bangkok were the wealthiest in town, he said. When we reached the Siamese capital he would entertain me as his guest. Like himself, his entire family had been educated, and were all good Christians. Now would I lend him five dollars? Or, if I wouldn't do that, wouldn't I at least make him a present of my shoes, or my camera, or my brown goggles?

I began to recall the words of an Englishman I had met several months earlier on my way to the Orient. He was a rubber planter from British North Borneo, who had had much experience with imported Chinese labor, and he made it a rule never to employ a Christianized Chinaman.

"I don't say, mind you, that there are not some honest Christians but I've never met one. The best Chinaman will no sooner desert their own religion for ours than we would desert ours for theirs. The majority of them pretend to accept it in order to get the education, to learn English, and that sort of thing. I wouldn't like to state it as a generalization, but it's my experience. The *deceitful* Chinamen affect Christianity, and I'd rather have an honest heathen. When any applicant for a job begins by telling me he's a Christian, I kick him right out of my office."

This Englishman, like many others I met, was antagonistic toward missionaries, and enjoyed belittling their work; he was biased, of course, yet I soon began to wish I had followed his example. Unlike the kindly heathen along the trail, this Chinaman had met just enough white men to regard them as "easy marks," to be fooled with oriental guile and blandishment. At half-hour intervals he repeated his requests for my money or my possessions, particularly for the brown goggles which seemed to have taken his fancy.

We stopped at noon upon the trail, and I brought out one of my cans of what I had thought to contain preserved fruit. It was put up by some Japanese firm, with Japanese inscriptions but with a picture of luscious strawberries upon the wrapper. I had forgotten to bring a can opener, but Gungha Dhin carried a huge sword-like knife which he used indiscriminately to chop coconuts, hack down the jungle, kill snakes, or cut bananas. I never noticed him manicuring his nails with it or picking his teeth, but had he ever performed such operations, he would undoubtedly have used the same knife. One chop opened the can, and revealed not strawberries, but four or five sickly little onions floating in a fluid which tasted not unlike kerosene. As my companions had brought no provisions, I opened the second can, which was decorated with a picture of appetizing slices of pineapple, and which contained two or three small carrots, also floating in the same vile-tasting liquid.

The Chinaman, forgetting the manners for which the Chinese are famous, promptly helped himself to the greater part of the contents. I had been growing more and more irritable since he joined me, and when at the conclusion of his very satisfactory luncheon, he produced the harmonica again, I snapped a curt order to him to stop his racket.

He surveyed me appraisingly from his keen slanted eyes.

"You give five dollars, can stop."

I did not have the five dollars, and I took the only other means of stopping it. I seized him gently by the neck, and followed the Englishman's advice by administering a slight push with my foot to indicate that he should betake himself from the vicinity. He was slow in absorbing the idea, but finally after the push had been repeated more vigorously, he seized his bundle of possessions from the pack horse and vanished into the jungle ahead at a coolie-like trot.

He was not easily snubbed, however. Two hours later I found him waiting for me upon the road, as friendly as though nothing had happened. He had something interesting to show us, and he led the party aside to the bank of a stream to point out the remains of a dead buffalo, half devoured by some wild animal. It was filling the atmosphere with a stench which only an Oriental could have tolerated, and when upon the strength of this exhibit, he repeated his request for my brown goggles, I was about to make a rush at him, when from a nearby cane-thicket there sounded a low snarl, and a big striped body leaped out and fled into the forest.

The girl screamed. Gungha Dhin drew his trusty sword. The Chinaman leaped to shelter behind the rest of us and began to blow frantically upon his harmonica. Undoubtedly the tiger was not a man-eater, yet even an ordinary tiger objects to having its feast interrupted. It must have been the harmonica which frightened it, and instead of repeating my kicks, I welcomed the Christian back into the fold.

IV

We continued for another day.

It was a hard uphill climb, particularly for the girl, but she paddled along on her bare feet, smiling when the trail was hardest.

Only one incident broke the monotony of the hike. As we were lunching again beside the road—upon bananas and rice which I purchased at the cottage where we spent the second night—four Chinamen rode out of the jungle on horseback. They were big rangy fellows, and appeared even taller in contrast to the shaggy little horses they bestrode. Each wore a knife at his belt, and each carried a rifle. If any Chinamen ever looked like pirates, they did, and I could see that my three companions were worried. I perched myself with my back to a tree, and reached ostentatiously toward my hip pocket as though it contained a revolver. But the four horsemen, after a brief talk with my own Chinaman, rode upon their way, and we continued upon ours.

We arrived at sunset in the first village in Siam.

It was merely a collection of thatched huts, but it included a large open shed built by the Siamese government for the convenience of travelers, and directly across from it was the barracks of the Siamese garrison. The soldiers, dressed in red or green pantaloons, were kicking a football across the parade ground with their bare feet, but upon seeing me, they hastened to their quarters, arrayed themselves in khaki uniforms, and came marching over to the shed with rifles loaded and bayonets fixed, led by a civilian official in purple trousers and a white coat.

They looked warlike, but their mission seemed to be one of peace. The object of their mission was not clear to me, and it seemed to be equally hazy in their own minds. Evidently the passing of a white man was an unusual event, and one which called for some sort of ceremony. Just what sort of ceremony no one seemed to know, for they halted in a line before me, and each looked at the other doubtfully, wondering what they ought to do next.

I solved the problem by opening Henri's flask of wine.

The civilian official thereupon made a speech. It must have been a good one, for my Chinaman's English vocabulary was not sufficient to interpret it. It lasted for twenty minutes, all in Siamese, and not wishing to be outdone in politeness, I responded for the same length of time in English. They were vastly impressed. They could not understand a word of it, of course, but they listened eagerly to the strange sounds, and were particularly fascinated by the rhythmic cadence of the multiplication tables, which I recited with eloquent gestures. Never in my life had I talked to such an earnest, delighted audience, and beginning to fell like William Jennings Bryan, I paid a compliment to their soldierly appearance, I dwelt upon the friendly relations existing between the United States and Siam, I expressed the high admiration which we of America entertained toward the Siamese people and the delight with which our circus patrons had viewed the Siamese twins, and in a final burst of eloquence, I voiced the hope that we might never be embroiled in deadly warfare but might always be as one, bound by inseparable ties of love and friendship, even as the twins themselves.

It was the best speech I've ever made, and when I closed by shaking hands with each soldier in person, they all marched home, entirely satisfied.

It was a memorable night in many ways.

I had no sooner finished a supper of rice, and had rolled myself in my moth-eaten blanket, when a troop of twenty or thirty dogs scrambled across the boards of my shelter to hunt for any scraps that might have been left. They were mangy, disreputable curs. The Buddhist religion, while it forbids the killing of these animals, does not direct that the people shall feed them, and these Siamese mongrels evidently gained their meager livelihood by stealing from the transient guests in the government shed. They were ravenous. No sooner had I chased away one than several others were nosing about in my baggage, and even threatening to nibble at my own toes.

Also, it was cold. We were at the top of the mountain ridge, and although the climate by day was sufficiently tropical, by night it was genuinely chilly. The Chinaman, unable to sleep, sat up beside me and commenced to sing in several languages. He was an accomplished linguist and was demonstrating the fact. "Burmese," he would announce, and his shrill falsetto voice would repeat about three discordant notes. Then, "Chinese," and he'd give the same three notes in the other language. Then, "Siamese," and he'd give them again.

I sat up myself and told him several things. He was a —— and a —— — and if he did not shut up his noise and go to sleep, I would further inform him that he was a —— ——. He understood the substance of it, and stopped singing. But no sooner had he stopped than the Annamite girl sat up. She also was cold, and she was going to tell the world about it, shouting at the top of her high-pitched voice as Henri's cook used to do, voicing her discomfort in a tireless stream of screeching complaint. The idiot promptly told her several things. He probably informed her in one of the native jargons that she was a —— and a ——, and told her that if she did not shut up her noise and go to sleep, he would further inform her that she was a —— ——.

Thereupon she stopped, but as though to express her annoyance at my desire for quiet, she began to throw grains of rice at me. First a grain hit me in the ear. Then another hit me on the cheek. I did not like it, but it seemed ungallant to rise and spank her, so I tried to pull the blanket over my head, but this merely exposed my feet. And when at length she hit me in the eye with a whole big lump of rice, I seized a shoe and hurled it at her. But her rice throwing had merely been a form of flirtation, and accepting my own action as a favorable response, she crawled across the floor, and crept under my blanket. Gripping me tightly with her arms, she raised her betel-stained lips toward mine.

I gave her the blanket, built a fire outside, and sat there until morning.

V

I had been advised against drinking the water along the trail, and I accordingly boiled some of it, and filled the thermos bottle which Henri had given me.

In the morning the Chinaman, as an indication of repentance, offered to carry it for me. But when the rest of us were preparing to set out, I discovered him at the barracks, proudly drinking its contents. He had no idea of the hygienic value of boiled water, since he habitually drank from mud puddles along the road, but he did enjoy sitting before the admiring soldiers and drinking from a bright, shiny nickel-plated receptacle.

I took it away from him, kicked him out of the party again, and we marched off without him. But he was first cousin to the proverbial cat, for we had not been traveling for more than an hour when he came tearing along on a horse which he had somehow obtained at the village, and galloped grandly past as though he never recognized us. And when we halted finally at a thatched cottage for lunch, there he sat upon its teakwood porch. In spite of his professed poverty he was buying a chicken. A semi-nude native chased it through the jungle for him with an old-fashioned crossbow. The chicken, like its several relatives that pecked and cackled about the cottage, was of the domestic variety, but was allowed to run wild and had to be hunted. The entire brood knew the sound of the twanging bowstring, and at the first twang went scattering into the brush, squawking in terror, with the native chasing them. But he came back, bringing an arrow-pierced rooster, and his native woman cooked it.

The Chinaman offered me half of it as though we were the best of friends. He was irrepressible, that fellow. But I was permanently and definitely through with him, and I bought my own chicken, for about twenty cents, which was probably more than the Chinaman had paid for his. Both Gungha Dhin and the Annamite maiden seemed to share my dislike for him, for while he took his afternoon siesta on the native's best piece of matting, they signaled to me to sneak away quietly.

Our trail was now descending steeply toward the coast. We were again approaching civilization. Groups of half-wild buffalo stood along the path, their long ears wagging to drive away the flies; at our passing, they would lower their heads and form back-to-back as though prepared to face an assault. Natives were burning down a field of wild cane somewhere ahead, clearing the jungle in this simple fashion preparatory to planting rice, and the cane crackled as though millions of firecrackers were being exploded. And finally we reached the open fields, where the sun blazed down upon us, and the parched sand gleamed white beneath the rice stubble.

Here at last the Chinaman overtook us. We had stopped beneath a palm tree to drink coconut juice. The idiot promptly dismounted, seized the nut from which Gungha Dhin was drinking, and drained it at one gulp. It was the crowning piece of impudence, and I immediately punched him in the nose. Instead of retaliating, he reached into his pocket and offered me a cigarette. I ordered him to move on, and when he hesitated, I punched him again. This time he offered me his horse. Thereupon I seized a stick. And this time, finally convinced that I was offended about something, he leaped upon the horse and disappeared in a cloud of dust.

We followed, slowly, trudging through the dried rice paddies. As night approached, we drew into a village—a real village, with a long street lined with Chinese shops, each a dim cavern with dryads and canned stuff upon its shelves, barely visible through the smoke of joss and pipes. The girl evidently had been here before, for she shouted greetings to the people we passed, and when at length we came to another Siamese garrison, the soldiers gave her an ovation.

Gungha Dhin led the way through the village to an open structure that looked as though it might be a lodging house. Several coolies were sleeping upon the floor, but above them, about four feet from the ground, was a wide shelf reserved for gentlemen. And upon the shelf, big as life, sat the Chinaman. He had opened his bag of possessions, and was exhibiting silk shirts which put my own dirty apparel to shame, while several other natives of all races and descriptions were admiring his clothes and listening to the fluent poetry of his poly-linguistic tongue. So this was the man who had begged for the brown goggles!

A Hindu arose from the group, and advanced to meet me. He was a gaunt, rangy man, his hairy body ineffectively draped in a long flimsy robe, but he carried with him an air of dignity that reminded me of Moung Ba, and he spoke English. It was not a lodging house. It was his home, but he knew Moung Ba, and my aged guide had brought word that I was to be treated as his guest. And when as my first wish, I expressed a desire for a bath, he led me to the village pump, and while Gungha Dhin drew up the water he himself poured it over me.

Afterwards he served tea, green tea in little china cups.

The Annamite girl, he said, had asked him to speak to me in her behalf. She liked me, he said, and wished to accompany me upon my further travels. She was a good girl, in spite of her profession. She would act as guide, cook, servant, and everything. If I insisted, she would wash the offending betel-nut from her lips.

While he discussed the matter, she sat near us, modestly turning her back, but fidgeting nervously as she listened to our voices. She was a likeable creature, and I did not wish to hurt her feelings. I asked the Hindu to express my thanks, but to tell her that I might soon be returning to America. That was all right, she said; she would walk there with me. But when I definitely refused, she arose and tossed her little head. Then she disappeared down the street in the direction of the garrison.

It was only two hours' walk from Chantaboun, where Gungha Dhin was to leave me. How I would reach Bangkok from there, I did not know. I slept upon the Hindu's raised platform, and when I awoke in the morning, the Chinaman had disappeared. So also had disappeared my brown goggles. The Chinaman may not have been a typical examples of all Chinese Christians by any means, but he was an excellent example of the sort of rice-Christians which the Englishman had described.

I am strongly tempted to point to the experiences of my hike as illustrating the fact that the only good Asiatics are the Asiatics of the interior who have not learned to impose upon white men and who still retain the virtues of hospitality and generosity, but as is always the case with such generalizations, something always happens to prove them wrong. For both Moung Ba and the Hindu had known white men, and had been educated in the white man's schools, and both treated me with far greater kindness than I would have treated them had they come straggling almost penniless into my own home in New York.

And when the Hindu refused to accept the coin which I offered him in the morning—my last remaining coin—I gave it to his little brown baby, and followed Gungha Dhin down the sandy road to Chantaboun.

VI

The road descended through wide rice fields, and brought us to a cluster of thatched huts surrounding a big Catholic mission.

There was hope in that mission. And if the mission failed, there was said to be an America in town, a Standard-Oil man. I would get to Bangkok somehow.

But just beyond the mission was a river, and at the end of the street lay a motorboat. Gungha Dhin bundled me into it, and waved me a farewell. Where was it going? He could not tell me, and I applied to a priest beside me. He was Siamese, but he had learned French from the other priests. Did I not know where I was going? Why, monsieur, this launch was about to meet a tramp steamer lower down the river, and the steamer was bound for Bangkok.

Out we shot into the brown current, past floating houses of cane and thatch and banks covered with palms.

To Bangkok? I hadn't a cent in my pocket, but if I could only make myself look respectable, I might persuade the captain to trust me. Unwrapping my long-neglected safety razor, I dipped my hand into the stream and wetted my beard. It was a painful shave, but I ripped those whiskers off. I found a matchstick and cleaned my nails. I turned my one soft collar inside out and made it look like a clean one. I parted my hair with my fingers.

The river widened, and we came upon a dirty little steamer.

I climbed up the ladder, and followed the company's native agent to the bridge. The captain was an English-speaking Dane. He wore a pair of Annamite pajamas, but the white uniform coat above gave him an air of authority.

"Captain, I want to go to Bangkok. I haven't a cent to pay you, but when—"

He did not smile.

"So you're another of these bums, are you?"

"Temporarily, yes. But when I get—"

"I've heard all that before. You're under arrest. Stand over there until I'm ready to talk to you."

Under arrest? What right did he have to arrest me? But perhaps, if he'd carry me as a prisoner to Bangkok, I could see the consul, I could wave the flag and make the eagle screech! And just then the company's agent retired over the side, and the anchor began to rattle on board. The Captain's face broke into a grin.

"Pst!" he exclaimed. "I couldn't give you a free passage in front of that fellow, but I'll be damned if I'd leave a white man stranded in that hole. We've just got time for a cocktail before lunch."

CHAPTER SEVEN

THE CITY OF THE GREAT WHITE ANGELS

I

The captain, once we had left port, discarded his high-collared uniform coat and lounged upon the deck in pajamas.

Having washed my one suit of clothes, I hung it upon the rigging to dry, while I joined him in my underwear. A previous writer, who happened to travel between other ports on this same steamer, described it as an "unkempt vagrant of the seas." To me, after my sojourn in thatched huts, it was a floating palace. And it was bringing me to Bangkok; the poet should already be awaiting me there, with my suitcase and my typewriter, my money and my clothes.

The "unkempt vagrant" plowed lazily across the Gulf of Siam, and crossing the shallows at the river's mouth, began to ascend the sixty miles of the palm-bordered Menam toward the Siamese capital. It was a quaint river, this gateway to Bangkok. Yellow-robed monks passed us in tiny dugout canoes just large enough for one passenger, paddling along the banks from nipa-shack to nipa-shack, the alms bowl perched in mute appeal upon the bow. Chattering Siamese women, their golden-brown arms shining bare in the sun, were rowing to market in sampans laden to the water's edge with fruit or betel-nut, standing at the stern and propelling the craft with a long oar, each stroke slow and graceful but ending in a twist that sent the sampan skimming across the murky water. Junk-like lighters filled with jabbering Chinese coolies swept past us on their way to the larger steamers anchored outside the bar. Fishermen in all sorts of strange craft hovered about their nets, their dark bodies naked beneath large wicker hats. Along the shore beneath the graceful palms the yellow robes of hundreds of the sacred Bo-tree, and the roofs of many Buddhist temples rose above the green vegetation, their inlaid glass and gilded spires shining and sparkling in the sunlight.

And then, as though to destroy the whole delightful barbaric picture, a great pall of smoke appeared ahead, the nipa-shacks and temples gave way to a cluster of European buildings—the structures with which the unsentimental European business man is constantly destroying the native beauty of all foreign lands—and the company's launch carried me shoreward, in my newly washed suit, to land me at the waterfront garden of a big modern hotel.

It was the hotel at which the poet had planned to stop.

A uniformed Hindu gateman, after staring at the unpressed suit, gave me a reluctant salute, and several English guests upon the wide-arched veranda, sitting one at each table and sipping whiskey and soda—evidently, since there was no one to introduce them, they simply could not meet one another, and were forced to sit alone and carry out English traditions by ignoring each other—looked at me and raised their eyebrows. In another ten minutes I too would have clothes and money, and could sit at a table, complacently ignoring other people. And then...

"No," said a Swiss clerk; "there is no Italian poet of that description stopping here."

For the first time since the poet and I parted company, I began to entertain a suspicion. He could not be so contemptible as to run away with my things after I had shared my money with him in Saigon, but he was a careless, improvident specimen of artistic genius, and it was possible...

I tried the other hotels, but he was nowhere in Bangkok. And finally, wringing wet with perspiration, and covered with dust, I made my way to the American consulate, to inquire whether the consul had an unoccupied desk on which I might spend the night.

"Foster?" inquired the clerk. "Here's a letter for you."

It was from Singapore. It read:

"*My friend:*

"I have meet one very nice woman. She is fine big woman. I come not to Bangkok because I am very busy. I am busy because I marry the fine big woman. I come when I have finish one honeymoon. Wait in Bangkok. Be good boy and do the nothing that I would not do. You understand, Foster, that a gentleman will need much clothes upon the honeymoon, and I hope you do not mind that I wear yours. Good-bye, Foster.

"Enrico"

II

I pawned my camera.

With the proceeds I cabled Enrico to forward my travelers' checks from my suitcase. Adjourning to the cheapest European lodging place I could find, I persuaded the Russian landlady to trust me for my board, and while I waited, I explored Bangkok.

Writers of the type who delight in comparisons—to whom every town with a café or cabaret is the Paris-of-Somewhere and every city with a steel mill is the Pittsburgh-of-Something—describe Bangkok as "The Venice of the East," but the description is inadequate, for the Siamese capital, with its 630,000 inhabitants of all races, is itself a hodge-podge of everything in the Orient, with not a little of the Occident included for good measure.

It straggles for several miles along both sides of the Menam. Through it runs a network of canals, tracing their paths across ramshackle alleys, across new modern streets, past slums, past royal palaces, their surfaces dotted with canoes, sampans, and thatched houseboats.

The Siamese themselves live mostly in these houseboats or in the thatched houses of the suburbs. Until recent years, the only trails through the 244,789 square miles of jungle that constitutes Siam have been the tropical rivers. The Siamese for generations have lived upon the water, and here they still prefer to live; they have their floating stores, as fully stocked as the native stores upon land; peddlers ply their trade in canoes; families move the home from place to place by simply poling it along the river or the canal and tying it to a new areca palm; the women sit upon the floating front porch and exchange gossip with the women next door; the men loaf in the shade of the trees along the bank and smoke rank tobacco wrapped in banana leaves; the children splash and swim and laugh and shout in the water; the geese and ducks quack about it; the water buffalo stand silently in the cooling water. Truly, it is an idyllic existence.

But this is only one phase of Bangkok.

In the downtown section, fronting upon the river, is the Europeanized business district, where the thatched dwellings are replaced by stone banks, consulates, embassies, stores, and office buildings. The district itself is colorless, but the traffic upon its streets provides plenty of color. Siamese walk about in gaily colored *panungs*—the strips of cloth which I had seen in Cambodia and upon the trail, wound about the waist and brought up between the legs to form a sort of pantaloon. Chinese coolies, their yellow legs bulging with muscle beneath the short drawers which constitute their only garment, thread their way with their rikishas through a maze of coaches and gharries driven by Malays in sarongs, of ox-carts driven by black-skinned Tamils from India, of bicycles and automobiles and everything else that rolls upon wheels. There are Siamese government officials, Chinese laborers and merchants, Hindu money lenders, Japanese dentists or photographers, European employees of foreign commercial houses, all mixed together in a jumble of dilapidated carriages and assorted humanity, a disconcerting mixture of the ancient and the modern, the native and the foreign.

Upon the main street—called in English, "New Road"—there is a tramway, a single-track affair with many switches. Aged-looking cars rattle along upon it, the clanging of their bells adding to the general racket of peddlers and hawkers and protesting cart wheels. Siamese motormen drive them in happy-go-lucky, carefree fashion, stopping for passengers when the spirit moves them. A Chinaman laden with bundles rushes to board one as it flies past; he misses it and turns somersaults along the road until stopped by a telegraph pole; the other pedestrians laugh at him in the unsympathetic manner of all Orientals; he rises and laughs with them—you can't hurt a Chinaman—and makes a rush for the next car. In little wooden stands in the center of the road, barefooted policemen loaf in khaki uniforms, molesting no one, for Siam, although an absolute monarchy with an omnipotent king, is quite the freest and happiest land in the Orient. The Siamese are such an indolent, pleasant, pleasure-loving race that the more industrious Chinese, pouring into Bangkok as they pour into all the lands of Asia where they are not restricted, now comprise half the population of the city.

The rickety tramway, leading northward parallel to the river, carries one from the European business district into the Sampaeng or Chinese quarter, a community of narrow lanes and smelly shops that reproduces Chinese Canton. Dogs, men, women, and children swarm through the twisting alleys, the filthiest of people in the filthiest of cities. Yet here is a throbbing of busy life unequaled in the other parts of Bangkok. Every Chinaman is carrying something, selling something, buying something, making something, doing something. Itinerant vendors cook horrible messes in portable stoves which they carry from place to place; perspiring coolies cease their labor long enough to perch upon their heels about the curb and shovel the unidentifiable messes into their undiscriminating mouths with chop-sticks or fingers. Funeral processions force their way through the crowds with much pounding upon gongs. Shopkeepers in the narrow booths haggle over their merchandise with prospective buyers or scream the virtues of their wares in shrill, unmusical voices at the passing throngs. Yet here in these dens of filth are the valuable products of the Chinaman's tireless labor—golden Buddhas, ornaments of emerald and jade, silks and embroideries, intricately designed boxes of silver, porcelain, and carved ivory. Here, too, are the opium dens, the gambling houses, the lottery agencies, the brothels, and the pawnshops—the last-named always situated near the gaming tables, suggesting that the Oriental would pawn his possessions in order to satisfy his craving for the games of chance. Where the Chinese live, in no matter what Asiatic city, will be found the noise and the stench and all that is vile, yet there also will be found the activity and the industry and the greater part of the city's commerce.

And finally, from all these drab and disappointing scenes, the dinky little tramway continues northward, passes through an opening in the ancient city wall—a wall that has been taken down in many places, so that only occasional patches of it still remain standing—and emerges into a strikingly different Bangkok, with wide shady boulevards modeled after those of Paris or Vienna, with parks and gardens and statues, with the handsome palaces of Siamese nobility, with modern office buildings to house the departments of the government, with marble temples surmounted by golden spires and glittering porcelain roofs.

Such is the hodge-podge of Bangkok—a network of canals where the lower-class Siamese live in carefree, contented poverty, a smoky European district where a few Europeans sit and ship their whiskey-and-soda and look vastly important, a filthy reproduction of China where old John Chinaman does most of Bangkok's work and takes most of its money, and finally this aristocratic section where royalty dwells among splendors that suggest the Arabian Nights. Comparisons are inadequate.

III

My lodging house was a small establishment which needed a coat of paint, but which was prominently situated upon the main street in the European business distract.

Its lower floor consisted mostly of a bar whose few bottles were spread across the shelves at wide intervals in an attempt to make a better display. In one corner stood a piano. Its loud pedal was permanently stuck. In the evenings an English lady of broken fortunes would play upon it for the entertainment of the mates or sea captains who drifted in from the little cargo boats in the river. When my landlady discovered that I also could play the instrument, and that my ragtime found more favor with the seafaring patrons than did the classical pieces performed by the English lady, my credit at the establishment became more secure.

I liked Siam and set out to find employment.

There were three daily newspapers printed in English. Considering their limited number of readers, none of them appeared to be very prosperous. All three, being edited by Englishmen, were much alike, with advertisements covering the front page. The contents consisted of ponderous editorial, a dozen cable dispatches so brief that they merely whetted the curiosity, and a column of personal items such as, "We are indebted to the East Asiatic Company for the gift of a very handsome block calendar which now rests on the editorial desk."

Nevertheless, I decided to try them.

The first editor seemed rather surprised at my informality in approaching him without an introduction. No, he explained, they did not require a reporter—never used one, in fact. The subscribers themselves supplied most of the copy—notes about their social doings, or the score from the cricket match. He did not go out looking for news. He rather implied that any paper which deliberately went out to hunt for news was an undignified sheet, and that I had insulted his paper by suggesting such a thing.

The second editor was busy, but he invited me to lunch with him. That seemed promising, but he had no job to offer; he happened to be the sort of Englishman who loves to back an American into the corner and tell him what he thinks about America, and this proved to be the principal motive of his invitation. He was a tall, well-built, handsome man, a thorough gentleman, but extremely important in bearing, referring to himself sententiously as a "journalist." He wanted to know who had won the war with Germany, and I tried to tell him. We sat at the table for the rest of the day, representatives of the world's two most conceited nations, and insulted each other in our best literary English, to the vast amusement of a Frenchman at the next table who smiled to himself and kept his peace.

Most of the Europeans in Bangkok, like the newspaper editors, were Englishmen. Siam welcomes all foreigners, but Siam is situated between French Indo-China and British Burma, and appreciates the necessity of humoring her immediate neighbors with especial courtesy.

The Englishmen in Siam, I discovered, like most Englishmen in the Orient, were antagonistic toward Americans. They regard us as intruders who have started to invade with our commerce a territory wherein they have so long held a monopoly that they feel entitled to continue monopolizing it. They particularly resent the fact that during the earlier years of the war, before America entered the conflict, our own merchants took advantage of the opportunity by trying to capture British trade in the East.

Possibly the newspaper editor mentioned me to his fellow-countrymen, for my lodging house became the nightly rendezvous of several young Englishmen—all, like the editor, with views about America which they wanted to tell to some American—and who forgot their natural English reticence after the fourth whiskey-and-soda, and seating themselves at my table would inquire:

"Well now, Yank, 'oo was it won the war?"

I liked most of them. The Englishman is the acme of national conceit and self-sufficiency, and his manners towards foreigners are not the best in the world, but he is absolutely honest and tells you what he thinks. Furthermore, he is always a sportsman, and respects you if you fight back. Considering that the people at home in New York were paying five dollars a seat to hear America criticized by visiting British lecturers, I figured that I received at least a hundred dollars' worth of abuse every evening.

But I found no job with the British concerns.

IV

My room at the lodging house was reached through the back yard and up a flight of steps to a balcony from which I could look into the houses next door.

On one side dwelt a Chinese family—pajama-clad girls in braided pigtails, and rawboned men with close-cropped hair. When I first arose in the morning, they were already at work, sitting at a table and making something with their hands—I could not see just what—but when I retired at night, they were still at work.

On the other side dwelt a Siamese family—*panung*-clad girls with long black hair falling gracefully over their shoulders, and plump indolent men who loafed in any old garment. When I arose in the morning, they were doing nothing, and when I retired they were still doing the same thing.

The Siamese have all the attributes of a tropical race. They are indolent, improvident, generous, carefree, polite, good-natured—a thoroughly lovable people if you happen to be lazy yourself. They came originally from the direction of China from the Shan-states of the interior, a people of Mongol origin and bringing with them a language which resembles the Chinese in its sing-song cadence and many tones with different meanings for the same word. But dwelling long in the warm countries, where nature provides them with food and makes clothing scarcely necessary, they have lost the industrious habits of their Mongol forefathers, and are now the very antithesis of the Chinese, possessing all the lovable vices which the Chinaman lacks, and lacking all the mean virtues—thrift, economy, and perseverance—which the Chinaman possesses.

In face, they rather resemble the Japanese, possibly because of an admixture of Malay blood, but the resemblance is merely superficial. The women are far more attractive than the women of Japan, their faces suggesting something of character and personality while the faces of Japanese women are mere doll-like masks. Their complexion is lighter as a rule than that of any of their neighbors, and they seldom disfigure themselves with powder and paint to the extent practiced by their Japanese or Chinese sisters. During the day they dab themselves with white chalk, but this is done for its supposedly cooling effect, and not to improve on nature.

Their dress is extremely alluring. Above the panung they wear either a thin silk chemise or a strip of cloth tightly wound about the breasts. Arms and shoulders are bare, and so are the legs. In figure, they are not the equals of the Annamites, for having lived so many generations upon the river, they have developed beautifully rounded arms by much rowing, while the lower limbs, seldom used in walking, have become comparatively thin; proportion is lacking, and in their walk, the knees seem to poke forward awkwardly.

The hair, according to the older style in Siam and still in vogue in Cambodia and along the trail I had traversed, was cut short. According to the legend which all writers upon Siam quote or copy one from the other, this style was instituted during a siege, when the women of the beleaguered city cut their locks and appeared upon the walls as men in an effort to fool the enemy regarding the strength of the garrison. At present, however, it is the mode in Bangkok to let the hair grow to the shoulders; instead of tying it into prim pigtails like the Chinese ladies or fashioning it into artificial coiffeurs like the Japanese, they let it fall naturally, so that it forms an attractive frame for their pretty oval faces.

There are, of course, many exceptions to the rule of Siamese beauty. Many of the girls chew betel-nut or blacken their teeth, as did the Annamites and Cambodians, for in the past even the wealthy nobles of Siam practiced this habit, and the King had his own golden betel-box inlaid with diamonds and other precious stones, but court circles are now setting the new style by condemning this habit. Even the pretty girls are inclined to lose their prettiness at an early age, particularly after they have once become mothers, for among the many superstitious customs of rural Siam is a most unhygienic one of building a fire beside a prospective mother and half roasting the poor lady. Older women in Siam almost invariably have drawn faces with parched lips protruding. But the younger girls are usually comely; theirs is the sensuality of the tropics, and lacking the Chinese girls' racial aversion toward foreigners, they do not hurry past a white man with lowered head, but survey him coolly and with frank, appraising interest.

The Siamese men dress also in *panungs*. According to the old traditions of Siam, a different *panung* of a certain prescribed color should be worn on each day of the week, but this custom is not often observed. The most popular color seems to be blue. Above the *panung*, they wear a white uniform coat of European cut, and below it, if they can afford it, white shoes and stockings. The whole ensemble makes a distinctive costume, different from any other costume in Asia, yet not distinctively Asiatic. They look rather like attendants at some mediæval court.

The Siamese delight in pomp and ceremony, and life in Siam consists in one ceremony after another.

One day, for instance, there came to my room the sounds of music and revelry from the house next door, and from my balcony I could see priests and guests assembling. Incense was burning before the statue of Buddha, food was being served, gifts were being received by the family, and in the center of the whole affair, upon a throne-like chair covered by a kingly pagoda-like umbrella, sat the twelve-year-old son of the family, little Dhip Borihar Pramonda Banaraks, or whatever his name was, all dolled up in skirts of rich brocade, his wrists and ankles so laden with ornamented rings that he could scarcely walk.

Little Dhip Borihar Pramonda Banaraks, it seems, was about to have his top-knot cut. It is customary to shave the heads of male infants, except for a little tuft of hair which is allowed to grow in the center of the forehead, somewhat like the pigtails that the Chinese used to wear, and when the youth reaches young manhood—at twelve years—this is removed in consummation of his adolescence, after astrologers have been consulted for a favorable day and hour, and friends and priests invited, and much ceremony has been performed. The celebrations next door lasted for three days, consisting mostly of feasting by the guests and recitations of Buddhist scriptures by the priests, but on the third day the three most distinguished relatives, one with gold-handled scissors, one with silver-handled scissors, and one with copper-handled scissors, made a concerted attack upon Dhip's top-knot, after which a professional barber came and finished the job which the relatives had botched, and Dhip became a full-fledged man.

This ceremony usually precedes the youth's entrance into the priesthood. Every Siamese, from king to peasant, spends a portion of his life in a Buddhist monastery—usually about three months of it—which accounts for the large number of temples and priests to be seen throughout the country. There are reported to be 10,000 monks in Bangkok alone, and over 100,000 in the whole of Siam. Presently Dhip will be dolled up again, and escorted to the temple, where the chief priest will ask him innumerable solemn questions as to his virtue, including such—

to us—ludicrous inquiries as, "Are you troubled with fits or leprosy?" and "Have you ever been bewitched by magicians?" and if Dhip hasn't, he will don the garment which has won for Siam its nickname of "The Kingdom of the Yellow Robe," and for three months or more will live the life of a saint, meditating upon the evils of the world, after which he will leave the monastery, return to civil life, and enjoy all the evils to the utmost.

The average Siamese, however, is said to have little knowledge of Buddha's teachings, and spends his time in the priesthood mainly because it is customary to do so. When he makes offerings to the mendicant priests, it is also from force of habit, coupled with a vague idea that in so doing he makes merit for himself, and saves himself from possible punishment in a future existence. Buddhism itself in Siam is coupled with many superstitious ceremonies picked up in remote ages from the neighboring Hindus or from heaven knows where, and most of these ceremonies, although conducted by the monks, have no inherent connection with Buddhism. The Siamese welcome the various religious celebrations not because they are religious but because they offer an excuse for another dearly beloved holiday.

A typical Siamese ceremony is the rice planting ceremony each spring, when half the population of Bangkok follows the Minister of Agriculture out into the country to watch him plow a field with a gilded plow drawn by white bullocks. If, during the plowing, his *panung* remains midway between the knee and the ankle, the people believe that the forthcoming rice crop will be blessed with good weather; if it rises to the knee floods are expected; if it drops to his ankle, a drought is threatened. Another ceremony is the swinging ceremony. In a prominent position in the aristocratic section of Bangkok there is an immense swing, about sixty feet high. As a part of the harvest festival, several Buddhist monks swing skyward upon this contraption and try to seize with their teeth a bag of gold suspended from another structure. All Bangkok enjoys this event; no one seems to know quite what its idea can be, but it offers another holiday.

The surest way of "making merit," if one can afford it, is to build another *wat*, or temple, and since the Siamese nobility has been doing this from time immemorial, Siam is overloaded with them, some shabby, some magnificent and filled with golden offerings that eclipsed even the displays I had seen in the Silver Temple at Pnom Penh. The Siamese are all spendthrifts; the lowliest coolie, unlike the economical Chinaman, if he has a few cents will not walk, but will call a Chinese rikisha coolie of no lower standing, and ride. And in a similar manner, Siamese, rich or poor, while the greater portion of their capital lies in contented squalor, delight in the pomp and splendor of their royal palaces and temples. The royal family itself has built or endowed many of the *wats*, and once each year the King visits the principal ones in person, for he is regarded by his subjects as the local descendant of Buddha himself. It takes him a fortnight to visit all of them, and to those upon the riverfront he makes his pilgrimage in a huge royal barge, seated upon a high throne and rowed by sixty oarsmen in costumes of red and gold, escorted by many other gaily decorated and richly ornamented barges, while the rest of Bangkok watches him from the shores, and the modern steamers in the river toot their whistles at him.

The Siamese, with their love of pomp, are very fond of grandiloquent titles. The river's full name is the Menam Chow Phya, meaning "The Grand Duke of Waterways." Bangkok's complete name signifies "The City of the Great white Angels." And the father of the present king was Prabat Somdetch Pra Paramindr Maha Chulalongkorn Patindr Tepa Maha Mongkut Pra Chula Klao Chow Yu Hua.

V

It was commonly remarked in Bangkok that one could not throw a stone without hitting a prince.

This was not surprising, in view of the fact that a late ruler first became a father at the age of thirteen, and later surrounded himself with some three hundred wives, concubines, and women servants. When his nobles, to gain the royal favor, kept sending him their daughters, he announced that while he did not aim to corner the beauty market in Siam, he would not offend his subjects by refusing any others that might be offered to him. Wherefore the Siamese directory today contains eight long pages of solid print merely to enumerate the King's immediate relatives.

Siam is a family-ruled nation, and most of the cabinet posts and other offices are held by princes. Wishing to see one of them at close range, I borrowed the consul's stationery, and wrote to General, His Royal Highness, Prince Purachatra, the Prince of Kambaeng Bejra,

Commissioner General of Siamese State Railways, asking the honor of an interview.

In due time my letter was answered. His Royal Highness would grant the interview at a certain hour in the office of the State Railways. To make a better impression, I had given my address at the leading hotel, but the answer came addressed to the small hotel at which I was stopping, suggesting in a delicate way that the Prince had investigated me and was not to be fooled by any of my pretenses.

I spent another day in bed while my only suit was laundered, and at the appointed hour found my way on foot through the suburbs to the Railway. The cars upon the tracks were ramshackle relics; like the rikishas and other vehicles in Bangkok, they had evidently found their way to Siam after being condemned by all the other countries of the Orient, but in the usual contrast that was never lacking in the Siamese capital, the station itself was a large ornate building that would have brought credit to many an American city.

Purachatra was reputed to be the high muck-a-muck among Siamese princes, and the most capable man in the country. When Siam entered the European war, it was he who took over the management of the railways from the German concern which had previously operated them, and it was remarked that he had operated them quite as efficiently as the Germans. Panunged attendants escorted me into his antechamber, and as though to prove his up-to-dateness, entertained me with a private moving picture show, exhibiting colored slides of scenes along the railroad interspersed with such Yankee-sounding advertising slogans as: "For comfort, safety, and speed, travel by Northern Railway."

And when at length they bowed me into the Prince's private office, I found it furnished with every modern instrument from telephone to dictaphone. The prince himself dressed not in silks and golden crown, but in English-cut military uniform of olive-drab and a Sam Browne belt, arose from behind his desk, extended his hand, and apologized in perfect English because he was five minutes late in according the audience. Then, with the air of a business man, he bowed me into a chair beside him.

The interview was desultory. The Prince knew in advance that I had no particular questions to ask him, and that I had come merely from curiosity to see how he would look and act. He was quiet, unassuming, and cultured—he had been educated in England and had traveled in the United States—and was perfectly democratic. He was modest and even reticent about speaking, particularly when I asked about his own achievements, and when at the end of twenty minutes, he shook hands and bowed me out, I had learned nothing except that Siamese princes are no longer the comic opera figures which I had expected to find.

I saw many more princes during my stay in Bangkok. On Saturday afternoons they came out, like the English residents, to the Royal Bangkok Sports Club to witness the horse races. Most of them had been educated abroad, they spoke English, and they conducted themselves in the manner of Europeans.

A national fair was being held at the time of my visit, and I was told that the King attended it each night. In fact, the fair opened upon the King's arrival, and closed whenever he went home, but all Siamese are great night-birds—most of the government offices are run during the cool evening while the officials sleep in the daytime—and since the King was the greatest night-bird of all, the fair was apt to last until the wee small hours of the morning.

I waited until almost midnight before I set out, and it was already started. It was held in a big field on the outskirts of town. For several blocks the approaches of it were lined with the automobiles of Siamese royalty, all of them big expensive cars with liveried chauffeurs. The fair, while open to the public, seemed to be a society event. Every man seemed to be in uniform or full dress. Each officer seemed to have designed his uniform to suit his own taste, for they were of all styles and all colors, with white predominating. Every one was saluting every one else with a snappy military salute; it was almost Prussian in its rigidity. Civilians doffed their high silk hats to one another. There was scarcely a native *panung* to be seen. Even the ladies were in European dress, in the latest Parisian gowns; they would have been more attractive in their own ancestral garments, yet nowhere in the East did I see such ravishingly beautiful girls as these royal princesses of Siam.

The exhibits consisted mainly of stores run by the local merchants, who evidently had received a royal edict to open booths here, since none of them acted as though they expected to sell anything. Only the shows and particularly the gambling games drew patrons. There was a Burmese opera, a Siamese drama, exhibitions of the Red Cross and the Wild Tigers—the last named organization being a form of Boy Scout

Movement instituted by the King—a European dancing pavilion, restaurants and drinking places, and even a Scenic Railway. But there was little merriment. The Siamese were holding a European entertainment, but they had learned their European manners from the restrained and dignified British, and they went about it in a solemn, matter-of-fact way, as though performing some rite.

I walked about, looking for the King, but could not find anyone who looked like him. Finally, I hit upon the idea of following one man, a particularly handsome nobleman in plain white uniform; he was the most important man present, and he had the most beautiful girl on his arm, wherefore I figured that sooner or later he would be calling upon the King. He walked quietly about, returning the salutes of his fellows, and I never suspected his identity until an old woman, evidently a scrub-lady of some sort, fell to the ground, wriggled across ten yards of dirt, and kissed his foot. I had been following the King.

And a few days later, through the American Embassy, I obtained permission to visit the palace grounds.

The permission also included the throne hall in a separate building. It was a handsome structure of marble, designed by a famous Italian architect, and considered the finest building east of Constantinople. Everything except the throne was done in European style; the marble pillars, the decorations, even the mural paintings of Siamese scenes were European in design. It was beautiful, but there was nothing Siamese about it, and I was preparing myself for further disappointment, when the panunged courtiers led me through a gate into the palace, and—

That palace surpassed all my wildest dreams. In all the world I doubt that there is a spectacle of barbarity to equal it. In its courtyard were gilded prachadees, towers and spires of inlaid glass, grotesque statuary, bizarre demons and monsters, marble elephants, temples and pagodas roofed with porcelain, all in a riot of brilliant color, all glittering and reflecting the sun from a thousand surfaces in a thousand sheets of flame. It was magnificent, astounding, bewildering, fascinating, and so on throughout the dictionary! No words could describe it; no painting could even begin to reproduce its blinding effect. It was barbaric spectacle which for sheer glory must surpass anything in Heaven and for sheer grotesquerie must eclipse anything in Hades.

For two hours the panung-clad attendants led me from court to court, and at every turn new sights burst upon me. Giant warriors, forty feet in height—hideous giants with dragon-like faces—scowled down upon me as they leaned upon their swords beside the palace gates, their faces as indescribably ugly as faces in a nightmare. There were fantastic goats with barbed tails curling in the air above them, animals with the faces of men, men with the faces of animals, huge stone watchdogs, roofs, towers, steeples, domes, curling gables, all culminating in one enormous prachadee plated with gold, real gold, rounded at the bottom but tapering skyward in a tall, slender spire, blazing in the sunlight.

Beside it was the temple of the Emerald Buddha, its roofs and towers inlaid with sapphire-colored glass, its interior laden with gold and jewels—the wealth of an empire laid at the feet of an idol—a small idol of solid jade, for the possession of which the ancient kingdoms of tropical Asia had waged war after war in ages past, and which now sat at the top of a high throne of gold, surrounded by golden Buddhas and golden ornaments of all descriptions, by diamonds and rubies and sapphires and emeralds. Seven life-sized Buddhas of solid gold, with costly rings upon their fingers, pointed upward to it from below, and everywhere about it were other priceless offerings of generations of Siamese kings. In Pnom Penh I had marveled at the wealth of the royal temple, but the Cambodian exhibits faded into insignificance beside these of Siam.

We came out again into the barbaric courtyard.

"Now," I said, "let's see the sacred elephants."

But according to my attendants, the last of the white elephants had just died. I learned later that this was not the truth. Possibly my escort was already bored with showing me about these familiar sights. Or possibly earlier European visitors had laughed at the sacred beasts. The Siamese are very sensitive about foreign opinion; every upper-class Siamese, even when he prefers his own manner of living, maintains in his house a European parlor, in which he receives European visitors with pathetic eagerness to make an impression; these educated Siamese no longer believe in the divine qualities of diseased albino elephants, and the King maintains them only from respect to the ancient custom. It used to be that when one was captured in Siam, the King would travel up the river to meet it, priests would chant scripture to it, nobles would welcome it to Bangkok with flowery speeches, and the entire city would declare a fête in its honor. But today, the Siamese have taken from their flag the distinctive emblem of an elephant, and adopted an ordinary banner of five stripes.

Eve3n the palace that I saw was but a showplace. The King now lives in a thoroughly modern European palace, designed and executed by European architects and builders. Educated at Oxford, he no longer rides upon an elephant, but in a big red automobile; instead of wearing silks and jewels, he dresses like Prince Purachatra in an English-cut military uniform; instead of maintaining a harem of three hundred concubines, as did his ancestors, he has announced his intention of marrying but one wife—the exceptionally beautiful girl whom I saw with him at the fair.

Verily the world do move, even as far away as Siam. Presently even the strange ceremonies, observed now only because of the old traditions, will be discarded. Then what will the travel writers find to write about in Siam?

I walked back from the palace, to find a second letter from the poet. It read:

"*Dear friend:*

"I send you one check. You know, Foster, the bridegroom need always the money. I have sign your name to the other checks and have spend them. When I get money from my publisher in Italy, I pay you back, but I go now for one honeymoon. Wait in Bangkok, Foster. Goodbye, Foster."

"Enrico."

From the check which he enclosed, when I had settled for three weeks' board, redeemed my camera, and paid my former steamship passage from Chantaboun, I had barely enough left to chase him, and I hated to interrupt a perfectly good honeymoon, but I started hot-foot for Singapore.

CHAPTER EIGHT

BY FREIGHT CAR TO THE MALAY STATES

I

I set out in the early morning while Bangkok was asleep.

A rickety trolley car—the first car of the day, operated by a yawning motorman and a dozing conductor—carried me through the darkened streets to the river bank, where a fleet of sampans waited to conduct passengers across the river to the station of the Southern Railways.

Many of the oarsmen were women. Back in Hong Kong, at the beginning of my wanderings, I had revolted at the idea of sitting comfortably in the stern while an aged female toiled and perspired for a few pennies, but I was growing callused to the sight. Anyhow, considering the many hours I had spent in the dim past at rowing the female sex up and down a lake at some summer resort, it really seemed my turn to ride, and while a stout lady in an abbreviated *panung* grunted at the oar, I sat and watched the roseate dawn—or whatever artistic people usually call it—tracing its crimson something-or-other upon the sparkling temple roofs behind me.

And then, reaching the Railway Station, I made an interesting discovery. My funds were just six ticals short of the price of a third-class ticket to Singapore. I tried to argue with the ticket agent. Anywhere else in Asia a merchant always asked more than he expected to be paid, but a railway fare, it seemed, was the one commodity that had a fixed price. The agent would not argue the point.

There was only one thing to do—become a tramp and ride the bumpers. I walked around and around the train, looking at the cars, and trying to figure out just what the bumpers were. I had always heard the term used in tramp literature, but the writers had never accompanied the term with a diagram. My strange behavior excited the usual curiosity among the natives, and a small crowd began to follow me, including two Siamese policemen. To steal a ride was an impossibility.

I stood there and watched the train pull out; then, shouldering my blanket and camera, I set out myself—on foot, walking the ties. At least I knew what ties were. And it was only 1188 miles to Singapore, down the long peninsula that curved southward between the Bay of Bengal and the Gulf of Siam, five days by train, and Heaven knew how many days by foot.

II

The track led across flat rice fields dotted with occasional clumps of bamboo or little patches of wood.

The natives, streaming into Bangkok to the market, the men empty-handed, the women carrying baskets of produce upon their heads, were vastly amused at the sight of a prosperous-looking European marching along with a pack upon his back. They paused to stare at me with open mouths; sometimes they grinned, the grin fading at my approach to reappear as soon as I had passed.

Now and then a Buddhist temple appeared among the patches of wood, its shabby plaster walls topped by the usual curving roof of glittering tiles. Occasionally the track led through a ramshackle village of bamboo walls and atap-thatched roof. Here, as upon the road, the Siamese women were at work while the men loafed in the shade. Only the Chinamen were busy, and not a village here—or anywhere else in eastern Asia—was without its Chinamen, some laboring as coolies, some keeping shop.

I passed one of them who was scolding his Siamese wife. She merely laughed, with the independence which I never had found among Eastern women as in Siam, and shrugged her beautiful bare shoulders, which seemed to irritate her Chinese lord and master. His thin lips curled back from his yellow teeth, his eyes narrowed to two oblique slits, and he hissed a stream of profanity at her. Certainly from its tone, it must have been profanity. They were mean, despicable specimens, these, Chinese, but they were industrious. Some of them along the way were husking rice in primitive fashion, sometimes with a homemade rotary machine of wood and rattan, which two men would turn, walking around and around as sailors in the old days might operate a capstan, but usually with an even cruder device, a mallet fastened to the end of a long sea-saw, upon the opposite end of which a sweating Chinaman would jump on and off, forcing the mallet alternately to rise and fall upon a basket of rice until the husks had been pounded from the grain.

Personally, my sympathies were all with the loafing Siamese. The sun was hot—far hotter than any sun upon my previous hike from Indo-China. I was closer to the equator, and would be heading toward it for many days to come, through one of the hottest countries in the world. The very thought of it made me thirsty, but the pools of water along the way, from which the undiscriminating natives drank, were mere mud puddles, and I sipped with forced moderation from the diminishing contents of my thermos bottle. The villages became less frequent, and the long, straight expanse of shining track ahead, with nothing to break the monotony of the rice fields or scrubby brown jungle of bamboo, seemed to blaze in two endless parallel lines of steel.

I began to burn inside. A dull feeling filled my head, and it seemed as though the upper portion of my cranium had dropped off somewhere along the road. My pack, light enough at the start, began to weigh heavily. And then, suddenly, the burning sensation was succeeded by a chill so that I shivered violently.

I understood at once. I had seen enough malaria victims in the tropics to realize that I had the fever. Mosquitoes had been thick in canal-intersected Bangkok, and I had been infected at this most inconvenient of moments. The thing to do was to find a resting place and lie quiet for the remainder of the day. There was not a village or dwelling in sight at the moment, so I selected a shady spot beneath a clump of bamboo.

Just then it commenced to rain. Or rather, it did not commence. It just rained. The black clouds covered the entire sky almost as though by magic, and the water fell in a torrent. The dry season was ended, and the rain-bearing monsoon from the Indian Ocean was beginning to blow northward, announcing its advent without any previous warning. The water was soft and tepid, but there was lots of it, and it seemed to heighten my alternate fever and chills.

Shouldering my pack once more, I forced myself onward along the track. Once I saw a ruined temple at the far end of a field, and made my way through the rapidly softening muck to seek shelter beneath its roof, only to discover that the roof had fallen, and to espy a moving patch of mottled black and yellow among its debris as a serpent writhed out of sight. I plodded back across the rice padi to the railway. There must be a village somewhere ahead. I stumbled along the uneven ties, mile after mile, moving without conscious effort, and wondering whether the empty-feeling spot at the back of my head was real or imaginary. The afternoon wore itself slowly to a close. I found myself indulging in that delightful mental pastime of self-pity in which fever victims so often indulge—picturing my funeral and wondering whether the news of my death would ever reach the people at home. It was rather enjoyable to speculate about the nice things that would probably be said of me by people who had never said anything nice before.

And then, as darkness was gathering, I saw far ahead a faint light.

It came from the open doorway of a tiny hut beside the track, and I quickened my pace, staggering toward it through the pouring rain. But as I reached the door, a woman rushed out, jabbering excitedly and motioning to me to go away. I was distinctly surprised. Along the previous trail the Siamese had been so hospitable and kindly. Her zeal, as she tried to drive me off, was almost fanatic. She chattered in her incomprehensible jargon, and barred my passage with her arm. But I was desperate; she might summon the whole neighborhood if she wished; I did not care particularly whether they shot me or cut my throat; I was determined to sleep upon her floor, and pushing her rudely aside, I entered.

The light was dim, but I could make out the bare interior, devoid of furniture save for a few cooking utensils and a piece of matting in the corner, upon which a man was sleeping, wheezing as he breathed, his face turned from the light. The woman pointed to him, trying to tell me something, and repeating her endeavors to thrust me outside. But I was accustomed to strange bedfellows, and crawling alongside him on the mat, I slept just as I was, in my soaking clothes.

But in the morning the woman's attitude was explained. For the man had turned over in his slumber, and a wisp of sunlight, seeping through the interstices of the bamboo walls, illumined his countenance. After one glance, I leaped to my feet, shouldered my belongings, and hit the trail again. The man was pitted and blotched with smallpox.

III

My fever was gone. Apparently I had the variety of malaria which comes upon alternate days, and would be ill in the future on Mondays, Wednesdays, and Fridays.

I was still a trifle weak, however, and my face, viewed in the reflection from a mud puddle beside the track, appeared sallow and pale. But I staggered along for an hour, until I came to a village. In a Chinese shop I breakfasted upon green tea, and discovered the most delicious concoction to be found in the Orient—rice soaked in coconut milk, stuffed in a hollow piece of bamboo, and baked in an open fire.

Refreshed, I was about to resume my march, when along came a freight train bound in my direction, and I promptly perched myself upon a flat-car. A brakeman interviewed me in Siamese, but when I offered him a few brass pennies, he accepted them and made no objection to my riding. I wondered what my acquaintance in Bangkok, the Prince of Kambaeng Bejra, would say if he knew that his recent interviewer was now stealing a ride on one of his freight cars.

It was a slow train, but it was better than walking. It crawled southward through a monotonous brown jungle of scraggly briars, passing several tiny stations that were mere sheds in a clearing, and stopping at two or three good-sized villages where crowds gathered to gape at me. At one of these villages, the freight was sidetracked to permit the daily passenger train to pass. It rattled by at tantalizing speed, affording me a glimpse of first-class compartments filled with dressed-up Europeans, second-class compartments filled with fat Chinese merchants, and third-class compartments filled with a motley horde of all sorts of Asiatics.

Late that night we overtook it to Chumphon. Only once a week is there an express that reaches Singapore in three days, running at night as well as by day. The other trains stop each evening at a village like Chumphon, where the passengers sleep at a government-regulated rest house. The house at Chumphon was a comfortable looking place where a Chinaman rented rooms and served meals at prescribed prices, but his rates, while comparatively cheap, were beyond my means, and I camped in a wicker steamer chair upon his veranda. Some natives in a neighboring Chinese shop, however, were having a wedding or a funeral or some kind of ceremony; their fiddles and gongs kept up a monotonous, ear-splitting racket throughout the night, and unable to sleep, I walked back to the railway station. Another freight was waiting there, and some coolies were loading it with pigs. Each pig was crated in a cylindrical wicker basket, through which its snout and legs projected helplessly, while the animal shrieked aloud with fright and discomfort. The coolies picked them up and tossed them onto the cars as though they were so many sacks of rice, caring not whether the pig arrived upside-down or right-side up; while the Buddhist religion forbids the actual taking of an animal's life, it does not enjoin the faithful to take any particular pains to preserve life or to make life comfortable, and the death of these animals en route would undoubtedly save the butcher from violating his religious creed. The Siamese, whose principal diet is fish, always defend their fishing on the ground that they do not kill the fish. If the fish is fool enough to die just because they remove it from the water, it is not their fault.

The last pig went on board with protesting squeals, the engine shrilled its whistle, a convulsive jerk communicated itself in turn from car to car—and I followed the pig. I was no longer particular where I slept, and the pigs did not seem to be afflicted with smallpox. They grunted and squealed with every lurch of the train, but their noise was less discordant than that of the Chinese fiddles, and spreading my blanket between two of them, I actually fell asleep, and slept until broad daylight, when a group of laughing Siamese train hands awoke me. Presumably, they wanted to know how I got there. Inspired with a brilliant idea, I made the signs of drinking. Then I sat up, looked at the pigs as though I saw them for the first time, and rubbed my head in a bewildered manner. I was trying to convey the impression that it was a "morning after," and my acting must have been good, for they all laughed uproariously and repeated my gestures of drinking. Drink, in the Oriental mind, explains many otherwise inexplicable performances on the part of Europeans, and the explanation seemed to establish my gentility.

There was no caboose on board, but the train hands, still laughing, escorted me to the top of a freight car where there were no pigs. My malaria came back on scheduled time, but I had swallowed several of the pills which Henri had given me many weeks earlier, and the chills were less wracking.

The ride was rather pleasant. Another shower had fallen during the night, and the landscape was ablaze with color. There were yellow fields of rice padi, groves of light green banana trees, patches of dark green coconut palms, all standing out in glistening relief against the background of tangled jungle. Mountains began to appear—the ridge that runs like a backbone through the center of the long, thin Malay peninsula—their slate-gray cliffs rising straight up from the verdant plain, with tropical vines and plants clinging precariously to every crevice.

In the wet fields stood herds of water buffalo raising their flat snouts to stare at the train. One old bull, tied to a stake, made ridiculous efforts to charge the engine, bellowing furiously and running around and around in blind circles at the end of his rope. Now and then there appeared against the many-shaded background of green the brilliant yellow robe of a Buddhist monk. And finally, to put the finishing touch to the most beautiful and picturesque of landscapes, there became visible through the palms in the east an occasional patch of blue sea, the Gulf of Siam, with the brown sails of a Chinese junk upon the horizon.

Beneath a cloudless sky, it seemed to be a pretty good world after all.

IV

Nightfall brought us to Surashtra Dhani—a thatched village of Chinese shops and Siamese houseboats upon a brown river.

As I tumbled off the car—the brakemen showed me by signs that we were going no farther—a native came hurrying forward with the air of a man who had been sent to receive me, and seizing my pack, started with it toward a launch moored at the river bank. He was a nice looking Siamese youth, clean, and dressed European garb save for his bare feet, and when I demanded explanations, he merely said, "All right, Mister," which exhausted his English vocabulary, but he kept on toward the launch, and paused for me to precede him on board.

Once before, in Chantaboun, I had climbed into a launch without asking where it was going, and had been rewarded with a free ride to Bangkok. Once again, I decided to take a chance. The "All right, Mister," sounded promising, and three other Siamese boatmen placed a steamer chair for me on the forward deck, as though they, too, were waiting specially for me. And accepting the seat I watched the coconut trees sweep past as we chugged downstream toward the sea.

It seems that the launch was from the lumber camp of the Danish East Asiatic Company at a port called Bandon; the boss had been expecting a European visitor on the passenger train; the visitor had missed the train; and when I dropped off from the freight, the Siamese boatmen, mistaking me for the man they had been sent to meet, were bringing me to the camp.

Two hours down the tropical river brought us to a big sawmill and a group of wooden cottages. The manager—or rather, the assistant manager temporarily in charge—was a massive Swede dressed in khaki "shorts," a species of knee-length breeches worn like running pants, which are commonly worn by white men on the Malay Peninsula. He was a good sport. The mistake amused him, and when I introduced myself as a vagabond author, stressing the "author" rather than the "vagabond," he showed me into a guest room, and entertained me at a seven-course dinner which might have been a social function save for the fact that we dined in shirt sleeves.

In the wilderness, one finds a ready hospitality that is lacking in settled communities. That Swede was a prince of a host. He gave me a gun the next morning and took me alligator hunting, and when we failed to find any alligators, he took me back to town to show me the jail. The town of Bandon, like the other towns of Siam, was rather shabby; it consisted entirely of Chinese shops, and its streets were paved mostly with rubbish and coconut shells, which were piled up against the sides of the ramshackle houses like snow drifts, but the jail was interesting.

The superintendent himself, a plump Siamese gentleman in a *panung*, escorted us through the yards, which were surrounded by insecure-looking wooden walls, and guarded by so few guards that one wondered how the prisoners were prevented from escaping, until one noticed the iron shackles upon their ankles. The prisoners were hollowing out logs to make canoes, or manufacturing tiles for the temple roofs. It is sometimes remarked by Europeans in Siam that the Siamese work only when in jail, but even here they were not working hard. Their accommodations, meager to the European eye, since they consisted of plain hard boards for a bed, and fish and rice for food, were in reality all that the inmates were accustomed to in their own homes, and they seemed contented.

At the superintendent's suggestion, I photographed his murder squad. He had an unusually large number of murderers awaiting execution at the moment, and seemed rather proud of them. At his command, they marched out obediently, and grouped themselves according to directions. One man, who had killed his own daughter because of her refusal to marry the husband of her family's choice, was accorded a seat of honor on a stool behind the others. All of them would shortly be executed with the sword. An execution in Siam is open to the public, and always draws a large and enthusiastic audience.

I might deviate from my narrative here, however, to remark that enjoyment of another fellow's suffering is characteristic of all Orientals. I had noted this fact in a small degree ever since coming to Asia. Whenever during my ascent of the river to Battambang, back in Indo-China, I bumped my head against the framework of the sampan's roof, the Asiatics had laughed uproariously. Whenever a Chinaman, trying to board a moving streetcar in Bangkok, had fallen off and collided with a telegraph pole, every pedestrian in the street paused to enjoy perfect paroxysms of mirth. In China, I have been told, crowds will attend a public flogging to enjoy the victim's suffering. Almost any book on China, with the exception of those written by professional optimists and literary Pollyannas who try to glorify the Chinese, contains illustrations of the inhumanity and cruelty of the Chinese: the story of a wounded soldier lying for hours in a public street, while other men looked at him but offered no help because he did not happen to be a relative; the story of a junk burning, while boatmen hovered about to rob the crew but not to offer succor; the story of a passenger falling from a riverboat and being allowed to drown by his indifferent fellow passengers who could easily have saved him but who did not happen to know him personally and felt no interest in him. The lower-class Chinaman in particular, because of the crowded condition of his country and the intensity of his struggle for existence, is probably the meanest and most indifferent to the sufferings of others, but the same despicable cruelty is found in varying degrees throughout the East. The Hindu of India will kill his own daughter by abandoning her as an infant in some jungle clearing, and even when he will not actually take life, he will—according to Herbert Compton's "Indian Life in Town and Country"—"watch it, unmoved, dying by inches in agony."

Personally, I found the Siamese people, taken by rank and file, the kindliest and most considerate people I met in the Orient, but they flocked in large numbers to the executions in Bangkok. The proceeding is spectacular. The executioner tilts his victim's chin in the air, marks with chalk the portion of the neck at which he plans to aim, seizes a large sword, and after taking a few preliminary swings, like a golfer, severs the neck at one blow. Picture post cards illustrating all the horrible phases of the exhibition were on sale at Bangkok.

When I facetiously offered to make my own photographs if the superintendent would have his squad executed on the spot, the official was apologetic. He was very sorry not to oblige me, but there were certain indispensable formalities which must first be observed. For instance, he explained, the murderers had not all been tried yet in court.

I should have returned to the railway, but the lumber camp manager's suggestion that I visit one of his jungle stations to see his trained elephants at work was too attractive to be disregarded. So he packed me into another launch, and sent me up a branch river, fringed with coconut palms. It was a wild river, a curling ribbon of brown water, with an occasional object which I at first took for a log lying half-submerged at the mud banks, but which disappeared quickly as the chugging motor approached, proving itself to be a crocodile.

The jungle camp consisted of a houseboat moored at the shore beside a group of thatched huts. Another Swede, a big man in shorts and shirtsleeves, welcomed me.

"So you wass a writer?"

He nearly broke my fingers in a powerful grip, and led me into the houseboat for lunch. He lived throughout the year in this floating home, moving farther up the river as his lumbermen denuded the forest, living alone with his native employees—Burmese or Cambodian mahouts, Siamese rivermen, and Chinese laborers—seeing other white men only when some other foreman dropped in from a similar houseboat for a day's visit. Another happened to be present at the moment, a young Dane, just out from home. Both these men, although from the almost arctic forests of the northern lands, seemed perfectly comfortable and contented in their new environment. The houseboat was fitted with chairs and tables, book and Victorola, but there was something of romance in the wall ornaments of tiger's skull and elephant's tusks, and just outside a huge elephant was snorting as it wrestled with a giant log, wading into the swirling river to load the log upon a raft.

And there was romance in the stories the foreman told me at lunch, stories of a Siamese bandit who had once ruled this region, capturing the Chinese merchants who used to ascend the local rivers in their junks to trade with the natives of the interior.

"He wass fine man—this bandit—but he do not have love for the Chinaman. He wass very big man, so big that his tracks, when he wass walked through the swamp, wass farther between than the tracks of any man in Siam, and the police wass more afraid when they have seen his tracks as they wass afraid of a tiger. When they killed him, it wass one day when he wass sleeping on a house, and the police have gone under the house to shoot upward through the floor."

He ended each story with an apologetic, "But that wass nothing."

"Do you see this thing?" he inquired, exhibiting what appeared to be a pebble, but which was the gall stone of a deer. "That wass good luck, so the Siamese think. My cook bought it for sixty ticals—many months' wages. Yesterday he come to me to say while he have this thing, nothing can hurt him, and he ask me would I take my gun and shoot at him to show that this thing is good luck. But he is goot cook, and I wass not like to kill him, so I put the thing in a bag of clothes and shoot a hole through the clothes. Now he would have back his sixty ticals, but the man who sell him the good luck say it is good luck against Siamese gun, not against European gun."

But that was nothing. Did I see that tiger skull? Always he had to watch his servants or they would chip off pieces from it, which would make them impregnable against the attack of living tigers. A former employee having implicit faith in the efficacy of this fetish, had crawled into a tiger's cave with only a knife as a weapon.

"But dot man," he explained graphically, "wass a former employee. He wass not any more."

After lunch, servants brought us three ponies, and we rode out to see the elephants at work. A dozen of them were rolling giant tree trunks around the jungle clearing, their own trunks stained red from the bark, their ragged ears twitching as they drove away a swarm of flies, their unwieldy bodies swaying from side to side. Their intelligence was marvelous. No other animal can even approach the elephant for understanding. If a dog can walk mechanically upon its hind legs, it is considered a marvel of cleverness, and a horse that can perform the same feat is admired in a circus. But these elephants, who looked so clumsy and whose tiny eyes showed nothing of the brain power within the huge head, were performing their daily work with scarcely a word from the mahout who squatted cross-legged upon their broad backs, and performing it quite as intelligently as human beings. Sometimes the mahout did guide them with a pressure of his hand, sometimes with a word, but usually not at all. Of their own accord, they knelt behind the huge logs and rolled them through the brush to a line of cars drawn by a tractor. Then, inserting their curved tusks beneath a log, two of the beasts would raise it and drop it on the cars.

The tractor carried the trees to the river, where the cleverest of the elephants promptly took charge. He was a big male, and he performed work that forty men could not have performed half so quickly. He would come and stand before the first car, while a native hitched him with chains. Then—with many loud trumpetings, as though protesting against this stupid and laborious task—he would drag the car almost at a gallop into the shallow water. But once in the water, the work required more use of his brain, and he seemed to enjoy it. The chains having been removed, he would walk around to the side of the car, brace his head against the log, and roll it into the water. The splash sent a shower into the air, and waves swept up the bank, so heavy was the log, but the elephant, promptly seizing it with trunk or tusks, would push it out into the deeper water, and since these species of wood here were too heavy to float, he would lift it and place it upon a raft of bamboo saplings. If the log became tangled with others, the beast would pause and look at the tangle, analyzing the trouble as quickly and efficiently as a man, select the logs which caused the jam, and proceed to remove them. And when the raft broke loose from its moorings, and drifted to deeper water, the elephant would swim out without his mahout, and bring it back. Then he would come and stand before the second car, ready to carry it into the stream, again with protesting trumpetings as though he resented this menial part of his work.

Lumbering in the hardwood forests of Siam is no simple occupation. This was not the famous teakwood that I saw here, but wood of a similarly heavy species, and the lumbering is much the same as in the teak forests of the north. The company first obtains from the Siamese government a permit to cut down a certain number of trees, usually ten thousand, in some particular locality. The trees, selected by a white employee, are girdled and allowed to die, a procedure which takes two years. They are then felled with the ax, trimmed of their branches, dragged by elephant or tractor to the river, floated downstream past the duty station which the Siamese government establishes to measure and assess the wood, to the sawmill where they are cut into planks. The whole procedure takes about four years, and were it not for the elephants, would take much longer.

The Danish East Asiatic Company—and it was not the largest of the several hardwood companies in Siam—owned altogether a hundred elephants of its own, and hired as many more, but they were distributed among many camps in many parts of Siam. So useful are the animals that the Siamese law forbids the shooting of wild elephants, although natives and sometimes white hunters violate the law in order to obtain the valuable tusks, the natives hunting the beasts in a characteristically cruel manner by first shooting one in the leg from ambush, and following cautiously until the swelling of the tender limb makes the animal incapable of charging them, when they surround it and kill it in comparative safety.

Theoretically all elephants in the Siamese forest are the property of the government, which issues permits for the capture of a certain number of beasts just as it issues permits for the cutting of a certain number of logs. No charge is made for the permit, but its recipient must pay a duty on the number of elephants captured. The hunt is an elaborate affair, begun with soothsaying on the part of native fakirs, who select a propitious place and hour; a large *keddah*, or enclosure, is built by erecting a circular palisade of poles ten or twelve feet high; a wild herd is driven inside by shouting natives and by tame elephants; the gateway is closed, the suitable animals selected—usually young ones, capable of being trained—and the others released.

The companies using elephants find it easier to buy newly captured wild ones from the natives than to breed them in captivity; the procedure is quicker, and the wild ones are stronger than those born in captivity. Beasts are preferred between the ages of two and nine. After being starved for a few days to make them weaker and more easily handled, they are started on their work with small logs. An elephant's life and development corresponds to that of a man; he is in his physical prime between twenty and thirty-five, and he dies at about seventy. A full-grown elephant in Siam costs about 10,000 ticals, or a little less than $5,000, but in the jungle his upkeep costs very little, for at night he is merely hobbled and turned loose to forage for himself. He can be worked steadily up to his death, and if worked less steadily is less susceptible to the period of ill temper or insanity know as "must," which is so often the cause of a loafing circus elephant's rampages.

Only one of the several elephants at Bandon was ill tempered. It was a huge, mean-eyed brute, and as it lumbered through the jungle, everyone gave it a wide berth. Only a few days before my visit it had picked up an incautious native wood cutter, and dashed his brains out against the trunk of a tree. Yet even this beast, knowing and fearing its own mahout, or native driver, would kneel obediently at his command, that he might scramble onto its back.

Females, as a rule, are better tempered than the males. They are smaller, but of equal strength in proportion to their size. The Swede foreman had recently read a book by an author who claimed to have been gored by a female elephant. Like all old-timers, he loved to pick flaws in books written by transient visitors to these countries, and he pointed out a female to my attention—a tuskless elephant.

"You see? The female neffer has tusks. If you wass going to say in your book that you wass gored by an elephant, make it a male elephant."

He led me back too his houseboat and served tea. The launch took me back to the sawmill where the manager served another seven-course dinner. He put me up again in his guest room, and on the following day sent me back to the railway station. And since, after receiving so much hospitality, I could not well disgrace my host by hopping another freight train, I bought a third-class ticket to the next station and left Surashtra Dhani as a passenger.

V

I was beginning to feel a peculiar satisfaction in being a hobo.

Many months earlier—way back in Montana as I was crossing the continent toward my embarkation port at Seattle—I had looked from a dining car window at three tramps who were cooking their dinner in a tomato can over an open fire, and the three of them had grinned at me with an air of conscious superiority which had set me wondering how such bums could possibly feel superiority to a man who traveled in a Pullman. But now, as I sat in a third-class car in southern Siam, perched upon a hard wooden bench among filthy coolies, I began to understand. It was the conscious superiority of a man who no longer requires such effete comforts as a Pullman.

Up forward in a first-class coach were three passengers—an Australian gentleman and his wife, and a plump-jowled young Englishman—all three of whom were complaining about the discomforts of travel. The young Englishman was particularly incensed. Never in his life had he endured such discomfort. The agent in Bangkok had told him that meals would be served on board, but the beastly train did not even stop at a restaurant! He simply could not go without tiffin—which is British for "lunch"—in fact, he made it a special point to eat tiffin every day. And grinning at him with the same conscious superiority with which the three bums in Montana had once grinned at me, I purchased from a wayside peddler a joint of bamboo filled with delicious rice and coconut milk, and had a most enjoyable tiffin, while he tightened his belt because there was no restaurant or dining car. It may be peculiar, but I gloated over him with the pride of a gentleman who has learned even to sleep with pigs.

The two Australians were tourists.

The man was very tall and slender, his hair prematurely gray, his features finely chiseled; one recognized him at once by his dignified bearing as a man of some importance at home, for in that bearing was the natural, simple, unaffected sort of dignity that distinguishes the man of genuine worth. His wife was plump, with peaches and cream complexion and the sweetest of smiles, but with the unfailing bad habit of the moneyed tourists—the habit of tossing coins to the natives along the way—the habit which, above all others, makes the old-time resident in every foreign country rail against the passing visitor. Her generosity may have been prompted by the very best of intentions, but it was something which the natives could not understand. At the local rate of wages, each handful of coins represented more than the day's salary of a grown man, and she tossed them to children. Begging was unknown here, and they simply could not understand it. They gathered about her window in a shy, curious circle, staring at her as though they considered her a lunatic. Finally one little urchin, bolder than the rest, advanced and picked up one of the coins, clinking it suspiciously to see if it were good. Then another followed, and another, all of them gaining courage, until every man, woman, and child in the village, who in their abundant tropical existence had never thought of begging, crowded about the window with outstretched hand. In two minutes at each stop she made mendicants of the entire population, and not another white man or woman from then until doomsday would ever pass through these places without being pestered to death with outstretched hands.

People at home might call her a kindly Samaritan, but the permanent resident would curse her. I was just beginning to understand a lot of things, and one of them was why the natives back on the Indo-Chinese trail, who had seen but few white men and not a single tourist, were the only kindly and polite natives that I ever met in Asia. Those who had met a generous lady like this Australian, not understanding generosity, had leaped to the conclusion that all white people were extravagant fools, whom it was the privilege of every Asiatic to cheat, swindle, and pester for alms. And still, one could not help liking that lady.

It was only two hours' run to the night's stopping place at Tung Song, another straggling village of Chinese shops, with a well-kept rest house for railway passengers. While the first-class passengers headed for the rest house, I strolled out into the jungle, found a shallow stream, shaved and enjoyed a luxurious bath, supped upon more rice and coconut milk, and walked back toward the station.

On the rest-house veranda the tourists were still complaining. The plump-jowled young Englishman was sipping a whiskey-stingah while a servant fanned him with a punkah, but he still complained about his discomforts. It seems that the bathroom attached to his boudoir contained merely a basin of water and a dipper, and he was going to write to the Penang papers because there was neither tub nor shower. Supper had been most unsatisfactory, the vegetables had been canned vegetables, and the chicken had not been sufficiently cooked, while the coffee had been execrable.

My sense of humor prompted me to build a fire on the road outside and make cocoa in the little stew pan which I carried; I found a bar of chocolate in a Chinese shop, and a can of condensed milk; its fragrant scent drifted straight toward the veranda. The young Englishman watched me at first with manifest disdain, then he began to fidget uneasily, and finally rising, inquired in a patronizing tone:

"I say, my good fellow, is that cocoa you're making?"

"Yes."

"Would you care too sell me a cup of it?"

"I'm not selling it, but if you'll join me, you're perfectly welcome. Perhaps you'll all come down?"

The Australian lady smiled.

"Let's do," she said to her husband.

And they came, the sweet smiling lady and her tall, dignified husband, squatting upon the lawn beside the fire, and enjoying it as though it were their own picnic. But the young Englishman bristled at the very suggestion of it, and remained coldly aloof.

There was a guest book upon the veranda table, in which visitors might write their suggestions for the improvement of the service, and the Englishman spent the evening writing in it. I had examined the one in the rest-house at Chumphon, and while American visitors had regarded it as an opportunity to become facetious, the English visitors seemed to take their task of criticism very seriously, inscribing such sentiments as, "The house is full of ants, and the nasty stinging kind, too," or "Why are there no towel racks in the bathroom?" or "Can't the whiskey-soda be served with ice?" I have always regretted that I neglected to ascertain what the plump-jowled young man wrote. I suspect it was something like, "Why are third-class passengers allowed to invade premises which should be reserved for gentlemen?"

VI

I slept that night in my blanket under the trees. My fever, which evidently was not a bad attack, had not reappeared, and I was beginning to enjoy my journey. In the morning, another freight train was standing upon the track, and allowing the passenger train to pull out with the other passengers, I made a rush to the station just in time to miss it, trying once again to establish my gentility in the eyes of the station police by pretending to come for the passenger coaches.

Having missed them, I gave a histrionic performance of tearing my hair in disappointment, and then climbed upon the freight as representing the next best means of locomotion available; the trainmen, with the usual easygoing courtesy of the Siamese, made no objection, but we had not traveled much more than an hour when I discovered that we were turning from the main line onto a branch that shot off westward toward the sea.

Selecting the softest-looking rice field I could see, I tossed my pack and leaped after it.

I landed in just the right place and at just the right moment, for along a road that wandered away into the jungle came a Ford, bouncing up and down upon the deep ruts, but driven by a white man, with another white man beside him, and the back seat filled with half a dozen kiddies—the most beautiful little golden-haired children I had ever seen—and the driver, seeing me land, put on the brakes and came to a grinding halt.

Miles, the Australian manager of a neighboring tin mine, was out driving with Dr. McDaniels, an American missionary, and the Doctor's children. Again I introduced myself as a vagabond author, stressing the "author" part of the title.

"Right-o," said Miles. "Better run up to my place. Everybody's welcome there, and there's no other place to stop here."

He ran me out past the mines—a large clearing in the jungle, where a big floating dredger cruised through the white sand, digging its own pond before it, sifting the sand for specks of tin ore, and filling the pond behind it with the residue from its huge shovels. A foreman, a fat-bellied Chinaman in a pair of trousers and nothing else, was directing a hundred other Chinamen at the work.

"If it were not for the Chinks," explained Miles, "this peninsula wouldn't be worth a cent. The Malays won't work any more than the Siamese. But those Chinese there will work eight hours a day, seven days in a week. The other natives don't like them, but we can't get along without them."

The day was past, however, when a Chinaman—at least in Siam or the Malay States—would work for a few cents a day. The experts here demanded at least a Siamese tical per day—about forty-five American cents, and had formed their own labor unions or guilds in the Peninsula. Miles drove on through the village of Rompibon, which consisted of the usual Chinese shops, and landed me finally at his own beautiful cottage among the palms.

It was a cottage built of teak, consisting almost entirely of screened veranda, since even the walls of the rooms would slide apart in Japanese fashion, and it was furnished with every comfort that the white man's ingenuity could bring out through the jungle to the isolated locality.

"The wife's away, so make yourself at home," invited Miles. "There's O'Leery, and here's Hill and Johnson."

O'Leery was the mechanic, the only other white man connected with the mine, a ruddy-faced New Zealander.

Hill and Johnson, like myself, were tramps, with the ambitious program of traveling overland from Singapore to London. They were a pair of tall, lean young Englishmen, clad in khaki "shorts" and undershirts, who, when the slump came in rubber, had sold their rubber estate farther down the peninsula, bought two motorcycles, and come this far on their long journey only to discover that there were no roads by which they could travel across Siam. O'Leery had built them an attachment by which they could run their motorcycles on the railway tracks, and they were now awaiting permission from the Siamese government to travel in that fashion.

Nationally, the British are supreme egotists; individually, the Englishman never brags about himself or his undertakings. When these two chaps reached the end of the railway, up in northern Siam, they would still have to cross Burma, India, Afghanistan, Persia, Mesopotamia, and various other strange lands, but in reply to questions, they remarked modestly that they hoped to reach London within five years. Yes, they rather expected some difficulty. So far, they had no trouble, except when obliged to ride through a large herd of wild cattle—and incidentally, I might explain that wild cattle are feared by hunters in the Malay Peninsula far more than wild elephants or tigers, since a buffalo bull is the only animal that will charge a man upon sight—but Hill had covered them with a rifle while Johnson rode through, and then Johnson had covered them while Hill rode through. Two other Englishmen who had previously set out with the same program had been treed by a rhinoceros on their first day upon the trail.

It seemed strange to hear such stories while I sat on Miles' comfortable veranda almost in sight of a railway track, but the track ran frequently through wild patches of jungle, and an old-timer had even told me of one occasion when a rhinoceros came out and charged full-tilt at the engine, to the complete ruin of both the engine and the rhinoceros.

McDaniels, the medical missionary, a little Iowan with a grizzly stubble of beard growing upon cheeks pale with long residence in the tropics, was just stopping at the mine on his way back to his mission at Nakon Sritamaraj, to which the branch line of the railway led. He was an energetic little man, with a deep booming voice that seemed ten sizes too large for his slender frame, and so interested was he in his work that he could not sit on Miles' porch for fifteen minutes without jumping up, looking at his watch, and exclaiming, "Guess I'll run over and give that

Chinaman some pills," or "Just wait a minute while I run over and cut that blacksmith's leg off."

In the beginning, he told me, he had found some trouble in winning the confidence of the natives. They were accustomed to their own fakirs and practitioners, who danced and beat upon tomtoms, and whose actual medical work consisted in sticking pins at random into the sufferers, or feeding them concoctions whose principal value lay in the confidence which they imparted by their nasty taste, but now that they knew him, they came in large numbers. He spoke Siamese fluently, and his popularity among the employees of the mine was evident from the broad smiles with which men, women, and children welcomed him wherever he stopped. And late in the afternoon, as he was about to depart, a Hindu guard from the mine came to express his gratitude for one of the doctor's favors by presenting his children with a goat.

"I can't say that I believe in missionaries," remarked Miles—and incidentally, I've never met a layman in any foreign country who did—"but that fellow McDaniels is an exception."

And the other three men nodded assent.

I have always felt that way about missionaries myself. I believe them to be wasting energies which could be devoted far more resultfully among the needy at home, and until the so-called Christian nations have proved themselves civilized and Christian-like it seems to me that we show poor taste in offering our religion and civilization to the heathen. I like to believe, as so many old-timers in foreign countries believe, that most missionaries are insignificant little fellows who, failing to make good at any other calling, discover that God has called them to preach the Gospel. And when I run across the really genuine, worthwhile missionary, who ventures far into the interior beyond the paths of any other white man, suffering hardship and privation, or one who manifestly is bringing happiness to the natives, as was McDaniels, I habitually classify him as an exception. And yet when I think over the missionaries I have met in various out-of-the-way places, it seems to me that there are more of the exceptions than of the others.

The mine employees crowded about the little grizzled Iowan, as he cranked his Ford. The golden-haired children shouted with delight as they seized the goat and bundled it into the already overcrowded back seat. The doctor waved a cheery farewell to us, climbed into his own seat, and with the children shouting and the goat bleating, and a troop of village dogs yelping in pursuit, he went rattling away in the ramshackle old car, still smiling and waving as he disappeared into the jungle.

CHAPTER NINE

ON THE BEACH—IN SINGAPORE

I

Having hoboed my way thus far, I could afford to travel as a passenger the rest of the way.

In the morning the weekly express came past Rombipon, and I swung on board a third-class coach. It was already crowded, and with a horde of Asiatic humanity which for variety surpassed any of my previous groups of traveling companions. There were Malays and Hindus, Siamese and Chinese, and even an Arab from the far-off deserts of the Near East, who wrapped himself in his voluminous white robes and perched upon his bench in fine disregard of the others. All of the coolies, unaccustomed to chairs, had drawn their feet under them and squatted upon their heels, lining the crude wooden seats like a row of Buddhas in a temple, save that the benignly grave expression was lacking. As usual, they watched my every move, discussing me with much amusement, but I had learned not to resent their mirth.

The express carrying me to Singapore, and in a few more hours I would see the poet who was responsible for my traveling with low-caste coolies. I devised various schemes of revenge, from beating to strangling, for my wrath, rising during the unpleasant nights in a native hut or a pig car, had become such as even a comfortable night at the lumber camp or at Miles' tin mine could not assuage. After purchasing my ticket, I had but a few dollars left; they would not carry me far in a city like

Singapore, yet if I could only reach that poet, I had no further plans for my travels. After accomplishing some of the schemes which I was meditating, I would probably be boarded and cared for by the police.

II

The express, in contrast to the freights, seemed a marvel of speed. In three hours it reached the border of British Malaya at Padang Besar. There were no passport formalities, since the British government trusts visitors to register of their own accord at the police headquarters in whatever city they alight, threatening them with a heavy fine in case they neglect the formality.

In the scenery, however, the change of government became immediately apparent. To appreciate the genius of the British as colonizers, one should enter their colonies after first seeing the French provinces. In Indo-China the officials had appeared content to disport themselves in their cafés and to let the rural districts take care of themselves. Even in Siam, despite the government's efforts to develop the jungle kingdom, there had appeared to be much more jungle than development. But British Malaya, as seen from the railway, had become a well-ordered and carefully kept park.

No other colonizers—except, perhaps, the Dutch in Java—can equal the thoroughness with which the British can take charge of a wild patch of tropical wilderness and make it a profitable, dividend-paying colony. Coconut trees flashed past my car window in even rows, each tree at a specified distance from its neighbors. Rubber estates lined the track for miles, the grayish trunks of the trees marked with tracery where the bark had been tapped; these trees, like the coconuts, also grew in regular rows at regular intervals, like so many soldiers on parade. Roadways appeared—macadamized roadways—winding off to other estates and plantations. It was a beautiful country, with bluish-gray mountain cliffs rising from the green orchards, and with fleecy white clouds outlined overhead against a brilliantly blue sky, so beautiful in fact that even the orderly precision of the trees—a precision never found in nature—could not destroy its beauty, nor could the hideous yellow-brown station buildings which the British had constructed at each stopping-place.

A previous writer has compared the Malay Peninsula for shape and color effect to a peacock's tail, and the comparison is excellent. The long ridge of vari-colored forests sweeps southward from the Asiatic mainland, for over a thousand miles, beginning with a width of thirty-five miles but spreading to two hundred, and growing more brilliant in its coloring as it approaches the equator.

Politically, it might be described as an anomaly. In the north it belongs half to Burma and half to Siam; then Siamese territory extends all the way across from sea to sea; then comes British Malaya, itself an anomaly. Of the 51,725 square miles of this division, only a small part actually belongs to Great Britain—the islands of Singapore and Penang, and two patches of territory on the west coast known as Malacca and the Dindings. Half of the remainder consists of the Federated Malay States of Peerak, Selangor, Negri Sembilan, and Phang, which are supposed to be merely a British Protectorate, although each local ruler has a British Resident whose advice and suggestions he follows as implicitly as the Kings of Annam or Cambodia follow the advice and suggestions of the French Residents in Indo-China. The other half of the remaining territory consists of the independent Malay States of Johore, Kedah, Kelantan, Trengganu, and Perlis, which also have British advisers. And wherever the British settle, the land begins to blossom and pay dividends. There are still miles and miles of undeveloped swamps and forest in Malaya, inhabited by savages or semi-savages and such animals as elephants, monkeys, tigers, wild cattle, or rhinoceros, but along the railway and the roads—the British have constructed 960 miles of the former and 3,000 miles of the latter—the country is thoroughly developed.

The coconut and rubber groves seemed endless, and where they did end for a moment it was simply to make way for a village or for a tin mine, a several-acre hollow of white sand where Chinese coolies in wicker hats were swarming up and down the slope with baskets, suspended from a pole across their naked shoulders, carrying out the ore in primitive fashion. Britain does not adopt states beneath her protectorate for sentimental or philanthropic motives, as we adopted the Philippines; she makes them pay, and if the natives—like the Malays—will not work and develop the land, she imports the Chinamen, who will.

The population of these Malay States was even more heterogeneous than the population of any of the countries through which I had yet passed. There were Malays in European garb or in sarongs—a skirt-like garment of intricately designed or flowered cloth, predominantly red in color, which slightly resembles the Siamese *panung*, save that it is longer, reaching almost to the ground, and not drawn up into a pantaloon effect like the *panung*. These Malays, like most Orientals, were short in stature, but fairly stocky, and the women were rather chubby. The faces of the men bore a slight resemblance to those of their Japanese relatives, yet there was a different quality, an expression about them which sometimes resembled the expression upon the countenance of a monkey. The women, who were a shade lighter than the men folk, seemed to lack this monkey effect, and were frequently very comely; they, too, dressed in the sarong, showing a preference for vivid color, and wore many ornaments, notably metal anklets and bracelets, so that they jingled when they walked.

But among the many other Asiatics who had come to share in the prosperity of British rule, the Malays seemed to be in the minority. There were Chinamen, of course, many Chinamen, and a great many Indians—Sikhs, Mohammedans, Hindus, and other varieties, some tall, some short, some fat, some lean, some swathed in white garments, some in European dress, some in turbans, some in a little cap like a Turkish fez, some with the head shaved, some with the head partially shaved, some with long black hair—every variety of the many races that make up the people of India. And Englishmen—tall, long-faced Englishmen—for whom all the others made way, and who strutted about with the lordly airs which no other Europeans can quite equal, the monarchs of the East.

You can take the most modest young Englishman out from home, the quiet reserved young man who will never brag about himself, and you can put him out in the East in an Asiatic colony, and he will strut just like that. But after seeing a garden spot like British Malaya, you can't blame him.

III

At nightfall, the train reached Prai, where a ferry carried the passengers to Penang, the second city of British Malaya.

Back on the road, I had taken secret pride in being a hobo, but as I stepped on board that ferry, the pride—for some reason which I cannot explain—suddenly evaporated. Perhaps it was because, traveling third class, I was neither a hobo nor a gentleman; perhaps it was the same feeling that a half-caste Eurasian must have when snubbed by both

Europeans and Asiatics; perhaps it was due to the sense of formality occasioned by the approach to a city.

A railing divided the first class from the third, and I tried to satisfy my remaining pride by taking a seat in the first-class section near the railing. But the ticket collector—a tall Hindu—promptly sent me back where I belonged, apologizing with oriental politeness on the grounds that one of the railway officials was on board and that he could not slight his duty, and I retired in confusion before the scornfully raised eyebrows of the Europeans and the laughter of the Asiatics.

A runner from a Chinese lodging house passed out handbills in mixed Chinese and English, advertising "Yom Kee Good Hotel," and I followed him through the Chinese section—a section almost as similar to Canton as was the Sampaeng in Bangkok. The British community may have been as charming as the British community in other cities, but most of Penang was Chinese, for the coolies imported in shiploads many years before as laborers had prospered and propagated, as Chinese will, and it was a Chinese city through which I followed the runner—a city of crowded, noisy, smelly streets lined with two-story plaster houses, of which the second story projected over the sidewalk and was supported by heavy square pillars of masonry, each house painted blue, green, or yellow. Yom Kee Good Hotel was one of these structures; in the basement, sweating rikisha coolies squatted about rice bowls, eating noisily; upstairs there were booth-like rooms separated by a five-foot partition topped by chicken wire, the walls of a nondescript shade of green which seems specially in vogue in fourth-rate lodging houses; the so-called beds consisted of pieces of matting spread across a board platform; and in accordance with Chinese tradition, the toilet was combined with the kitchen. The only recommendation I could give the place was that it was cheap. I spread my blanket upon the wooden couch, but I could not sleep. Across the way was a more elaborate restaurant, with a Chinese orchestra which pounded upon gongs and sawed upon squeaky fiddles throughout the night; the streets resounded with the clacking of wooden clogs and the jingling of rikisha bells, the cries of peddlers and the various toots upon horns or clicking together of sticks with which they called attention to their wares.

And then, to add to my increasingly grouchy state of mind, on the following day as another express carried me southward on the last twenty-four hours of my journey, my malaria returned. I had but five dollars left, but I paid it to the Hindu conductor to smuggle me into a second-class sleeping coach that night. It was an improvement upon the crowded third-class hovel, but by no means comfortable.

Across from me was a Hindu with his wife, and incidentally she was the only Hindu woman I ever saw, since the Hindu, except when traveling, keeps his women-folk locked up at home. She, like the Malays, was laden with ornaments, and had a little god button with an inset pearl stuck through one nostril. Her complexion was almost as dark as that of a negress, but her nose was aquiline. When I tried to study her face, however, she drew a shawl over her head, and her husband glared at me with dark, tigerish eyes, as though he felt that I was invading the sanctity of his marital relations. Two other Indians, evidently from different parts of India, were conversing in English; their conversation was entirely about the money they had just made or expected to make—a favorite theme of the Indian merchants, I am told—and they talked dollars, rupees, ticals, and piastres throughout the night. Perhaps they, like the several fat Chinese merchants in this second-class coach, were far more wealthy than the dressed-up Europeans in the first-class, but they were traveling with the typical Asiatic economy.

Night came, and the rattan seats were slid together to make shelf-like berths, but they were almost as hard as the beds in Yom Kee Good Hotel. In the third-class cars, windowpanes had been lacking, and there was at least some fresh air; here there *were* windowpanes, and every one shut them at night; the lights were left burning; the enclosed car became stuffy with the rankest of native tobacco smoke, and the odors of unwashed feet; and not the least odorous were the feet of a French Catholic missionary who shared my improvised bunk—a pair of feet encased in vivid red socks, which he always contrived by some kind of squirming to poke into my face.

I landed in Singapore in the morning, prepared to commit murder when I found the poet. I felt like a wreck, and certainly looked like one. I needed a shave. I was yellow with fever. My clothes were stained and wrinkled from sleeping in the sooty car. Even my sun helmet and my camera failed to give me any semblance to respectability.

A native policeman directed me to the leading hotel, the Raffles, from which the poet had written, and I made my way through a Chinese section like that of Penang, to a waterfront lined with broad driveways, and parks, and big European buildings. If I had had a few coins to jingle in my pocket, I might have retained some slight feeling of self-assurance; as it was, I felt like slinking through the streets, but I had to find that poet, and I forced myself toward the big hotel, an unkempt figure with a pack on my back.

The Raffles was not difficult to find—a big building facing the harbor. Its veranda was filled with English people, girls in summery creations of silk, men in spotless white linen, grouped about wicker tables, laughing, chatting, playing cards, smoking gold-tipped cigarettes, sipping whiskey-stengahs. I had never felt quite as insignificant in my life as I did when I walked up the driveway toward that veranda.

The Sikh gateman—a brown man in white uniform, with a sash across his shoulders, stationed there to flatter the guests by saluting them as they entered—did not salute me, but barred my passage.

"What do you wish?" he demanded.

His tone was irritating. I named the poet. What right, I found myself asking, had he to stop the guest of a guest in this manner? The question came unconsciously—a survival, I suppose, of the pride of the white race—and coming from one so unkempt it must have sounded ridiculous. A lady on the veranda surveyed me amusedly through her lorgnette. Another lady giggled. A young man stepped to the veranda rail to obtain a better view of me, and said "Ha!"—just one brief "Ha!" delivered as the English comedian might deliver it in a Broadway musical comedy, as though I were not quite deserving of a complete, "Ha! Ha!" I recognized him as the plump-jowled young man in the railway cars several days before.

I reddened through my sallow coat of tan. I could feel my ears burning. My blood boiled. So this was where the poet had enjoyed luxury at my expense, leaving me to stand at the gate like a ragamuffin, the recipient of a brief, "Ha!" In two minutes now I would have that poet by the throat!

Then the Sikh returned from the desk.

"The gentleman is no longer here," he said. "He left with his wife yesterday for Java."

IV

Presently I found myself walking the streets, walking mechanically.

I must find employment somewhere, but I knew the necessity of a good appearance. If I could go somewhere to shave and to wash my clothing, I might be able to do something, but in a city like Singapore there was no place where I might perform such operations.

Singapore was a big, bustling city, and it had no use for strangers.

I walked along the edge of the harbor. Chinese junks, hundreds of them, lined the beach, their masts rising in a perfect forest. Beyond them dozens of steamers lay at anchor, small cargo steamers flying all the flags of the earth, most of them with strange Oriental names printed in English upon the bow, steamers that plied the local seas to strange ports—to Rangoon, to Zamboanga, to the Celebes and the Moluccas, to Banjermassin and Macassar and Port Moresby, to Papua, New Guinea, and Australia. And beyond them lay the big passenger liners, British, French, American, Dutch, Japanese, bound for the big places, for Hong Kong, Suez, London, and Frisco. Singapore, lying at the end of the very long peninsula, was a port of call for every vessel that passed from West to East or from East to West. Perhaps, had I gone to the consulate, the consul could have arranged for me to ship homeward on some steamer, but I wanted to remain in the Orient until I caught that poet.

I continued to walk mechanically. I passed along wide avenues lined with the big hotels and government buildings, where dressed-up Europeans like those at the hotel swept past me in rikisha or automobile. I crossed the Singapore River, where sampans of many hues filled the stream from shore to shore with a blaze of color. I walked through the business district, where the streets, lined with big stone banks and office buildings, might have been the streets of any European or American city, were it not for the Chinese coolies that thronged the driveway. But there were not only Chinese, for every variety of heathen filled those streets—sleek-looking Japanese in kimonos, dark-skinned Tamils or Klings from southern India, tall bronzed Hindus in gaily colored turbans, Malays in sarongs, Boyanese, Burmese, Javanese, Bengalis, Bugis, Dyaks, Filipinos.

Finally, wandering back again into the two-story region of pink, green, and yellow Chinese dwellings, I ran across a small lodging-house kept by a Russian woman, and applied for a room. She stared at me suspiciously.

"You got money?" she demanded.

"Not now, but—"

"I think so when I see you. I should give away my rooms? Go to the sailors' home—go to the Boustead Institute."

That was an inspiring suggestion, and I began to inquire for the institute. At length I found it, way out at the end of town, in a region inhabited by Indian ox-cart drivers. It was a three-story brick building, its lower floor furnished with pool tables and other amusements. Several Englishmen of the seafaring type were shooting billiards or reading magazines; most of them appeared to be in the same condition as myself; their faces were very red, and their clothing little better than mine. As I entered, several of them looked up hopefully, as though seeking some sailor in better fortunes who might stand them a drink, but upon seeing me, they returned immediately to their play or their reading.

"Are you a seaman?" inquired the clerk to whom I applied.

I tried to lie gracefully.

"Well, I've knocked about the sea quite a bit."

"Have you a seaman's papers?"

"No."

"Then I can't do anything for you here."

I stood outside for half an hour. It was useless to ask any one for a job while I looked as I did. I had already seen enough of the Orient to know that it was the land of bluff, where appearance counted for everything, and that a white man who could not look like other white men was an object of derision even to the yellow race. And Singapore was full of disreputable-looking hoboes like myself.

Suddenly I remembered the words of that beachcomber back in Hong Kong—"Just knocking about? That's 'ow I got my start." There was only one way to get my next meal—walk up to some other white man and beg for it. During all my self-supported travels in South America, I had taken special pride in the fact that I had never had to ask for anything, and I hated to do it now. I stood in indecision while three lordly-looking Englishmen hurried quickly past me as though they guessed my intention. I determined to stop the fourth. And yet I didn't. For as chance would have it, he proved to be that plump-jowled chap from the train, and I would have starved first. I would stop the next, whoever he might be. He was an odd-looking fellow in a khaki suit, and his hard face suggested that he, also, had known how it felt to be hungry. He seemed a likely prospect.

"Excuse me," I said, "but can you spare a few cents for a cup of coffee?"

He did not hurry past. Instead, he stopped and looked at me.

"You're a new one—ain't you?"

I began to wonder whether I had stopped a police officer. Beneath his sun helmet, his face defied reading. It was a peculiar face wherein no two features were in harmony. His eyes popped forward; so did his nose, and his jaw. It was as though each feature were trying to make itself more prominent than the others.

"Yes," I admitted, "I'm new."

He grinned.

"Then let me tell you something. Don't bum a man like you was afraid of 'im. Act like you'd push 'is bleedin' fyce in if 'e didn't 'and out somethin'. And 'ere's some more: I know where you can sell that bloody camera you're carryin' and then we'll both 'ave a cup of coffee."

V

It seems that I had met "The Kid."

He pawned my camera for six dollars at a shop kept by a Hindu; then he led the way to a waterfront saloon, a long narrow room with a bar in the center and a dilapidated piano at one corner. Several other bums were lounging at one of the plain wooden tables.

"I sye, Kwong!"

Kwong, the proprietor, a young English-speaking Chinaman, came hurrying forward.

"Kwong," explained the Kid, "is the whitest Chink in Singapore. Ain't you Kwong? Any time I need a bloody dollar, 'e's the man'll give it to me, ain't you, Kwong?"

The Chinaman was reticent about committing himself to any such promise. Evidently the Kid was only too frequently in need of the dollar. But today he displayed my six dollars with an air of great pride, and Kwong, immediately rubbing his hands together and bowing, sent out for a big bowl of chop-suey, and brought us a couple of whiskey-stengahs.

"I mye be down now'n then, but I come up again, eh what?" explained the Kid. "Ain't that right?"

A little Scot at a neighboring table nodded affirmation.

"Aye. You're down now'n then."

The Kid glared at him.

"D'ye mean to sye I don't come up again?"

"I did na say you did na come oop, did I?"

but the Kid's coat was already off, and he was glowering at the little Scot.

Kwong came hurrying forward.

"There, there, boys, let's not fight. Let's all have another drink and forget it."

And as he hurried away to get the drink, both the Kid and the Scot favored me with a grin.

"S'easy," said the Kid. "S'only time Kwong'll set 'em up—when he thinks you might break up 'is furniture. You stick to me, and I'll show you 'ow to get what you want in Singapore."

I was not keen about sticking to the Kid. For a roughneck, he was not unlikable, but there was something peculiar about the eyes that I seemed to have remembered about the eyes of convicts back in Sing Sing when I was a newspaper reporter in New York. At the moment, however, I could not choose my company. The other bums gathered at my table—hard-faced men in clothing as disreputable as my own, professional vagabonds all of them, who made their living by telling hard-luck stories to the passing tourists, and who wouldn't have accepted employment if they could have found it. Kwong brought the drinks. The whiskey was strong, with a raw burning taste; it helped to smooth away the scruples that I had about mixing with these bums. The gathering became a party—with me as host—and chop suey for the banquet.

"Bring me the banjo, Kwong!" commanded the Kid, and Kwong brought a dilapidated instrument with a badly battered head, and one string missing. But the Kid could play two or three tunes upon it, and did so. The piano over in the corner attracted my attention, and I made it a duet. I could play ragtime by ear, not always with the correct bass, but always with good rhythm and considerable violence. There was a loose board in the floor in front of the piano upon which I could beat time with one foot, while I kept the other on the loud pedal, and what I lacked in technique I supplied in enthusiasm. It was not an artistic performance, but it delighted the audience.

" 'E ought to be on the styge," said the Kid.

A party of sailors coming up the road from the wharves stopped to listen, and finally came inside. Kwong nodded his approval to me. Then another party of sailors came along and dropped in. Kwong beamed, and set up the drinks again for the Kid and myself.

"Fine, boys," he said, "keep it up."

The Kid turned upon him.

"Look 'ere, Kwong, what'll you give us to do this every night?"

Kwong shrugged his shoulders. His was the conservatism of the Chinaman, and he did not like to increase his expense account.

"I sye, Kwong, if you 'ad me for a manager and this lad for a pianist, we'd mike a bloody fortune for you. Someone to go onboard the ships and bring 'em 'ere, and somebody to entertain 'em when they come. What d'you sye? We'll do it if you'll pass the bleedin' 'at for us. Won't we, young feller?"

I nodded.

And Kwong's conservatism melted.

I banged the piano with new vigor, and the Kid began waylaying passers-by in the street, leading them in with promises of a riotous night. In they came—sailors on their way up the long street that led toward the red light district, stopping to quench their thirst, and remaining to sing and dance. Night gathered, and they came in greater numbers, until the long narrow grog-shop was filled with European seaman, mostly Cockneys. It was a big night for Kwong. He, with his half dozen Chinese bartenders, kept hurrying from table to table, dispensing liquor. The crowd had an insatiable thirst not only for drinks, but for American ragtime. No sooner would I finish one piece than someone demanded another.

"'E don't always 'it the right note," said the Kid, "but when 'e does, 'e 'its it awful 'ard."

They liked the noise. They all sang. Some sand the piece I was playing; others, having heard only a few notes and mistaken it for something else, were singing what they thought I was playing. But everybody sang. Some danced. One sailor jigged, his heavy shoes pounding upon the boards while his friends beat time upon the wooden tables with their glasses and beer bottles. A big, awkward Scandinavian stoker staggered up from one of the seats, grinning like an imbecile, staring at the dancer as though fascinated, and clumsily tried to imitate him. Others rose in pairs and began to fox trot. Demands were made that Kwong send out for women partners. He protested that they were not obtainable, and that the police might object, anyhow.

"T'ell with the police!" exclaimed somebody.

They grew noisier. Two men, arm in arm, began to gallop up and down the floor. Others whirled around and around. They crowded about me, naming their favorite selections. A gnarled, barrel-chested little man with a dent in his head which he claimed to have received in the Boer War, but which looked suspiciously as though it had been made by a boat hook, demanded that I play "There was never such another wench as sweet as Mary Anne." He was going to sing it. The others immediately drowned him out, but he stood beside the piano, bawling his sentiments into my ear in a throaty bass voice, meanwhile contorting his gorilla-like face into the most frightful grimaces. All were insistent in their demands, threatening to beat up those who wanted something else, or to pound me to a pulp if I did not comply.

The Kid was in his element. In his new nominal capacity as manager, he strutted belligerently about the place, ready to eject the unruly patrons, welcoming the newcomers, patting them on the back and assuring them that in the future this would be the liveliest resort east of Suez, bidding them come back on the morrow and succeeding nights, and contriving to sit down with them whenever any one was treating the crowd.

It was a noisy mob, but it spent money with the proverbial recklessness of the drunken sailor. The grimiest and sootiest spent most freely. They sent drinks to me until the whole top of the instrument was lined with them—glasses of all sizes, filled with every variety of intoxicant. They sent whatever they happened to be taking themselves—beer, whiskey-soda, gin, vermouth, cocktails, highballs, liqueurs—an array that would have been worth a fortune in the United States, and as fast as I could, I dumped the stuff beside an open window beside me.

And at length, someone started a fight. Two dancers had knocked over a table, upsetting several bottles of beer, and the incensed owners of the bottles had promptly retaliated by heaving them at the dancers. The Kid, as manager, rushed into the fray and began to remove his coat, very slowly and deliberately, with the air of one who is conscious of his own power and is in no hurry to kill the other fellow. The Kid, who professed to be an ex-pugilist, as he was an ex-everything-else, had considerable reputation in local beachcombing circles, and the habitués of Kwong's resort were said to avoid arguments with him, but these sailors were new to the locality and were not daunted by his confident deliberation. They were all rushing forward to fight him, when Kwong himself intervened.

"There, there, boys, let's not fight. It's time to close up, and the police will be along in a minute."

"T'ell wi' the police!"

But peace was finally established. The clock struck midnight, and Kwong, assisted by his Chinese bartenders, began to urge the reluctant patrons outside, cajoling them with promises of more fun the next night, and repeating many times his fear that the police would be around shortly. At length, when the door was shut behind the last staggering sailor, the bar resembled a wreck with overturned tables and broken glass, but Kwong grinned broadly as he looked at his cash drawer.

" 'Ow about it? Is it a steady job?" demanded the Kid.

And Kwong nodded. He sent out for more chop-suey, and gave us both a midnight supper, after which I spread my blanket upon the flat top of his bar, and stretched out for the night beside J. Clancy Scruggs, my new partner, otherwise known as "The Kid," or by the self-awarded title of "King of the Beachcombers." The passing of the hat had brought us twelve dollars.

CHAPTER TEN

IN A WATERFRONT GROG-SHOP

I

I became a permanent fixture at Kwong Bee's piano.

Kwong was not particular about his patrons, and his patrons were not particular about their music.

Each morning the Kid would visit the ships in the harbor to drum up trade. The Kid had the gift of gab, and he knew how to talk to sailors. If they went to the Maypole Bar, he told them, they were sure to be shortchanged; if they went to Robbie's Bar, they were likely to have their pockets picked; if they went to the Happy Tar or the Square Deal Saloon, well, he didn't like to talk about other people, but every one of the bartenders in both these resorts was afflicted with leprosy.

In fact, according to the Kid's convincing story, there was only one really decent place in town, and that was Kwong Bee's place—good liquor, big glasses, cheap prices, honest treatment, the best pianist east of Suez, and they could sing or dance all night and have as many fights as they wanted, just as though they were in their own homes.

He brought them down in droves—grease-covered oilers and soot-covered stokers, grimy deck hands and neatly dressed stewards, square-jawed bucko mates and grizzled old sea captains, men from the four-masters and men from the big liners. Night after night I pounded the piano for them. No sooner would I finish one tune than some rough-neck—perhaps some fellow beachcomber whose companionship I would have scorned a few months earlier—would command, "Give us another, Jack," and I'd keep on playing. Stewards of the type that had often waited upon me with an air of servility and had accepted the tips which I offered with condescension, came into the resort in far better clothes than I was wearing—in fact, in their conversation, they mentioned tailoring establishments in New York or London whose world-famous names I vaguely recalled—and after adding their own commands to "Give us another, Jack," would offer me a tip, also with an air of condescension.

It was not an elegant position, but I earned a living, and was not required to join the other beachcombers in begging for a livelihood.

II

Kwong's place had only one redeeming virtue; it was a laboratory for the study of odd characters.

There was the little barrel-chested sailor with the dent in his head, who was commonly known as "The Gorilla." He was exceedingly proud of his dent—and indeed it was quite an achievement for any man to continue alive with such a gash in his cranium—and he would go from table to table exhibiting it to new guests in a mute appeal for admiration and applause. Kwong was not pleased to have him loafing about the establishment, but never dared to throw him out. And occasionally "The Gorilla" did come in with money to spend across the bar. Where he obtained it, he never explained, but he had a suspicious habit of wandering out into the less-frequented streets at night and coming back with a roll of it.

Another constant habitué was the big, square-headed Swede who had recently been thrown off his sailing ship for boozing. He had a little cash left, and as long as it lasted he had no intention of seeking a new berth. If asked what he was doing in Singapore, he would reply, "Chust drinkin'." He was a great admirer of my low-brow type of ragtime, and if no one else would dance with him, he would seize protesting Kwong Bee, drag him upon the floor with the threat, "You don't dance with me and I punch you the nose in," and would force the apologetic Celestial to hop up and down with him. His great favorite was "The Merry Widow Waltz," but he never could distinguish it from any other piece, and while I was playing it for him, he was quite apt to stop me and threaten to punch my own nose in if I didn't give him "The Merry Widow." He swore that Caruso couldn't play ragtime half so well as I could, and was always ready to fight any one who argued the point; since he was the huskiest brute present, that settled my status as a musician.

Most of Kwong's regular patrons were beachcombers of this type. The upper-caste Englishmen of Singapore avoided the place, but there was one exception—Jimmie Brown.

Jimmie was a nice-looking, fresh-faced young man, of exceedingly innocent and harmless appearance—one of those easy-going, generous, likeable youths whose friends feel it incumbent upon them to advise and protect. So much had they annoyed him with their well-meant and much-needed attentions that he would run away from them and come down to Kwong's to cause them further worry by throwing his money away. He held a well-paid government position, and always came in waving a roll of bills in the air—a decidedly foolish thing to do in that part of town. And when his friends came rushing after him, whispering excitedly, "Shhh! Put that out of sight! Do you want to be murdered?" he would merely smirk in his silly-ass manner, and order drinks for every bum in the place.

The Kid, in his new capacity of "manager," always welcomed Jimmie, and would interpret his general order as meaning champagne. If Jimmie protested, he would say, "Well, didn't you ask for champagne? Sure, you did! You know you did!" Jimmie knew better, but he had come here for the specific purpose of being a fool, and smirking again, he would toss his roll to Kwong with instructions to let him know when more was needed. Once he did raise a small row, saying that a hundred dollars had disappeared from his pocket, but when his friends threatened to call the police, Jimmie smirked once more.

"S'all right. Forget it. What are you having to drink?"

"But it's not all right, Jimmie! They've robbed you! Don't be such a fool!"

"S'all right. I'm the fool. You're not the fool. What you having?"

The only possession about which Jimmie was particular was his sun helmet, and as soon as he had partaken of a few beverages, he would begin to accuse everyone about him of having stolen his hat.

"S'all wrong. Nobody ought to take my hat."

Thereupon some one would remind him that he was wearing it; he would remove it and examine it, smirk again, and order another round. But he was extremely generous, giving away or lending his possessions to any friend who might ask for them. When he informed us that one of his friends to whom he had lent an entire suit of clothes had not merely failed to return them but absolutely refused to do so, we were so indignant that the Kid and the Swede promptly seized upon the man, disrobed him, and sent him home in a rikisha through the crowded streets in his underwear.

That incident brought a police official into Kwong Bee's
"I say," he protested. "It's not the thing to do, you know. You can't send your guests 'ome nyked."

"But the bloody stiff 'ad Jimmie's clothes."

The official examined the clothes.

"Are these yours?" he demanded, turning to Jimmie.

Jimmie also examined them, and smirked his silly smirk.

"No; s'all right, officer; I've got my clothes on, I think. S'all right. What'll you have to drink?"

But the officer was not appeased.

"You're miking a bloody nuisance of this plyce," he warned us. "Any more of these funny jokes, and I'll close it up."

As he stumped indignantly out of the saloon, Jimmie nudged me and showed me a hundred dollars.

"S'all right; didn't lose the money. Just like to worry my friends. What are you having?"

But probably the strangest specimen that ever invaded Kwong's was a giant of a man who strolled in one afternoon. He was evidently a sailor, for there was an anchor tattooed upon one ham-like forearm and a mermaid upon the other. He was past middle age, and his legs were bowed, yet there was tremendous power in his drooping shoulders, and thickly matted hair upon his cavernous chest. His face, an enormous face, was seamed and scarred and wrinkled; it was a strong face, the face of a man who had suffered adversity, but there was a kindly humorous twinkle to his eyes.

"Have a whiskey-stengah?" someone invited.

He shook his massive head.

"No, boys, I'm going to give a party of my own here, and it'll be better than whiskey."

" 'E's goin' to buy champagne," whispered the Kid.

But the giant bought nothing. Instead, he began to tell funny stories of experiences in strange ports—in Djibuti, in Benguela, in Nigger

Bay. How that man could swear! Even the Swede and the Gorilla listened to him with admiration, and the other beachcombers began to form a circle about him.

Suddenly the stranger picked up the Kid's banjo and commenced to strum it. Then he sang. His voice was a mellow tenor, as sweet as the voice of an angel; coming from that rugged frame and that profane mouth, it struck one with amazement, like an unexpected punch in the jaw.

"Pull for the shore, sailor,
  Pull for the shore."

"Come on, boys, let's all sing it," he directed.

"I neffer heard dot chantey before," objected the Swede.

"Sing it anyhow, damn you," roared the giant, and we sang it. It seemed appropriate to that seafaring circle. So did "Throw out the life line." But there were sentiments in both these songs which were not commonly heard in Kwong Bee's, and we began to exchange questioning glances.

"My God!" exclaimed the Kid. "It's a bloody 'ymn!"

"Yes, boys, it's a bloody hymn, and now you're going to listen to a bloody sermon."

He began to preach. And how he swore! He had conviction, and he could quote the bible, but he could not express himself in the language of the pulpit. He preached on personal purity. He talked of the brothels, their evils and their dangers; he talked of drink, and its terrible results; he cussed the prostitutes and the purveyors of liquor, and he cussed his congregation, but he knew whereof he spoke. He laid bare his own soul, and spared not his own past. He held himself up as a horrible example.

"Now, boys, we'll close with the Lord's Prayer."

"I don't know it," someone protested.

"Then you'll learn it, damn you. Altogether!"

Some of us repeated it after him. Some hesitated, but after an accusing and threatening glance from the deep-set eyes of that amateur parson, everyone made a pretense by mumbling something.

When he had finished, he walked out and left us. He never returned. Presumably he was passing through on some ship. The Kid, as manager, was incensed about the visit.

"If 'e ever comes back," he announced, "I'll 'eave 'im through the bloody window."

It was perhaps fortunate for the Kid that he didn't come back.

III

The popularity of Kwong's place increased.

On some nights, of course, when there happened to be few ships in the harbor, or when the sailors had spent their money on the previous evening, receipts dropped abruptly. On such nights, the seamen would gather merely to sing and dance, rather expecting Kwong to return their last evening's generosity, by "setting 'em up" for the crowd, and in case he refused, showing a tendency to break up the furniture. But in general, the receipts increased, as did the contents of the hat which Kwong's assistants passed for my benefit whenever the boys were spending freely.

Not liking the atmosphere of the saloon as a place of residence, I found a room at a neighboring lodging house run by an Italian and his wife. They regarded me suspiciously, and demanded each day's board money in advance, but I was always able to pay it, and to turn over a few extra dollars for Kwong to lock in his safe.

I considered myself rather fortunate.

Singapore at the moment was overflowing with human derelicts. Some were professional beachcombers. Some were well-meaning but weak-willed sailors who had missed their ships. Others were discharged employees from the rubber estates or the tin mines, for with the slump in rubber and tin—the principal industries of the Malay States—many better-class Europeans were finding themselves stranded. Nowhere in my travels had I ever found a city so full of the down-and-out as was Singapore at that particular moment.

In Latin America, where I had drifted about for two years, it was quite easy to find employment. Many victims of the wanderlust knocked about from one place to another, finding jobs as mechanics and typists, and holding the jobs just long enough to earn the price of passage to another place. Firms there were accustomed to these tramps, and usually had positions for them. The Latin Americans, if they had sufficient education for these positions, were usually too proud to work, and the firms had to employ someone.

But in the Orient, conditions were entirely different. Chinamen filled the mechanical and clerical jobs, and the only employment for the average European was in some executive capacity, for which a drifting vagabond is not fitted. The whole scheme of the British was to maintain racial supremacy and prestige by employing white men only as managers. And these managers came out from home on contract. Even if there were a vacancy in some minor position, and a white man were willing to work for the same low wages as a Chinaman, the firm would not lower white prestige by employing him beside the Chinese.

Hence, in any British colony in the East, there were only two general classes of Europeans—those who were on top, and those who were on the bottom. There were many grades, of course, in the upper class, and officials receiving three thousand a year would not associate with those receiving fifteen hundred, for a British colony is unsurpassed for snobbery. But there was no place for the tramp who would support himself by temporary employment during his wanderings, unless he happened upon a vacancy at the top and was capable of filling it, and such vacancies were scarce. If one did not come out on contract, to join those who were on top, there was only one place for him, and that was on the bottom. Just previous to my arrival, two stranded Englishmen had tried to earn a living by opening a bootblack stand; the Chinamen in Singapore were delighted at the opportunity to have their shoes polished by white men and began to flock to the establishment; the British officials promptly closed the place, informing the two English bootblacks that shoes were not being shined by white men in the Orient.

It is the only social scheme that would work in the East. No one values "face" or appearance more than the Asiatic. The Indians are accustomed to a caste system; the Chinese, when they become wealthy, love display; all Orientals are impressed by pomp and ceremony. The Englishmen aim to hold their respect by dressing like millionaires, riding about in automobiles or rikishas, stopping at palatial hotels, traveling first-class on steamship or railroad, and their system works, as I had early discovered when I tried to travel steerage back in Indo-China and was immediately ridiculed by all the Asiatic steerage passengers. The East is the land of "swank." Men and women who are nobodies at home will come out on some government position, and immediately begin to assume the airs of royalty. It is the only thing for the white man to do in the British colonies.

But if they can not do this, they must go to the other extreme, and beg for a living from their more fortunate fellows. Since beachcombers do not keep up prestige, the British government tries to send them home as quickly as possible, securing berths for them on British ships, and when this fails, even giving them a free passage on a passenger steamer. But at the moment of my visit to Singapore, the beachcombers were accumulating faster than they could be sent home. And there were some, like the Kid, who did not wish to go home.

The Kid was a fair example of the professional bum.

He loved to recount his history for my benefit, commencing with his arrival in Singapore by being thrown off a steamer.

"You see, I didn't like the second mite. I 'and't 'im no 'arm, but 'e was always raggin' me. I'd 'ad a bottle of gin in me bunk, d'you understand—I was a bos'ain, d'you see—an' I 'ad a couple of drinks, d'you understand, and the mite come walkin' in, and 'e sez to me—'e was a young fellow, d'you see, and too young for 'is bleedin' job—and 'e sez, 'Bos'ain, you're drunk.' And I wasn't drunk, 'aving the bottle in me bunk, and it wasn't nobody's business but me own if I 'ad 'ad a few drinks. And I sez to the mite, 'Blast you, I ain't doone no 'arm to you, mite.' And 'e sez to me—'e was young, d'you see, and too inquisitive for 'is bleedin' job—'e sez, 'Bos'ain, d'you know what you're doing? You're talkin' insolence to your superior officer.' An 'e goes an' gets a pair of 'andcuffs, an' I sez to 'im, sez I, 'Mite, of you're a man, put aside 'em bloody 'andcuffs an' fight it out like a man.' Well, 'e puts aside the bloody 'andcuffs, an' I 'it 'im one crack in 'is bloody mouth, an' knocks 'im clean over the side of the bloody ship."

At this point, the tale was always subject to variations. When inspired by a large audience, the Kid would proceed in turn to be attacked by the first mate, the engineer, the second engineer, and other officers, whom in turn he would hit in the bloody mouth and knock over the side of the bloody ship, and when he was finally subdued, it was only by the combined efforts of the captain and the entire crew. The ending, however, was stereotyped:

"And so they dropped me 'ere on the beach, just because I 'ad a bottle of gin in me bunk, only I wasn't drunk, only 'aving 'ad if I 'ad been drunk, it wasn't nobody's business but me own, an' 'ere I was on the bloody beach without a bleedin' tuppence to me nime."

But the Kid had thrived at beachcombing, and now called himself "The King of the Bums." He had wheedled alms from every white man in town from the Governor and the Colonial Secretary down to passing tourists, and even from the wealthier Chinese. Twice, during the six years he had been here, the government had given him a ticket home, and on several occasions the government had boarded him at the public jail, but he was determined to remain in Singapore until the return of the Prince of Wales. The Prince was the only man, he said, who had passed through the town whom he had not succeeded in "bumming." When the Prince returned, the Kid was going to walk straight up to him and say:

"Look 'ere, Prince, they give me a ticket 'ome, but they don't give me no overcoat. Are you goin' to stand there with your pocket full of money and see a fellow Britisher go back to London without a bloomin' stitch on 'is back. "Ow'd you like to go back that way yourself?"

But even after bumming the Prince, the Kid was doubtful about going back. Life was easy in the Orient if you knew how to play the game, and had no pride. If I would stick with him, between my musical ability and his brains, we would conquer the world. But I was not keen about such a partnership. I meant to remain at Kwong Bee's just long enough to obtain the price of a passage to Java. Then I would start after that poet.

IV

Kwong, the proprietor, was a clever Chinaman.

He was a Macao, or Chinaman born in the Straits Settlements; he had gone to school, and spoke better English than nine-tenths of his patrons; although he was less than thirty years of age, he already owned an automobile and a handsome residence in another part of town; yet each morning at daybreak, he would be at the saloon, working in his shirtsleeves or his undershirt, and would still be on the job at midnight when a Sikh or Malay policeman dropped in to suggest that the closing hour had arrived.

The Kid, as the nominal manager, strutted importantly about the establishment; Kwong, the real manager, stood meekly and quietly behind the bar, raking in the cash.

The Kid, although he made a valuable runner and publicity man in the morning, when he was quite likely to be sober, became more or less of a nuisance in the evening when he was certain to be drunk. Then his old habits of bumming people would assert themselves, and even while he strutted from table to table, welcoming the guests, he could not check his impulse to borrow money from them, nor could he resist the temptation to sit down at any table where someone else was buying drinks for a group. The patrons began to resent his behavior, and not a night passed but someone threatened to "bash ís bleedin' fyce in!"

When so threatened, the Kid would rise in his impressive manner, and begin to remove his coat—very slowly and deliberately, after the fashion of a professional bruiser who is confident of his ability to obliterate his opponent with one wallop, and who wishes to give that opponent a fair chance to apologize or flee. He removed the coat with such extreme deliberation that I sometimes suspected him of procrastinating in order not to spare his opponent, but to spare himself. And Kwong always intervened, hastening forward with pacifistic meditation, slapping both contenders upon the back and assuring them that it was all a misunderstanding.

Kwong had the Chinaman's aversion to physical violence, especially since such violence might result in the wholesale destruction of his furniture, and a possible loss of his license. He himself was constantly insulted by his patrons, who summoned him with, "Come 'ere, you bloody Chink!" but he concealed his resentment. Although in his intelligence and his manners he was infinitely superior to those who called him, he would come forward at a little trot and obey their commands with cringing humility. But after the last patron had been cajoled out into the street at closing hour, Kwong would send out for a large bowl of chicken, rice, and vegetables, and while the Kid and I sat with him and his bartenders over this midnight supper, he would sometimes express his real sentiments:

"Yes, Foster, I do not like to be called 'bloody Chink.' But that is the way of the White Man. If I were to resent it, I should lose his trade. And so I let him talk to me as Master to Servant. But all of his money, Foster, is coming into my cash-drawer."

Kwong's was the way of all the Chinamen in Singapore.

"Listen, Foster, according to statistics, less than five hundred Chinese paid an income tax this year, and yet I know for a fact that at least a thousand own automobiles. Believe me, Foster, these White Men whom you see at the Raffles or the Europe are not the wealthy men of Singapore; the millionaires here are Chinese, but they keep their wealth hidden in the little Chinese banks almost hidden on side streets, and they do not make ostentatious display like the White Men. And many of these White Men here who live like millionaires, Foster, are posted at the clubs for not paying their dues or their gambling debts."

I read one day in a newspaper of a Chinaman who began life in the Straits Settlements as a rikisha coolie, and who, when he died in Kuala Lumpur, left a fortune of nearly three million pounds. A Chinese sugar king in Java was reputed to be worth seven million pounds. There were many wealthy Chinese of lesser degree in Singapore, and some did live ostentatiously in magnificent homes, but most of them lived simply and obscurely, continuing to work meekly like Kwong, allowing the Europeans to strut about and put on the "swank," and profiting from the lordly, overbearing White Man.

Only once in twelve months did the Chinese observe a holiday, and that was on the Chinese New Year, which fell during my sojourn in Singapore on January 28th.

It was then that I realized how important were the Chinese in the industrial and commercial life of Singapore. The entire city ceased to move. Shops were closed. Ships could not be loaded or coaled for want of stevedores. In my Italian lodging house, which advertised a "French chef," my Italian landlady, like many another European housewife, was forced to cook her own meals, for even the so-called French chef, who looked suspiciously like a Chinaman anyhow, was celebrating the holiday. Only the very poorest coolies were at work—the rikisha coolies—and they were scarcely numerous enough to carry the wealthier Chinamen on their rounds of visits and calls upon relatives and friends.

In every doorway firecrackers were exploded to frighten away the devils, and in every Chinese home incantations and incense were offered to the spirits of the departed. Even Kwong, with all his European education, rubbed honey upon the mouths of his kitchen gods, which go to Heaven at this season to render an account of the household's conduct; the honey was to sweeten the account, which, coming from Kwong's place, was sadly in need of sweetening.

Every Chinese home was decorated with strips of red cloth over the door, and with red placards upon the walls, bearing some Chinese inscription in black or gold lettering, perhaps the equivalent of "God bless our happy home." Everywhere was the flag of the Chinese republic—an artistic abomination of five horizontal stripes of red, yellow, blue, white, and black—much less distinctive than the ancient dragon.

The stores, although closed for business, were open for the entertainment of visitors. Passing them I caught glimpses of food and tea offered to fat, happy-looking Buddhas, of carved chairs of black wood inlaid with pearl and ivory, and covered with red and gold silken draperies, of tables laden with soda and liquors and fruits and nuts and other refreshments for the guests. The Chinese orchestras were hurrying from house to house, and all Singapore resounded with the shriek of fiddles and the clanging of gongs. Chinese women, who ordinarily were clothed in black pajamas, were now arrayed in gay pajamas of pink, blue, or green; their braided pigtails, usually so plain, were decorated with colored tinsel and elaborate ornaments set with many-hued pieces of glass that sparkled like the temple roofs of Bangkok. And everywhere were prosperous-looking Chinese merchants riding about in the largest and finest of automobiles.

New Year is the great season for collecting or paying debts, and for giving presents; the Chinese, usually economical, are then in an extremely generous mood, and the Kid, who never missed an opportunity to approach anyone in such a mood, came back to Kwong's upon the following day with fifty dollars in his pocket.

"S'easy if you know 'ow," he boasted. "A chink'll give you 'is socks if you know 'ow to talk to 'im."

All the other beachcombers crowded about him to demand the secret of such colossal success, and the Kid was not reticent about telling the story. He did not share the British national pride in keeping up white prestige, and he had gone begging to the palatial residence of the Honorable Eu Sing Tang, a wealthy Chinaman whose title came from an honorary position in the local government.

Hindu guards had stopped him at the gate, but the Kid had talked his way past them and into the private office of Eu. Inspired with unusual eloquence, he had pointed at the silken draperies of the apartment.

"Look at all them things!" he exclaimed.

Then he pointed at Eu himself.

"Look at your 'andsome, well-nourished body."

And finally he pointed to his own figure.

"And just look at me own skinny frame, and me unfed belly, and me ragged shirt. You're a Chinaman, Honorable, and you're a better man than I am, but you've made your fortune from Europeans, and I'm a

European. 'Ow about lending me a few dollars?"

The Honorable, like Kwong, spoke perfect English.

"Why don't you go to your own people?" he asked.

"Because, Honorable, I know that you Chinamen are the whitest men in Singapore."

That pleased the Honorable Eu Sing Tang. It flattered him, perhaps, to have a specimen of the lordly, overbearing race cringing before him. He called his servants, gave the Kid a bath in his own bathtub, presented him with a new suit of white linen, fed him and gave him a glass of whiskey, and finally thrust fifty dollars into his hand, and bowed him from the house.

"S'easy," concluded the Kid. "Just tell 'im 'e's the whitest man in Singapore. 'E's a yellow devil, but 'e likes it."

There was an immediate exodus of beachcombers from Kwong's. They raced for the home of Eu Sing Tang. The Gorilla won the race, and when the Hindu guards sought to stop him, he floored one with a ponderous swing to the jaw, and rushed straight into Eu's private study. What transpired there I could deduce later from the Gorilla's story:

Eu looked up from his books and his ledgers with an expression of surprise and annoyance, but the Gorilla plunged into a repetition of the Kid's plea.

"Look at them heathen things!"

"Look at your fat belly!"

"Look at me, with a hole in me head and nothin' in me own belly."

Eu gave him the bath and the change of clothing, the food and the drink, but did not offer him the fifty dollars.

"Look 'ere," protested the Gorilla, "ain't you goin' to give me no money? They said you was the whitest man in Singapore, but you're the yellowest——"

He could get no farther. Eu Sing Tang's servants seized him, removed the new clothes, threw him out into the street, and hurled his old breeches after him. He came raging back to Kwong's, accused the Kid of having deceived him, and gave the Kid a trouncing. The Kid, despite his many boasts, was no match for the little Gorilla, who dragged him out into the backyard where Kwong kept his empty bottles, and knocked him about the enclosure until it was a mess of broken glass.

Immediately three other bums, who had always wanted to lick the Kid, but had been overawed by the Kid's boasting, came rushing forward, demanding to be allowed a "go at the blighter." Kwong dissuaded them, and established peace by giving them all another drink, whereupon everyone assured him that he, and hot the Honorable Eu Sing Tang, was the whitest man in Singapore.

V

The Chinese were so numerous in Singapore that the Malays themselves seemed comparatively scarce. The Malays, like the Siamese, were an indolent tropical people, and preferred to dwell in the rural districts of the Peninsula rather than endure the strenuous competition of their more industrious invaders in the big cities.

Next to the Chinese and Malays, the Indians were the most numerous.

One old beggar used to spend his days on the sidewalk before Kwong Bee's. He would come in his bedraggled and tattered rags, and crouch upon his bare heels at the curb, expectorating into the gutter until he had formed a small pool. Then he would squat there for hours, staring at it, as though his own reflection provided material for philosophical meditation.

Kwong's place was situated in a section of town populated almost entirely by Tamils, or Klings, from southern India. They dressed sometimes in flowing white robes of thin material, sometimes in a loincloth; in neither case did the clothing conceal their repulsive animal-like bodies. Some tied their black hair in a knot at the back of the head; others let it fall in kinky array about the shoulders.

Most of these Tamils were drivers of ox carts. Their beasts of burden were carabaos, hump-backed cattle, white or tan in color. The horns of the beasts were fantastic, and no two of them seemed to have horns alike; some were short, some long, some curled forward, some curled backward, some outward, some in spirals, some stuck straight up. Frequently the horns themselves were not mates, one curling forward and one standing straight. And as though nature had not been sufficiently fantastic, the drivers had painted the horns various colors, blue and red, red and green, red and yellow, and had put little brass ornaments upon the points or strung coarse beads from horn to horn.

More imposing Indians were the Sikhs, big, black-bearded men from a more northerly clime, dressed in European clothing save for the turban wrapped around and around the head. Their skin was brown, but of fine texture; their noses were aquiline and their features those of a Caucasian; there was a natural dignity in their bearing which no White Man can duplicate. They were, as a rule, soldiers or guards or policemen, and no race was better fitted for these professions. Huge men and fighters, they were always cool and capable in managing the traffic. They took particular joy in making the Chinamen step lively, and although they were polite and courteous to Europeans, they were firmly insistent in the performance of their duties. Of all the policemen on earth, including the Irish cops in New York, I have never met any who inspired me immediately with more respect for their authority than these Sikhs whom the British have imported to police all their colonies in the East.

And there were many other species of Indians in Singapore, unidentifiable to the newcomer. They were mostly shopkeepers and money-changers. They squatted cross-legged in their booths sandwiched in among the more imposing European stores, slim brown men wearing the Mohammedan fez. Always polite, yet shrewd and intelligent, they figured exchanges in strange monies of which I had never heard, computing and counting so swiftly that I could follow neither their mental processes nor their moving fingers.

The Indians, like all Orientals, were great gamblers. It is said that one may walk into any Hindu Bazaar, offer to bet the proprietor any amount of money that it will rain tomorrow, or that it won't rain, and without a moment's hesitation, the Hindu will accept the proposition. In the neighborhood of Kwong's place, the Indian coolies, when not at work, would sit upon the sidewalk in strange groups—each caste by itself, so that one wore long robes, another loin cloths, another European clothes, while one group had shaven heads, another partially shaven heads, and another heads swathed in turbans—playing some native game, so fascinated by their gambling that as day faded into night they merely bent lower and lower until finally they lay flat upon the sidewalk, with faces close to the game, still playing.

But three times each day—at sun-up, midday, and sundown—there came, for the Mohammedans, a moment when they ceased whatever else they were doing, and kneeling upon their prayer rugs, prostrated themselves for several minutes. From the old tattered beggar to men in European garments, these Mohammedans observed the rites of their religion. I used to watch them with the respect which any man feels for the fellow who is not ashamed to pray in public, even though the religion be one of blood and lust. I understood the Indian least of any race in the Orient; there was always an unfathomable mystery behind his dark smoldering eyes; but I carried away a higher respect for the Indian than for any other Oriental.

VII

Weeks passed. The proceeds from the passing of my hat accumulated in Kwong's safe, until I had sufficient to carry me to Java. And just then I picked up a Singapore newspaper to read in the Personal Column:

"Mr. Enrico ———, the young Italian author who recently spent several weeks in Singapore, passed through the city yesterday with Mrs. ———, en route to Manila. The author has been sojourning for some time in Java, but is now returning to his newspaper work as correspondent for the *Messaggero*, of Rome."

I looked hastily through the shipping news. The poet's steamer had sailed that morning, and I had missed him. There was another boat for the Philippines two days later, but it was scheduled for Zamboanga, in the southern Philippines, via Borneo.

"Why don't you see the Swede?" inquired the Kid. "'E was telling this morning as 'ow 'e'd shipped on some boat—I think it was for Manila."

"Where is he now?"

"'E went to the Yoshiwark."

I leaped into a rikisha. The runner took me where he usually took Kwong's patrons when they left the place in the evening. He jogged through the dark streets of the deserted business section, across the bridge, along the waterfront where lights blazed from hotel porches on one side while on the other a hundred red and green lamps twinkled from a forest of masts outlined against the stars.

Then he turned abruptly into a narrow street lined with Chinese shops, illumined only by the dim light from the smoky booths. It was a crowded street, filled with Chinamen who paddled softly with a slap-slap-slap of cloth slippers; slant-eyed faces appeared out of the darkness, leering at me, and drifting back into the crowd; other rikishas loomed up before me, their runners and mine exchanging sharp cries of warning to avoid a collision, and then they faded away into the sea of humanity.

The dim booths were opium joints. I caught a glimpse of long wooden benches, of Chinamen curled beside a lamp, of other Chinamen lying upon their backs, a pipe still in the mouth, their eyes closed, their minds enveloped in dreams. At some of the doorsteps sat girls, black Tamil women with thin, sharp features, and a hopeless worn-out expression in their eyes; Malay girls, plump and chubby, but with pudgy faces that lacked the beauty of Malay faces in more respectable communities. And then Chinese brothels, more brilliantly lighted, with tiny mites of children in pink or blue silk pajamas sitting in a circle and smiling at the prospective buyers who surveyed them from the open doorways. The faces were so thickly enameled and the lips so brilliantly rouged that they seemed unreal, like tiny little dolls.

Leaping from my rikisha, I hurried from house to house, examining the crowd for a glimpse of the Swede. Chinese and Hindus, wandering from doorway to doorway, discussing the relative merits of the inmates with much laughter and comment that must have injured most brutally any pride or sensitiveness that the inmates retained, grinned at me and joked about me in their own languages. It was futile to inquire for the Swede; the loiterers spoke no English, and the Madames could say only, "Come inside." Some of the fat Madames seized me, and tried to drag me in, but their girls quickly averted their eyes or surveyed me with manifest loathing. If the white race has a sense of repulsion for the yellow, the yellow, with the exception of the tropical Malays and Siamese, reciprocates it tenfold.

My rikisha runner took me across Singapore's principal street, however, and into another district. This district was considered of higher class than the other, and was more familiar with the white men. Here were the Japanese houses, ornate structures with much latticework, the interior tastily decorated with flowers, mirrors, prettily carved woodwork, the ornaments few but always artistically arranged. The girls, in kimonos, sat upon little platforms, each girl busily engaged before a mirror in rearranging her elaborate coiffeur and repowdering her little snub nose. But the Japanese girls were not numerous; in years past, old-timers say, the entire Orient was filled with Japanese prostitutes, until the Japanese had much the same reputation as the French have in foreign cities elsewhere; but a few years ago the Japanese government through its consuls sent most of them home, presumably to avoid the further spread of Japanese reputation.

The Chinese places were better populated. There were gaudy booths in this section, with draperies of flaming red, and with many nicknacks before a most inappropriate statue of Buddha. The girls here, more accustomed to Europeans, would greet me with a flutter of beckoning hands that reminded me somehow of the flutter in a bird's nest when the parent arrives with food. It was a loathsome district. Runners and procurers followed me through the crowded streets, plucking at my arm, and speaking pigeon-English:

"Chinee girl no good. Me savvy plenty girl—Portugee girl, Russian girl, Malay girl."

And then in a little Chinese drinking place, with four bamboo chairs and a filthy table sandwiched in between the resorts, I found the Swede.

"No," he said, "dot boad don' go to Manila. Dot boad go to Java."

My rikisha carried me back toward Kwong's. When I passed the Raffles, the upper class European colony was dancing. At the wicker tables upon the wide veranda sat men and women in evening dress; an English orchestra was trying to play ragtime, and couples were dancing stiffly in the British fashion, seemingly with little enjoyment, as though merely performing a rite required by society. It was here, I reflected, that the poet had spent many delightful weeks at my expense—wherefore I was now the official pianist in Kwong Bee's saloon.

And then I arrived back at Kwong Bee's. About the doorway was the usual crowd of curious Hindus and Chinese, which gathered nightly to laugh at the antics of the European sailors inside. And along the curb waited forty rikisha-coolies, waiting—I also reflected—to carry Kwong's patrons back to the brothels I had just seen.

I was inclined to turn away, but some one saw me, and a dozen sailors rushed to seize me and carry me inside.

" úrrah! 'Ere 'é is!"

The place was crowded. A big P. and O. liner was in the harbor, and the Kid had succeeded in bringing the whole crew along, promising them music and entertainment. They were already unruly. A burly seaman had stripped off his shirt, revealing a wealth of blue tattooing, and was threatening to lick the Kid.

"Yuh told us there'd be music! I don't 'ear no music!"

They crowded about me, and I began to play. It was the noisiest night in the entire history of Kwong Bee's. Sixty lusty voices roared the songs, the songs I was playing, the songs they thought I ought to play, any songs at all. Men danced in pairs. One pair was trying to kick as high as possible. Another pair galloped around in circles. Two other pairs were having a pushing match. Twice, through collisions, I was knocked off the piano stool. Tables and chairs went over. There were several arguments, of which I caught brief snatches. The sailor with the tattooing was threatening to lick poor Jimmie Brown:

"You sye I took your bleedin' 'at, and you've got it on yuh bloody 'ead!"

The Kid was accusing one man of failing to pay for a bottle of beer, and was backing up the accusation by removing his coat. He removed it slowly, in his deliberate, impressive manner, unintentionally revealing a shirt beneath it which was already torn and tattered by many previous combats. The sailor with the tattooing, having forgotten Jimmie, was now trying to reach the Kid; he had no idea what the argument was about, but he wanted to hit somebody. A wild-eyed youth struggled through the crowd, and rested a sweat-dripping arm upon my shoulder, leaving greasy thumbprints all over my collar.

"You a Yankee? So'm I. We're two Yankee boys here together, and we're going to make every damned Lime-juicer stand up and sing 'The Star Spangled Banner!' You with me? We'll lick every Britisher in the house!"

Then there came a crash. Someone had thrown the Kid clean over the bar and against the shelves of bottles. The bottles rocked, toppled over, and fell with a succession of crashes. Liquor dripped from shelf to shelf—little red drops of port wine, green drops of crème de menthe. Someone, catching the spirit of the occasion, began to seize other bottles and hurl them against the ceiling. Everybody was pushing or pummeling his neighbor, all for no particular reason. Kwong, crying for them to stop, was seized by the neck, and came hurtling over the top of the piano, to fall in my lap, and send me to the floor.

Then the police came—a British officer and several Sikhs—and the fight stopped.

"What's all this bloody row?"

No one answered.

" 'Oo's the boss 'ere?"

The Kid strutted forward, trying to look important despite a rapidly closing eye and a cut lip.

"I'm the manager," he announced.

The officer turned to me.

" And 'oo the 'ell are you?"

"I'm the pianist."

"Well, you've mide a bloody nuisance of your managing and your piano. Get the 'ell out of 'ere." And to Kwong: "If you let those two beachcombers in 'ere again, I'll tike your license."

I was no longer a fixture at Kwong's piano.

CHAPTER ELEVEN

BY CARGO BOAT TO THE PHILIPPINES

I

Once again I set out in pursuit of the poet.

Although there was no steamer leaving immediately for Manila, I discovered that the *Kajang*, a blackened freighter with accommodations for a few passengers, was sailing for Borneo, whence it was possible that I might catch a second steamer to the Philippines.

Having drawn my savings from Kwong's cash drawer, washed my one suit of clothes, redeemed my already much-redeemed camera, and purchased a first-class ticket, I seated myself upon the small portion of the Kajang's deck which was not littered with derricks and donkey-engines and miscellaneous freight, and watched Singapore fade into the distance with its memories of vice, iniquity, and general rough-house. Once more, for the time being, I had become a respectable gentleman.

For three days the little steamer lumbered eastward through the China Sea. Each night a full moon, directly overhead, tinged the rising clouds with streaks of blazing silver, and tipped the horizon with a faint glow, but left the sea darkly mysterious save for the globes of phosphorescence which tossed and twinkled in its depths. There was something of romance about a cargo boat which the passenger liner can not supply—the romance of a darkened ship upon a darkened ocean, the romance of creaking spars illumined only by the reflection of a pair of red and green lamps, the romance of a weird snatch of Malayan chantey from the steerage passengers huddled upon the forward hatch, the romance of the pat-pat-pat of bare feet across the silent decks when the tolling bell called the Chinese crew to change the watch.

II

The other half dozen passengers were all Englishmen.

I shared a diminutive stateroom with the drummer from a Singapore wholesale house, a stout gentleman with florid complexion who might have posed for the original cartoon of John Bull.

He was the life of the party. As we first sailed out of Singapore harbor, he amused the others by pointing to the fading shoreline and remarking facetiously, "Oh I say, do you see that chappie over there with the diamond stick pin?" To which the others, after a moment of severe mental strain, would reply with similar jocularity, "Do you mean the beggar with the mosquito on his neck?" Then laughter would be affected by all—not hearty laughter prompted by enjoyment of the jest, but a formal sort of laughter prompted by an Englishman's desire to prove to everyone present that he has grasped the point of the witticism.

The drummer had several unalterable British ideas about Americans. He believed that all Yankees are extremely provincial, chew tobacco, talk nasally in a high-pitched key, and repeat such phrases as "I reckon" and "I swan." Whenever he addressed me, he first pretended to shift a chew to the southeast corner of his mouth; then he spoke through his nose in what he believed to be the typical American drawl, repeating these two phrases, and adding various improvisations of his own which he fancied to be American slang. In retaliation I was forced to plaster a fifty-cent piece in my eye and exclaim, "Ha!" or "Bah Jove!" after the manner of the musical comedy comedian whom most of us provincial Yankees imagine to represent the typical Englishman.

With one exception the other passengers proved surprisingly sociable, yet in their conversation there was none of the romance that one might expect on a steamer bound for Borneo. Instead of discussing wild animals or headhunters, they talked of sport and club life. The well-bred Englishman is not only extremely shy about mentioning his own personal adventures, but has a perfect horror of being considered sentimental or sensational, and in the farthest corners of the earth his conversation is the same as at home—about his sports and his club.

The one exception to the rule of sociability was an official of the British North Borneo Company. The inflated sense of importance which most Englishmen in the Orient show by their manners, if not by their speech, is most noticeable in officials. This gentleman remained aloof not only from myself but from the other English passengers—who were mostly rubber planters—and he descended from his stateroom behind the bridge only at mealtime, when he sat upon the right of the captain. He was a tall man, with the long, clean-cut face of the born executive, and with level gray eyes that examined everything critically and judicially—a cool, practical man, supremely self-assured. Once he did deign to speak to me, when he learned that I was writing.

"So you're an American journalist, are you? I suppose you'll spend half an hour in Sandaken and write a whole book about Borneo. That's what most American journalists do."

III

On the third day Borneo loomed upon the horizon.

Not a habitation nor a lighthouse nor another ship was to be seen—only an unending stretch of white beach beyond the blue water, and behind it a tangle of vines or a grove of trees that might have been the tropical relatives of fir or pine, backed by verdant mountains that rose into the fleecy clouds.

There was scarcely a ripple upon the sea, and the waves that rolled shoreward turned over so gently at the beach that they showed not a speck of foam. Not a tree moved. Not a living creature was to be seen. It was difficult to believe, as I sat there upon the deck and mopped the perspiration from my brow, that these forests were the haunt of rhinoceros, orangutans, poisonous reptiles, and head-hunting savages, or that this island—the second largest island in the world, with 190,000 square miles of wilderness more impenetrable and dangerous than any wilderness in darkest Africa—was any different from any other island.

Still, at each of the nondescript ports where we stopped, I watched for the Headhunters. According to all my conceptions of Borneo, they should have swarmed about the ship in whole fleets of war canoes, but they didn't. Nothing could have been more disappointing than Borneo, as seen from the seacoast, and the ports-Miri, Labuan, Jesselton, Kudat, and Sandaken—were but hodge-podges of tin roofs, thatched roofs, shingled roofs, and tiled roofs bordering the shore, and populated not by head-hunting Dyaks but by Malay fishermen and Chinese laborers imported by the English overseers, who had built their bungalows and clubs and golf courses and cricket grounds and race tracks, as Englishmen always do, and who, when questioned about native customs, would reply briefly in a manner of extreme boredom and promptly change the subject to sport.

The Dyaks are not the only savages in Borneo. There are several tribes of similar racial characteristics—Bajows, Muruts, Dusuns, and others—but the Dyaks, while in the minority, are the physical and mental superiors of their neighbors, as well as the least tamed. It is the Dyaks of whom one hears most and whom one expects to see in Borneo, but to see them, one must venture into the interior.

At Kudat I did see a party of Dusuns, who came into town in dugout canoes with bamboo outriggers. They were tiny little people. The men were clad in pajamas of drab blue, with a brilliant sash tied about the waist and a handkerchief twisted about the forehead; the women dressed in any old collection of rags, as though they had picked up whatever the Chinese or Malays had discarded. The women tied their greasy black hair into a knot but into a clumsy knot which allowed the hair to drag over the shoulders; their features were small and rather pretty, the nose being less flat than that of most Orientals, but their persons were as filthy as their garments and their mouths, like the mouths of most tropical Asiatics, were stained with splotches of betel juice.

I saw but three Dyaks. They were young boys, of magnificent physique, short in height, but symmetrically and gracefully developed, and absolutely naked save for a loincloth so small and tight that at first glance it was not noticeable. Their earlobes are distended to hold black wooden ornaments that resembled spools; their skin was golden brown; their bodies were tattooed from neck to ankle with blue tracings; their foreheads appeared to be partially shaved, but behind the forehead the hair rose in a high black pompadour which suggested the mane of a horse. They carried themselves with conscious pride—and strode past the Chinese and Malays with an air of superiority unsurpassed even by that of the English.

When I unslung my camera, they paused. It was their native superstition, I was later informed, that in taking their picture the photographer was stealing their souls for some diabolical purpose which they did not understand but which they did not welcome. The boys were too proud, however, to run away, and after pausing a moment in indecision, they strode manfully past my lens, their heads very erect, their eyes straight to the front as though they did not see me. It made a beautiful picture except for the fact that, as I later discovered, I had no film in the camera. And before I could insert a new roll and take a second snapshot, they had disappeared.

"You won't see them again," explained one of the local residents. "You really won't see anything along the coast. The Dyaks are not afraid of white men, but they don't care for civilization and seldom come out to the towns. Oh, yes, they still practice headhunting, if you go into the interior. The governments discourage that sort of thing, naturally, but the native women make them do it. A Dyak girl wouldn't think of marrying a man who couldn't supply a few heads to furnish the living room." He glanced hastily at his watch, as though fearful that I might ask for further information. "My word, it's cocktail time, and I'm due at the club. Hope you have a decent voyage. Cheerio."

And there's the English empire-builder! He seems so little interested in his exotic surroundings that I never cease to wonder why he ever comes out to strange lands, to places where he sweats and swelters, where mold gathers upon his clothing and mushrooms grow overnight upon his boots, where cockroaches eat the bindings from his books and ants get into anything that isn't kept in sealed tins, where mosquitoes force him to spend most of his time behind a net, where lizards crawl about the walls of his room, and snakes invade his privacy. And still he does come out to such places, the world's champion adventurer who never mentions his adventures, and having built his empire, he settles down at his club and talks cricket. Wherever he settles he builds a golf course; if there are two or more horses in the neighborhood he builds a race track; if there is one other Englishman within ten miles, he builds a club, and establishes a soda factory to supply the wherewithal for his whiskey-stengah.

Wherever you find him, he is every inch an Englishman. He may dress in khaki "shorts" during the day, but he is always cleanly shaved, and at night he always appears in white linen, and possibly in evening dress. He rules the natives with a tolerant regard for their customs and particularly for their religion, but he rules them firmly, and holds himself superiorly aloof. It is just this aloofness that makes him the world's greatest empire builder. He has such a supreme respect for himself that others have to respect him.

"I admire them," a Standard Oil man confided to me, "but they get my goat. They're so damned superior in manner, even to another white man. When I first came to the East, it amused me, but I've been here a good many years and I've met a lot of them, and that superiority of theres is getting under my skin. After you've lived constantly with them, and been treated by all of them as though you were an inferior creature, you sometimes get to feel almost as though you were. I can see how it impresses the natives with a sense of servility, and raises the British to the plane of little tin gods. The system has certainly worked."

Personally, I did not dislike the English, although I was constantly aware in the East of their patronizing attitude toward Americans, and not infrequently of an attitude that might be described as one of hostility. Particularly in Borneo there was a strong feeling against American writers. Major E. Alexander Powell had just published an article in *The Century Magazine* in which he charged that the British North Borneo Company, which rules the northern portion of the island, was exploiting the natives. Borneo, like the Malay Peninsula, is a political anomaly; in the southern part of the island are the Dutch possessions; then in the strip of British protected territory that fringes the western and northern coasts, there is the independent state of Sarawak, ruled by the famous White Rajah, James Vyner Brooke, whose English father became Rajah after assisting the natives in defeating neighboring tribes; above Sarawak is another independent native state known as the Sultanate of Brunei; and in the north is this British North Borneo, which originally belonged to the Sultan of Sulu, the Moro chieftain of the southern Philippines, who leases the territory to the British North Borneo Company for five hundred pesos a month. It is not a British colony, but a company-operated territory under British protection, the company having free rein in governing and commercializing the country as it sees fit. Powell had charged, among other things, that the BNB, as the company is commonly called, denies the natives an education; that it permits its soldiery, largely recruited from the wild tribes, to decapitate prisoners when suppressing an insurrection; that it imports hordes of Chinese coolies as laborers, and holds them through indenture and indebtedness after their contracts have expired, taking back from them through its licensed opium dens and gambling houses all that it pays them in wages, and sending them home finally as broken wrecks.

While no one seemed to point out any errors in Major Powell's statements, every British official I met was inclined to ridicule American writers in general, and after a few days in the capital at Sandaken, I was relieved when a second steamer carried me northward again toward the Philippines and out of the chilling atmosphere of an English colony. But as always, when I have tried to make generalizations about national characteristics, something happened to prove the generalizations entirely wrong, for just as I had embarked and decided to describe all Englishmen as snobbish and churlish and generally disagreeable, two young English passengers slapped me upon my back and asked if I wouldn't join them in a whiskey-stengah, a jovial British Major on diplomatic service came up and introduced himself, and the British captain sauntered down from the bridge to join the party. The Scotch engineer brought out his bagpipes, the Major produced a mouth organ, and all of us sang "Beautiful Ka-a-a-ty" in the most sociable good-fellowship imaginable.

IV

The *Selangor*, which picked me up in Sandanken, was even smaller than the *Kajang*, but its boards were spotless, its rails gleamed as though the crew consisted of Dutch housewives instead of Chinamen, and rumor suggested that its skipper would put in irons any passenger who dared to defile its decks by dropping a cigarette butt.

Captain Campbell prided himself both upon neatness and promptness, two qualities which one scarcely expects to find in such outlandish ports as those of Borneo. The steamer was scheduled to leave Sandaken at 5:30 p.m. At 5:29 the skipper strode from his cabin in spotless white uniform and signaled for visitors to go ashore. At $5:29^1/_2$ he signaled to haul in the gangplank. At $5:29^3/_4$ he signaled to cast loose the ropes. And at 5:30, on the second, the *Selangor* slid out from the wharf.

The voyage northward through the Sulu Sea was the most beautiful voyage imaginable. At night the full moon, now low upon the horizon, traced a wide golden path across the water, through which the tiny waves crept toward us in a succession of little black streaks. By day every white cloud in the bluest of skies was reflected in the bluest of seas. The breeze was soft, and laden with the indefinable scent of the tropics. We twisted through a maze of little islets, diminutive tropical atolls, each a perfect circle of palms framed with a rim of white coral. Nothing I had ever seen could equal in beauty that Sulu Sea, or these atolls of the southern Philippines. And much as I always despise the type of Yankee who boasts extravagantly about all things American, the sight of that fairyland sent a thrill of pride up my spine, and I felt like poking my fellow passengers in the ribs and telling them, "Do you see *that?* That belongs to *us!*"

At noon, a day out from Sandaken, the island of Jolo loomed before us, a massively mountainous island among the smaller atolls. Along the shore the coco-palms grew in riotous profusion; above them the dark green forests were interspersed with lighter patches that indicated clearings, and spirals of bluish smoke indicating that more clearings were being made. Clusters of thatched villages rose upon stilts at the water's edge, and the tiny old Spanish town, enclosed by a crumbling wall, lay in the foreground. It was all so quaint, and picturesque, that even the modern pier and the Chinese village could not destroy its attractiveness. Brown Moro children in outrigger canoes swarmed about the ship, calling to us in English to "Throw a penny, mister!" and we watched them dive after the coins, all of them going overboard as the penny flashed, their frog-like kicking visible in the clear water until they were far down in the depths where only the whitish soles of their feet could be seen.

We were scheduled to arrive at midday. The skipper came marching to the bridge just in time to signal "Stand by" to the engine room, timing his act so precisely that I suspected him of having waited in his cabin with an eye out of the porthole in order to achieve the effect. The clock in the dining salon indicated two minutes past twelve, but such was the faith of the Chinese steward in the punctuality of his captain that when he heard the anchor chain rattling, he immediately set the clock back to the hour.

All passengers hastened ashore with the Scotch engineer as a guide. Jolo was reputed to be the smallest walled city in the world. Years before the Spaniards first invaded these islands, this was the capital of the Sultan of Sulu, and from this stronghold the Moro pirates would sail in fleets of a hundred or two hundred galleys to raid the villages of the other Filipinos in search of slaves and loot. Even the Spaniards, although they built the walled town, seldom ventured beyond its walls, and never completely subjugated the pirates.

The Moros, who are of Malay origin, came to these islands from Borneo, bringing with them the Mohammedan religion which they still observe. They, of all the mixtures of peoples in the Philippines, resented most the fanatical efforts at conversion made by the Catholic Spaniards, and upon them the missionaries had no more effect than did the soldiers. Toward the Americans, who have lacked the fanaticism of the Spaniards, they have been somewhat less stubborn, but Jolo, even after the American occupation, was long a dangerous city for the white man, mainly because of the old Malay custom of running "amok."

This custom, locally known as "juramentado," has been found among all the Mohammedan Malays in varying degrees of frequency. Since the Mohammedan religion teaches that to die in slaying Christians is to ensure heavenly reward, the Moro who becomes disgruntled with life commits suicide in dramatic manner by first clipping his hair, shaving his eyebrows, paring the nails of his fingers and toes, girding up his loins, and then rushing into a crowded street with his bolo, to chop up the pedestrians until someone succeeds in chopping him.

Efficient policing in Jolo has done much to discourage this practice. To be disarmed by a cop, and formally executed, appeals less to the Moro sense of drama than to be slain in battle. Also, the American authorities have discovered that by burying a pig with the body of a man who had run amok they could inflict a most humiliating punishment upon the pig-loathing Mohammedan. Yet even today, according to one old-timer I met—a lean, lanky New Englander who had come to the islands as a soldier—the cry of "Juramentado!" would send inhabitants of Jolo scattering for shelter behind a barred door.

The Moros who thronged the city were strong, agile men, rather short, but well built. They were darker in complexion than most of the Malayan races; their hair was black and abundant; their eyes were small and keen. They dressed in skin-tight breeches that came to the ankles, and in little jackets that failed to meet in front. Nowhere in the whole colorful Orient had I seen such a blaze of color, for even the lowliest fishmonger in the marketplace was apt to be dressed in bright green trousers lined with silver buttons, and perhaps in a purple jacket, with a brilliant handkerchief tied in turban fashion about his head and a blazing scarlet sash about his waist. From each sash protruded the shining steel blade of a bolo, and there was something in the demeanor of these Moros which suggested that they might not hesitate long about using the weapon if a stranger provoked them.

When we had passed through the city to the wall, the old-timer stopped us.

"If you go outside the town," he said, "you go at your own risk."

"I have an automatic," objected the Major.

"Then don't go. A Moro can slice your head off before you can draw a gun—and if he sees the gun and wants it, he's more likely to do it."

I had planned to point out to my English companions the superiority of American rule in the Philippines to that of the British in Borneo, but this information put a slight damper upon my intentions. The walled city, however, while small, was very neat and orderly, and its streets and buildings were better than anything in Sandaken, but my companions were out to criticize. They laughed at the club, which, since Americans are less ardent club men than the English, was deserted. They ridiculed the absence of a race course or football field, and when we finally came to a baseball diamond where Filipino youths were playing the American national game in an idyllic setting of coco-palms, they were not impressed.

"It's rather odd," commented one of them, after watching the game for a few minutes. "Why is it that you Americans have never been able to learn cricket?"

V

At the club, the Scotch engineer ordered "Whuskey." He was a droll individual, that Scot, and having partaken of several more portions of "Whuskey," he suggested that we call on the Sultan.

In days past, when the Sultan of Sulu ruled with authority of life and death over the most warlike race in the East, he was a man of unquestioned power. Today, although the American government allows him to continue being Sultan, just as the French and British allow the local potentates in Indo-China and Malaya to continue being potentates, he is a comic opera figure and a butt for the humorous comments of visiting travel writers. It happens that His Majesty, Haji Mahomed

Jamalulhiram, is somewhat of a spendthrift and a waster. Once each month he goes across to Sandaken to receive the five hundred pesos which the British North Borneo Company pays him for the lease of its territory. The British meet him with a guard of honor, and escort him and his comic opera retinue to the hotel. Since the American government does not allow him to gamble at home, he remains in Borneo until he has lost his monthly five hundred pesos to the Chinese croupiers at Sandaken's government-licensed gambling houses, whereupon the British guard of honor lines up once more outside his hotel as a gentle hint that his welcome has expired and that he need not come back until another monthly payment falls due.

The Scot led the way to the royal palace. It was situated in the native quarter outside the city walls, a two-story barn-like structure of some color so drab that I failed to note it. Several barefooted flunkeys in bizarre Moro costumes of purple, blue, green, yellow, and crimson, each with a bolo in his sash, barred our entrance until an English-speaking Chinaman appeared. He proved to be the royal interpreter and he informed us that the Sultan was not at home.

"That's verra strange," mused the Scot, scratching his head. "I understood he'd be here to receive us. We'll leave our cards."

We all searched our pockets. Only one man could find a card. It contained his English address, one of those extremely long English addresses, somewhat like: "T.A. Gilbert, Limejuice Manor, Hydebank, Dumbledown Terrace, Jolly-well-on-the-Thames, London, W.C., England." It made a remarkable impression. Possibly the royal interpreter mistook the directions for titles, for he and the flunkeys all began to bow to us, and after a hurried conference inside the palace, the Chinaman reappeared with the information that while the Sultan was absent, the Sultan's niece was at home, and would be honored to receive us.

The Scot said that to see the Princess was an even greater honor than to see the Sultan. The Princess was unmarried, was reputed to have diamonds in her teeth, and since the Sultan had once paid Alice Roosevelt the compliment of proposing marriage, this would be an excellent opportunity for me, as an American citizen, to return the courtesy by asking for the hand of the Princess.

The attendants ushered us through the doorway, through a darkened basement, up a flight of rickety steps, halfway around the upper floor by way of a balcony that ran around the outside of the house, and into a reception hall. It was, to my surprise, a room neatly and tastily furnished, with nothing to suggest wealth nor the expected grotesquerie of a Sultan's palace. It was merely a parlor such as one might find in the middle-class dwelling of a Spanish-Filipino family.

For half an hour, while the Princess was dressing, the Chinaman entertained us. He was a big, raw-boned Celestial in thin silk pajamas, and he had the oriental habit of giggling rather nervously both at our remarks and at his own, with an ingratiating, half-apologetic little giggle. And in due course the Princess appeared. She was short and stout, about forty years of age, dressed in a costume that was half European and half Oriental, and with the promised diamonds sparkling from her teeth when she smiled. She seemed even more embarrassed than the Chinaman, advancing almost timidly to shake hands with each of us, but looking fixedly at the floor while she did so. Behind her came a troop of handmaidens, Moro girls in Malay sarongs, with a wealth of brass anklets jingling upon their bare legs.

After a moment of indecision, the Princess took a chair, and the rest of us, after glancing in similar indecision at one another, also sat down. The Princess, according to the interpreter, spoke very little English, but if we would deliver to him our message—

Now it was our turn to become embarrassed. What message had we for the Princess? The Scot fixed his eyes upon me with an expression that meant, "Speak up, Yank," but I pretended to be so engrossed in the beauty of the handmaidens that I did not notice. All of us shifted uneasily in our seats, and someone crossed and uncrossed his legs. Each of us cleared his throat encouragingly, but no one cared to become the spokesman. The Scot, who was responsible for the whole situation, calmly helped himself from the Sultan's box of cigars.

It was the Major who came to our rescue. He was a diplomat of first rank, that Major was.

"Ask the Princess if she is enjoying good health," he directed.

The interpreter began a five-minute consultation with Her Highness, in which both jabbered back and forth with much animation.

"Yes," he said. "She is very healthy."

There followed another uneasy pause.

"Ask her if the Sultan is enjoying good health."

Another five-minute conference. They jabbered back and forth again with increased animation.

"Yes."

It seemed that the entire family was doing remarkably well, and the Major assured the Princess that we were delighted to hear it. After this, conversation lagged again, and the interpreter suggested once more that he would be glad to explain our message to Her Highness. Apparently the royal audience was drawing to a close. The Princess was fanning herself nervously with a Spanish fan, and the rest of us were constantly clearing our throats and then lapsing into silence. Only the Scot, who seemed to like the Sultan's cigar, was enjoying the interview.

"Why—er—we have no message exactly," stammered the Major. "We—er—just wanted to present our respects to the Princess. Awfully jolly time, I assure you. Perfectly ripping call and all that. Tell her we've enjoyed it immensely."

The Scot stuck a handful of cigars in his pocket, and we all exited backwards, bowing majestically.

VI

We were walking toward the ship, when we met an American girl with a Moro husband. She was a slender, pretty young thing, scarcely out of her teens. The husband, also youthful, was a nice looking man in European clothes of college style, but he was manifestly an Asiatic.

I had seen other cases of the same kind. In a Sunday newspaper supplement at home there had been the pictures of a Chinaman and his American bride, with the bride's statement that if any girl wanted a really nice hubby, she should be sure to pick out a Chinaman. But I had seen the two of them later in Asia, where the yellow race was ostracizing them as completely as the white. I had met many of the half-caste offspring of such unions, outcasts from both races. The East is East and the West is West, and if the twain ever do meet, it is a sorry day for both, and a sorrier day for the offspring.

"That pair was married at college in America," explained the old-timer, indicating the American girl and her Moro husband. "I suppose he told her she'd be a Princess out here, for he really is related to the Sultan. She thought she'd have pearls, and sit on a throne, and be worshiped with all sorts of pomp and splendor. But you saw the Sultan's palace, and you can guess the kind of palace he's taken her to. It might be fit to keep horses in, but not good horses. Serves her right, but I pity her. She's just arrived, and thinks it's romantic. She hasn't learned yet that he already has a native harem."

VII

Through the moonlight tropic night the *Selangor* steamed northward amid another fairyland of atolls. In Borneo, which was operated by a company for profit and not for progress, scarcely a lighthouse had graced the dangerous coast; here in the Philippines, which was operated by a government as a philanthropic hobby, a light gleamed from every rock.

I was entering the Philippines through the back door, but it was the most attractive entrance, for Zamboanga, where the *Selangor* dropped me the following morning, was the garden spot of the entire Archipelago, if not of the entire Orient. It was a quiet little city in a beautiful setting of coconut palms. Its piers and its streets were lined with potted ferns; parks and plazas were to be found at every crossing, and among the flowering shrubs were coral-encrusted fountains that sparkled in the sunlight. At night the piers and streets were illumined with clusters of softly glowing electric bulbs, and the fountains played above colored lights artistically hidden among the corals. It was altogether so charming that one of my English fellow passengers admitted, although a trifle reluctantly, that the Yanks *had* made a rather decent sort of place here after all.

The influence of the American occupation was everywhere apparent. Upon the hotel sidewalk sat a half a dozen old-timers—sun-browned veterans of the campaign against Aguinaldo, who had remained in the islands as merchants and tradesmen—tilting their chairs at a comfortable angle, chewing tobacco and drawling nasally in the manner which the Britisher considers typical of all Americans. In the British colonies every white man, except the beachcomber, wears faultless white linen; these old-timers, with American democracy and love of comfort, sat there in shirtsleeves without collars. And after surveying me and deciding that in spite of my British sun helmet I was one of them, they all nodded genially and said "Howdy!"

After so many months among Englishmen, such informality was almost disconcerting. The Englishman is never glad to meet you until you've proved that you're quite all right; the Yankee is glad to meet you until you've proved that you're not all right. A hotel clerk reached out the "glad hand," and introduced me to a young man who in turn introduced me at the club, and within half an hour after landing I knew more people than I had met in half a year in the British Orient. The incoming English passengers were similarly welcomed, and after they had recovered from their shocked surprise and convinced themselves that the welcome was not some species of Yankee bluff concealing a Yankee dollar-chasing scheme, one of them made the further admission that Americans really were not as bad as they seemed.

VIII

I might have spent an enjoyable twenty or thirty years in such a place as Zamboanga, but the poet had to be pursued while my new funds lasted, and after a couple of days an inter-island steamer—an aged relic of the Spanish days—carried me northward toward Manila, rambling upon the way among the many strange islands that comprise the Philippine Archipelago.

We passed big islands and little islands, mountainous islands and flat islands, wooded islands and almost barren islands. On some of them the sun was shining, on some the rain was falling, on some the vegetation was luxuriant with moisture, on some the trees had withered from drought. The stay-at-home who merely reads about the Philippines can scarcely comprehend the diversity of scenery, and climate, and people, and languages, which exists in these Pacific possessions of ours. There are 7083 islands, 114,400 square miles of territory, 10,350,640 inhabitants, and the dialects spoken are estimated or computed by different authorities to number from 35 to 51. In general, for purposes of classification, the people are divided into Christian races and non-Christian races, sometimes described by old-timers as Pagans and Filipinos, but each division has its subdivisions, and many of the subdivisions have their sub-subdivisions. Even the Filipinos, or Christianized natives, while all of Malayan origin and more or less similar in appearance—with small stature, slender frame, brownish-yellow skin, and oriental features—are separated by language into Tagalogs, Bicols, Ilocanos, Pangasinanes, Pampangans, and Cagayanes. The Pagans are separated into their subdivisions not only by language, but by religion and customs, and even by race, for among these peoples with a preponderance of Malayan ancestry are to be found also the Negritos, the original settlers of these and other south sea islands and also of the southern Asiatic mainland—little dwarf-like natives with flat noses, kinky hair, thick lips, big feet, and black skin, miniature stragglers from the black race. Intermarriage has added the Spanish-mestizo and the Chinese-mestizo. And while the main body of Filipinos is becoming slowly fused through the Spanish religion, the American education, and the English language, there still remain large Pagan sects—notably the formerly head-hunting Igorotes of the north and the Mohammedan Moros of the south—who still have little in common with their neighbors.

IX

The approach to Manila was less attractive than the approach to Zamboanga. There was the rugged Gibraltar-like mountain at the entrance to Manila Bay, the fortress which guards the entrance, the wide stretch of Manila Bay itself, the towering skeletons of the wireless stations at Cavite, a huge pall of smoke hovering over a dusty city, and the steamer docked in the brown Pasig River beside an aged Spanish fortress.

Manila might be described as Spanish-Asiatic-American.

On the south bank of the Pasig, the original Spanish city has been changed but little by the American occupation, save that trolley cars clang though its narrow streets. Where once was a moat there is now a golf course, but the walls and battlements still stand, and within them one finds two-story Moorish houses with overhanging balconies of carved wood. One finds also the two-foot-wide sidewalks which characterize the old Spanish cities of Mexico and Peru, and which always suggests to my mind that the Spaniards who built them must have been pretty thin themselves after their long voyages of conquest. But the most striking reminder of Spanish rule, not only in the walled city but elsewhere in Manila, is the great number of Catholic churches. Wrinkled old women sell candles upon the age-cracked pavements before them; Filipino *señoritas* pause at the doorstep to adjust a Spanish lace mantilla over their dark hair before they enter; religious processions march the streets on *fiesta* days with images of the Virgin; and at all hours of the day or night the bells are rung, not softly and sweetly like the bells of Buddhist temples, but loudly, rapidly, aggressively, imperatively, until one suspects them to be operated by trap-drummers specially engaged from a jazz orchestra.

Upon the sidewalks the native Tagalogs rubbed shoulders with Spaniards and Chinamen and with American sailors, soldiers and civilians. Among the Filipinos, however, there was none of the vivid color found among the Moros. The upper classes copied European fashions, exhibiting a truly Spanish pride in the neatness of their white linen. Among the lower classes, a shirt and a pair of trousers constituted the favorite male costume, but the women dressed in picturesque native garments consisting of a shirt-waist with puffy collar and sleeves of delicate lace, and a skirt which nearly dragged upon the ground but which was pulled up at one corner to show the end of a lace petticoat. They were rather petite, these Filipino girls, small but very shapely, and graceful.

Despite the restriction upon the immigration of Chinese, old John J. Chinaman was noticeably among those present. Upon the north bank of the Pasig, he had his own community. While John may always be found in the farthest outpost of civilization, he is essentially a gregarious creature, and swarms in every Oriental city. The American health authorities had not allowed him to surround his community with the filth and vileness which he seems to love, but he had his typical Chinese stores, block after block of them, narrow booths that contained an amazing stock of silks and dry goods. And despite the Filipino antagonism to the Chinese, Filipino girls had married John, as the native women marry him everywhere else, not because of his blandishment so much as because of his reputation as a worker and provider, and John had left his stamp upon Manila in the shape of a horde of slant-eyed half-breeds exceeded in number only by the Spanish mestizos.

But the American influence was not lacking. The main business streets were lined with big stone banks and shops and innumerable American bars with patriotic names, for the Philippines are not affected by Volsteadism and are wet enough to make up for the dryness of half a dozen States. There were American restaurants placarded with such announcements as "Sugar Cured Virginia Ham", "Boston Baked Beans", and "Roast Maryland Turkey." Filipino orchestras, excellent orchestras of mandolins and guitars, were playing American ragtime in fine jazzy style, and the toddle which had just reached Manila had been accepted with such acclaim by the Filipinos that the waiters fairly hopped up and down while they served dinner. Out at the Ball Park, Filipino nines regularly worsted the teams from the American regiments, and in the boxing arena the native sons were regularly knocking out Australian lightweights. While the majority of the Filipinos, notably the upper-class mestizos, still spoke Spanish by preference, the younger generation was speaking English.

X

What impressed me most in Manila, however, was the democratic relationship between Americans and natives.

In the British colonies, an Englishman would give but a curt order to his waiter; in the Philippines, the American was inclined to drop into his seat with a friendly greeting of "Hello, Juan, how's every little thing today?"

As a result, the Filipino had little of that respect for the Americans which other Asiatics had for their European rulers. The American is not designed by nature to command native respect. If his manners are not too easy and familiar, they are too brusque. He lacks that superior aloofness which makes the Englishman a little tin god. In the very beginning of White Rule in the Archipelago, the Spaniard descended to the level of the conquered by cohabitating extensively with the native women, but he did instill into the Filipino something of his own politeness and courtesy and respect for the upper classes. As a result of the American occupation, the Filipino is gradually losing these qualities.

The Filipino is not an unlikable individual. He is lazy, of course, like most other dwellers in the tropics, and his favorite occupation in Manila seemed to be that of driving a dilapidated hack, which enabled him to sit and wiggle his bare toes and watch a horse do the work. But like most lazy people, he is cheerful and contented, good-natured and friendly. Some American residents disliked him, described him as a "thief," referred to him habitually as a "skunk," and treated him with contempt, but in general they liked him, and treated him with friendliness. This democracy was something which the Filipino of the coolie class could not quite appreciate, any more than the Filipinos as a whole appreciate the unusual magnanimity and philanthropy with which our government is ruling the islands.

In the European colonies no Yellow Man was ever permitted to hold office above a White Man; in the Philippines American lawyers were pleading cases before Filipino judges, and American patrolmen were serving under Filipino police captains. The American government was educating the Filipinos for Independence by placing Filipinos in office wherever possible. Except for the Governor General and Lieutenant Governor and the heads of educational, scientific, and technical bureaus, the officials were natives. And the Filipinos, instead of thanking the American government for a kindly treatment which they would have received from no other government in the world, took it as their due. When, during my stay in Manila, an American was appointed Chief of Police, the Filipino press was loud in its indignation at what it considered an abuse of Filipino rights.

They clamored for complete Independence. Every Filipino with whom I talked—and I talked with lawyers, schoolteachers, shopkeepers, waiters, and hack drivers—wanted independence. The only exceptions were the Moros, who had never liked the other Filipinos, and whose difference of religion made their attitude comparable to a second Ulster question. Having come to the Islands with the typical American belief that only the politicians were clamoring for Independence, I was surprised to find the sentiment so general.

"Your belief was both right and wrong," explained an American newspaper man whom I met in Manila. "They all want Independence, but it was the politician who told them to want it. Very few of those who want it have the least idea what it is. They think it means freedom from taxes. Now you may also have the belief, like most other Americans, that the United States is paying for the development of these Islands, but except for the purchase of the Islands from Sapin and the cost of supporting our army and navy here—which isn't any greater than the cost of supporting them elsewhere—we haven't spent anything to speak of; the Philippines are self-supporting, although they pay us no dividends. Now these Filipinos like the development, but they don't like taxes. When we build a new post office or a new road, the native politician goes to his constituents, and says, "See what I've done for you!" but when the tax collector comes around to collect for the new post office or the new road, the politician says to his constituents, "See what the Americans are doing to you!" Most of these natives have an idea that the tax money goes into the United States Treasury; if they could only have Independence, there will be no more taxes, and they can all quit work and sit in the shade of a coconut tree and tickle a guitar and watch the wife take in washing. And those who do know what Independence really means are the intelligent fellows who expect to boss the other fellows. Their aspiration is the natural aspiration of any race; no race likes to be bossed by another race; but mighty few of them know what they're cheering for."

The Americans with whom I talked in the Islands were opposed to Independence, and agreed with the Wood-Forbes report in their opinion that the Filipinos were by no means ready at present for self-government.

"Wood and Forbes knew what they were talking about," said an American ex-judge in Zamboanga. "The Filipino politicians tried to show them the best side of conditions, but they went into every nook and corner of the Islands and couldn't be fooled. I was with General Wood, for example, when he visited Melita, over on the island of Davao. We were sitting on a veranda there when along came a young Filipino, followed by a whole crowd of other natives. The young fellow started a speech for Independence; it was in excellent English and it was a good speech, and at appropriate moments the other natives would cheer. But Wood knew perfectly well that half of those natives couldn't understand a word of the speech, and he just called the speaker to him. 'Young man,' he said, 'your address is splendid, but I wish you'd tell your friend behind that coconut palm to stop signaling to the others when it's time to cheer.' And that's the whole situation; all the Filipinos are cheering for Independence, but somebody is telling them when to cheer."

The Americans in the Philippines who oppose Independence have their own personal interests, of course, and most of them admit it.

"If it were not for these interests," said one man, "I'd say to turn them loose and let them go to smash if they want to. They only half appreciate what we're doing for them. We as a nation get nothing from these islands except a naval base in the Pacific and the self-satisfaction of feeling that we've played the part of good Samaritans. But we who live here came over as soldiers and fought the Spaniards; then we settled down and invested our money in business; we have a right to expect that the United States will not leave us here under a native government until the natives can run a good government.

"And they are not ready to run a good government. If they were all like Osmeña and Quezon and the rest of the leaders you meet in Manila, it would be different. But there are some who are not even completely civilized. Look at this morning's paper. Here's an Ifugao who became the father of twins; he didn't want twins, and so he buried one of them; when the police arrested him he was indignant; he hadn't known that there was anything wrong in his act. And some time ago, a Moro tribe killed an old maid; it hadn't rained in their village for several months, and they thought the gods were angry because this woman wasn't married, so they took her out and killed her with appropriate ceremonies. The Chief was mad as blazes when we arrested him; it seems that it had rained immediately after they killed her, and that proved that they were right. Now, just as horrible crimes happen in other countries, even in the United States, but here's the point. Men who commit such crimes at home know that they're committing crimes, but there are still people in these islands who don't know that such acts are wrong.

"The Filipinos who are civilized are improvident. I'm not afraid of unfair treatment under a Filipino government; I've always received a pretty square deal from Filipino officials. But no matter what wages you pay a Filipino, he's always in debt. He spends it on dress or gambling or cockfighting just as soon as he gets it. Turn the Islands loose, and the government will be in debt in no time. Japan would own them in less than ten years; the Japanese bankers and their merchants would be down here, smirking their oily smirks and rubbing their hands together and offering loans, and they'd soon own the islands without raising a sword or landing an army. If we were to give the Philippines their Independence with an American protectorate, we wouldn't be able to keep them out of trouble, but we'd be called upon to come to their rescue as soon as they got into trouble."

I ran across two American residents who disagreed with these opinions.

"We've promised them Independence," said the first, "and we can't go back on our word. We residents in the Islands have known *that* from the beginning. If any American here believes that Independence means a business panic, he's had plenty of time to move elsewhere."

"I'm heartily in favor of Independence," said the second. "The Filipinos are as enlightened as the natives in many of the Central American republics. And if the Filipino government is as inefficient and as corruptible as some of those Spanish-American governments, I've figured out a scheme that will make me a millionaire inside of three years."

But the general opinion was something like this:

"We've started something here, and it's up to us to finish it. We're preparing the Filipinos to run a good republic. We may be forcing kindness on a man who doesn't fully appreciate it, but since we've started this thing, let's make a good job of it, and not turn them loose until we're sure that they'll run a good republic."

Personally, I'd like to suggest that having trained the Filipinos for Independence, we make a really good job of it by training the Esquimaux to run a good independent republic in northern Alaska, and then to do ourselves proud, that we buy Africa, Tibet, and a slice of the Gobi desert and do the same thing there.

"You Americans are the most ridiculously sentimental people in the world about your Philippines," an Englishman once told me. "You think the Filipino is your little brown brother. He's an Asiatic. An Asiatic doesn't understand kindness. You send your missionaries to China, and the average Chinaman thinks they're secret agents who are trying to get control of his country. It doesn't pay. If these islands belonged to the British, we'd make a profit from them; if the Filipinos wouldn't work, we'd import Chinamen. And we wouldn't tolerate impudence either!"

And still, I like the Filipino. I think also that while he respects us less, he probably likes us a little more than the natives of the European colonies like their rulers. Furthermore, the day is approaching when the White Race will cease to dominate the world, and will be forced to treat the Yellow Man as his equal. When that day comes, I wonder whether our record in the Philippines will not stand out as some of the decent chapters in this rapidly ending era of White Supremacy?

CHAPTER TWELVE

A TOURIST IN JAPAN

I

In Manila I found no trace of the poet.

Evidently he had not disembarked in the Philippines, but had continued to China or Japan. As I had exhausted the funds saved at Kwong Bee's resort, it appeared that I must bring my narrative to a thrilling conclusion by swimming northward from port to port through shark-infested waters to capture him in the final chapter.

I did nothing of the kind. A much-forwarded letter overtook me in Manila, bringing a check from a magazine editor at home. It was not a fortune, but it raised me temporarily to the status of a tourist, and I completely ruined the thrilling conclusion by embarking in ordinary passenger style for Yokohama. It seemed useless to hunt that poet throughout all the main cities of the Orient, but such was my intention. I was determined to catch him in the last chapter.

II

My steamer was a Japanese steamer, and most of my fellow passengers were Japanese.

They were friendly, but very formal. They introduced themselves to one another with much ceremony. First they smiled. Then they bowed several times. Their eyes narrowed to a pair of tiny slits above the prominent cheekbones, and their lips drew back to display scrupulously white teeth. They bowed with their feet together, their hands upon their knees, their bodies folding stiffly as though consisting of two sections joined by hinges.

At the dinner table, all of them proved to be proficient in English, and each showed his friendliness by asking the same questions:

"Do you go to Japan?"

"Ah, I see. Do you go for business?"

"Ah, I see. Is this the first time you go to Japan? I hope you will like Japan."

Their extreme courtesy, and stereotyped formality, made it impossible for us to converse with genuine candor. As with every other Oriental I had met, I had the feeling that there was much behind their mask-like faces which they would not share with a White Man. When I asked questions, I received only the answers which they knew would please me. Questions regarding their opinions of America, or their ideas on international relations, which would have brought from any Englishman a frankly outspoken criticism, seemed to embarrass them, and they replied with evasive flattery. When I asked whether they, who had been obliged to learn English when they came to an American possession, did not resent the fact that so few Americans made any attempt to learn Japanese when they came to Japan, they merely shrugged their shoulders and smiled:

"Japan is little country; America is very big country."

It sounded almost unpatriotic on their part, but it was merely oriental courtesy, which prescribes that one must belittle himself and flatter those to whom he speaks. Their manners contrasted noticeably with those of the American salesman beside me. He was the type of superpatriot who constantly tells all foreigners about the superiority of the United States. Even when the rice was served, he explained to the Japanese in condescending manner that the Americans had learned to eat it with butter and sugar instead of curry, and urged them to try to eat it in the American style, as though the Orientals had not already had sufficient experience with a rice diet to know how they preferred it. To his long-winded account of the life of George Washington, and his many boasts about American progressiveness, they all listened politely, even when he told them what America would do to Japan in case of war. No one offered an argument, but each seemed to be making quiet mental reservations.

In reality, no one is more patriotic than the Japanese, whose Emperor is his God and whose first duty is to the Empire, but the Oriental does not quarrel when nothing is to be gained thereby. If the White Man chooses to strut and brag, the Yellow Man merely smiles inwardly, confident of his own superiority as is the White Man, but more polite.

III

Early one morning the steamer crept into the harbor of Yokohama. Through the mist the sun came up like a great red ball, like the emblem upon the Japanese flag. A vague outline of low hills appeared, topped by the snow-crowned peak of Fujiyama, the snow shining like silver, the base of the mountain hidden by clouds so that the blazing peak seemed suspended in the sky.

Out of the fog that hung thickly over the water loomed the bulky figures of clumsy junks, their brown sails cut in peculiar patterns and hanging at peculiar angles, each sail lined with tiny wooden ribs, like the latticework upon a Japanese paper lantern. But everywhere in the changing Japanese Empire one finds a mingling of the ancient and the modern, and among these junks loomed the bulkier figures of many big steamers, while a chugging launch came out to meet us, bringing a score of newspaper reporters whose picturesque Japanese kimonos were offset by brown derby hats. Merchants came on board, and spread out their wares of silk, ivory, tortoise-shell, and porcelain upon the deck, smiling at us and begging our patronage with a coaxing politeness for which the Japanese merchant is unexcelled, and so irresistible was his bland, persuasive smile that all the American tourists promptly filled their trunks and suitcases with souvenirs which, like most Japanese products, were destined to fall to pieces before they could be carried home.

The first glimpse of Yokohama showed the same mixture of the Oriental and the Occidental as did the harbor. The steamer moved alongside a big stone wharf surmounted by huge sheds of corrugated iron, which made an absurd setting for the kimono-clad Japanese who peopled it. Several hundred rikishas were awaiting the passengers, the runners dressed in skin-tight blue pants and loose blue-and-white coats—a grotesque, goblin-like costume. If I had taken an airship to the Moon, I should expect to be met by a reception committee of just such creatures.

They swarmed about me, bowing and smiling in their irresistible fashion, most of them speaking English, and although I had firmly intended to walk on foot, I presently found myself inside on of their man-power carriages.

The runner loped through Occidentalized streets lined with red brick office buildings that bore the names of English and American firms, turned a corner, crossed a dirty canal filled with crude wooden rafts and lined with drying fishnets, and plunged into the Japanese section. So sudden and complete was the transformation that it was bewildering. Impressions came too rapidly to be remembered—impressions of tiny shops, strange wares, strange people, odd customs, mixtures of Japanese lettering with occasional signs in English—in quaint English, wherein "Butchery" indicated a butcher shop, or "Headcutter" indicated a barber shop, and a cannery was labeled "The Kitsutani and Company, every canned foods"—a vision or series of visions of kimonos and derbies, of elaborate feminine coiffeurs, a mixture of strange sights, strange noises, and strange smells.

Yokohama, like all Japanese cities, stunk to the Heavens, for in this land of economy sewers are unknown, and manure of every kind is saved and carried from the homes in little carts for use upon the rice fields, the "honey wagons," as the carts are called by European residents, polluting the atmosphere on their constant journeyings through the streets. A newcomer cannot but wonder how the Japanese, who are so clean personally and so esthetic in their tastes, can tolerate the stench which characterizes the neatest and prettiest of their streets and homes.

For the homes which lined these evil-smelling lanes were spic-and-span. They were tiny little homes, entirely open to the gaze of passers-by. Along the sidewalk were the lines of clogs and shoes belonging to the inmates, religiously removed when their owners entered the dwellings. The matting upon the floors was spotlessly white. One felt that he was gazing into toy houses, inhabited by toy dolls. The girls, their faces immobile, their hair coiffeured in formal, artificial style, resembled waxen figures. The men, usually a merchant and his customer, seated upon pillows with their feet doubled under them, bargaining ceremoniously across a table that rose only a foot above the floor, seemed but part of the tableau. Everyone sat upon the floor. One girl was reading, her book flat upon the matting, her body bent over it in a position of which no European would be capable, yet she seemed perfectly comfortable. Seeing these people at home, one understood why it was no effort for them to bow themselves into right angles, and why they walked habitually with a looseness of the knees, the legs seeming to sag slightly at each step.

Everything was tiny. The houses were gingerbread structures, with frail-looking walls of latticework covered with paper. No two houses were exactly alike in design, their cornices and roofs projecting at all heights and angles, yet they all seemed to harmonize with their neighbors. The streets were narrow, the shops and houses jumbled together in the economy of space which marks all Oriental cities. Everywhere were advertising streamers, hanging on housefronts, or suspended upon wires draped overhead across the roadway, and as we turned a corner, we came upon a long procession of men in single file, marching along with big placards bearing Japanese inscriptions, and led by an orchestra of four men, of whom one played a three-note ditty upon a reed pipe, one beat upon cymbals, one pounded upon a small drum, and one upon a bass drum.

The rikisha man fell in a the rear of the procession, and bore me like a King through Theatre Street, where the many advertising streamers were supplemented by gaudy pictures of scenes from the Japanese drama, and cinema halls were fronted by life-sized statues of Charlie Chaplin. This street, save for its pedestrians, might have been a street in Coney Island. But it was crowded by Japanese. Rikisha runners picked their way through the dense throng with shouts of "Hi! Hi! Hi!" to warn others from their course; and Japanese on bicycles, with kimonos trailing behind them, whizzed past the pedestrians at alarming speed, dodging one another by a quick turn of the handlebars.

It was quaint, charming, fascinating, bewildering, but over it all hung that disgusting stench. A guidebook which I purchased informed me that the ideal time to visit Japan was during the cherry blossom season, and I agreed with the statement. The human sewerage system, consisting sometimes of a man drawing a cart, sometimes of a man with two buckets swung on poles across his shoulder, announced his approach by ringing a handbell, but such announcement was unnecessary. Oh for the fragrance of the cherry blossoms!

IV

Neither in Yokohama nor in Tokyo could I find any trace of the poet, although I consulted newspaper files, hotel registers, steamship records, and police reports.

I must start back toward China, seeking him at the other ports, but on the way I wished to see something of Japan, to live like a Japanese for a few days in some out-of-the-way city which was not besmirched by the unpicturesque modernity of a European section.

Accordingly I took the train for Kyoto, once the ancient capital of Japan, and still the center of Japanese art and culture.

The railway coaches were as diminutive as everything else in Japan. Each bore a placard in both Japanese and English to announce its destination. First-class coaches were designated by a white stripe along the outside, second-class by a blue stripe, and third-class by a red stripe. In all three, there were but two longitudinal seats running the length of the coaches, and the Japanese passengers, having left their clogs or slippers upon the floor, drew their feet up under them and squatted cross-legged upon the seats in their own favorite manner.

Everything ran with efficiency. The conductor tooted a whistle form the platform, the engineer answered with a blast from the engine whistle, and we slid out of each station on exact time, to arrive at the next station at the very minute indicated in the schedule.

Rural Japan was even more quaint than the cities. The entire countryside was cut up into little square rice paddies by paths that resembled the latticework upon the sides of the houses. Not an inch of space was wasted, the fields coming to the very edge of the railroad track, and climbing to the summits of the terraced hills. Men and women were working together, carrying armfuls of yellow grain, or preparing the ground for a new crop, the man plowing behind oxen, while the woman followed with a queer tool that looked for all the world like a harp, but which served the less artistic purpose of breaking the coarser lumps of dirt overturned by the plow. Occasionally the vista of yellow fields was varied by a shallow river between low banks, where men were poling little skiffs laden with produce, or by a mountain gorge red with maples and green with pines, with a temple perched upon the cliffs, its pagoda roofs rising one above the other, to crown the whole delightful landscape.

Then, as though to carry out the Japanese program of ruining native picturesqueness with European adaptations, the train rumbled at nightfall into a big modern station, and dropped me at Kyoto.

In the gathering dusk a score of goblin-like rikisha men crowded about me, jabbering in pigeon-English, and I selected at random a stocky little individual with the oiliest of smiles and the fattest of legs.

"Japanese hotel," I directed.

He grinned doubtfully. American tourists went not to Japanese hotels but to one of the two or three hostelries which catered to Europeans.

"You mean hotel like Japanese go?"

"That's it."

"Oh, yes. You go Japanese, take off shoes, sit on floor?"

His grin broadened into a laugh at this unusual desire on the part of an American visitor.

"Mebbe-so, Japanese hotel no can spik English?"

"Mebbe-so. No give damn," I said. "Let's go."

And we went, to stop finally before a two-story bric-a-brac structure, where two servant maids in kimonos conversed with the rikisha man, and giggled at me, and summoned an elderly gentleman with a tuft of goat-like whiskers upon his chin, to whom the rikisha man said something in Japanese which, being interpreted, probably meant, "I've brought you another sucker." The price named for a room was several times what the guidebook had led me to expect, but after my many months of bumming, I felt affluent with my new funds, and I nodded assent.

The entire hotel staff and most of the guests promptly assembled to witness my initiation into Japanese custom.

At the entrance was a series of three wide steps. On the bottom step a row of wooden clogs belonging to the people inside suggested to me that here my own shoes should be laboriously unlaced and removed. On the second step was a row of straw slippers to replace the shoes, and I tried vainly to put them on. Japanese socks are so cut that the big toe has a separate compartment, and the thongs of the slippers are designed to fit through the divide between the big toe and the other toes. My own socks were not so designed. I took one step in the ill-fitting footwear, started to lose my balance, reached out a hand to support myself against the wall, and stuck the hand straight through the wall, which consisted of paper.

This mishap seemed to displease the old gentleman with the goat-like whiskers, but he promptly supported me on one side, while the rikisha man supported me on the other, and feeling somewhat like an inebriate whose friends are putting him to bed, I started up a winding staircase which was about two feet wide, with steps about six inches wide, led by a troop of tiny serving maids whose gaily colored kimonos and pillow-like *obis*, or girdles, gave them the effect of winged butterflies, and followed by another troop consisting mostly of the other guests, whose curiosity could not be appeased until I had arrived in my room without further damage to the paper-walled establishment.

It was a tiny room, delightfully Japanese. The floor, covered with spotless white matting, was devoid of furniture, save for a bureau top without any bureau, which stood in one corner, just high enough for one to make his toilet while sitting on the ground. The walls, while simple, were most ornate, and no one of them was like another. Two of them opened in sliding panels into adjoining rooms. On one the panels were fronted by a silver screen; on the other the panels were ornamented with a design of white flowers. The third wall was covered with woodwork, from which opened tiny sets of drawers and diminutive closet doors, all so minute that they did not seem designed for practical use, and all decorated with the most intricate carving of pine trees and temples, or with strips of paper upon which dainty landscapes had been sketched in black and white. The third wall, also consisting of sliding panels, opened upon a balcony with a carved railing just high enough for a European to trip over. Below it was a tiny backyard of the sort which in any other land might have been utilized as a place for ashcans and refuse, but which here had been converted into a garden planted with dwarfed trees—one of those typical Japanese gardens with toy lakes and paths and bridges. And looking across the garden, I could see through the opened panels of another house into another dainty room where a pretty young Japanese woman was playing with two tiny children. So small was the mother and so small were the children and so small was their dwelling that I could imagine myself looking into a nursery where a little girl played with her dolls.

A serving maid brought me a toy teapot, and placed it upon a toy volcano of live coals in the center of a wooden box full of dead ashes. Another maid brought a pair of mattresses from somewhere and spread them for me upon the floor. The rikisha man cemented an agreement to take me sightseeing upon the morrow, and withdrew through sliding panels, followed by the maids, leaving me alone. In the house across the garden, someone slid the windows shut, and the latticework stood out in artistic shadow-relief against the paper. Beyond it, as I looked over the city, were other latticed windows similarly outlined, and from the eaves of the roofs hung Japanese lanterns of all shapes and colors, giving the whole city the appearance of a fairyland.

I sat like a Buddha upon the floor behind my simmering teacup, a wisp of smoke rising from the live coals before me like incense before an idol, and I gloried in the charm of the whole picture until my cramped legs went to sleep. At length, deciding to follow their example, I undressed, turned off the light, and stretched out between the two mattresses. Through a crack between the sliding panels I could see the flock of serving maids stretched out upon the floor in the same kimonos they had worn throughout the day, their light still burning, their heads resting upon wooden blocks with a curved groove for the neck, which kept their elaborate coiffeurs from becoming disarranged.

For my own head I found a round bundle of hard straw covered with a white doily, which I promptly threw into the farthest corner, substituting for it one of the cushions upon which I had sat. The teapot rattled faintly as it simmered over the glowing red coals, but the rattle was distinctly Japanese; it harmonized satisfyingly with the clatter of wooden clogs upon the pavements outside, and with the complacent snores of the serving maids. Through the opened window, I could see the fairyland of twinkling lanterns. It was all so delightfully picturesque, I could not help regret that this charming land had ever adopted such incongruous things as bicycles, red brick office buildings, steam engines, and brown derby hats.

V

In the morning I was awakened by the sound of sliding panels, as the partitions were being opened throughout the hotel.

Peter, as I had decided to name my rikisha man, was already waiting for me. So also was the proprietor of the hotel, a studious-looking young Japanese in spectacles, who came up with paper and pen to register the information which every landlord must furnish the police about his guests—information which included my name, nationality, destination, permanent residence, reason for visiting Japan, age, state of marriage or bachelorhood, profession, and countless other details.

The landlord had learned a small amount of English at school, and was very timid about speaking it, yet he evidently felt it his duty as host to sit with me and make some effort at conversation, speaking brokenly with long pauses between remarks, and nodding as though he understood my answers whether he did or not.

"You are write for paper?"

"Sometimes. I also write books."

He nodded, and stared into space, very ill at ease, but trying to collect enough English for another effort.

"O'Henry is write books," he said.

"Yes. Have you read his books?"

He nodded politely, not meaning that he had, but to show his agreement with whatever I was saying.

"O'Henry is dead," I added, trying to break the painful silence.

"Thank you," he replied.

But at length, having fulfilled the requirements of Oriental courtesy, and incidentally having collected my board for a day in advance, he bowed many times and withdrew, leaving me to the care of Peter.

"Please, where you likee go? I show you," announced that individual.

What I desired most at the moment was a bath. If there is any one thing for which the Japanese are famous, it is their cleanliness. The hotel contained a tiny room furnished with a square wooden tub, but I had heard so much about the big public bathing houses of Japan, that I wanted to see one.

Peter grinned, and placed both hands upon his plump stomach—a habit of his when vastly amused.

"You go upstairs—get kimono."

But when I reappeared, carrying the kimono which the goat-whiskered night clerk had lent me for sleeping purposes, Peter's amusement increased.

"No, no. You changee shirt upstairs."

Supposing that the bathing establishment must be just across the street, I accordingly donned the kimono and rejoined my guide. A maid provided me with a pair of wooden clogs—plain pieces of wood cut foot-shape and raised above the ground about two inches by wooden cleats—and off I started behind Peter. Around the corner he led me, but no bathing establishment was to be seen. As though conducting a parade, he chose the center of the street, and his bland smile became the proud smile of a showman who introduces to the public some new specimen of freak. All traffic stopped. My stature, although not great, was greater than that of the Japanese costume commanded immediate attention. Crowds of small boys on their way to school promptly formed an escort. The only traffic which failed to stop was that of the trolley cars, and whenever I was forced to jump over the tracks before them, I quite expected to jump out of my ungainly wooden clogs. The line of march was through the main shopping street for several miles, with the escort of school boys growing in numbers at every crossing.

But at length we arrived.

Peter ushered me into a wooden building, where a lady cashier collected five sen—two cents and a half—and instructed me to doff the kimono, an operation in which she nonchalantly assisted. While the Japanese is ordinarily extremely modest and has selected his kimono costume because it effectually hides the figure, he seems curiously inconsistent about the bath, which he regards as a necessary and normal function, and therefore one in which his usual modesty may be discarded. In this establishment a partition had been erected to separate the sexes, but it was only four feet high, and upon the other side of it an elderly woman in the costume of Eve was industriously soaping an infant, while the cherubic faces of several younger women stared interestedly at me from the tubs in which their persons were soaking.

On my own of the partition, four or five tubs were sunk below the wooden floor to a depth of three or four feet, and in one of them several Japanese youths, sitting contentedly in the water, surveyed me with similar interest. Peter had warned me that it was Japanese custom to soap and rinse oneself from a small bucket before climbing into the main tub, and I did so laboriously and thoroughly. Since all eyes were focussed upon me, I felt that American reputation for cleanliness was at stake, and that upon me rested the good name of a nation. Word of my arrival seemed to have spread across the partition to the feminine contingent, and the cherubic faces which had first glanced at me from the tub were now examining me over the top of the wall. Trying with difficulty to appear unconcerned, I soaped and soaped and rinsed and rinsed, the spectators growing numerically greater with each new soaping.

And at length, feeling that I had done sufficient credit to the reputation of the United States, I leaped with joyous relief into the sheltering water of the big tub. Ye Gods! I almost screamed. The water in which the Japanese gentlemen were basking so contentedly was boiling hot. The flush which, despite my strongest efforts of will, and already reddened my face, neck, and ears, now spread uniformly to my toes and the sweat came out in thick drops upon my forehead. How any living creature could endure the scalding heat was incomprehensible, but there the Japanese were basking with manifest satisfaction, parboiling themselves with glee. My impulse was to jump out, but American reputation for cleanliness was still to be maintained. I must stand it as long as did the Japanese, and since they had already been there for considerable time, it was to be hoped that they would soon exhaust their two-and-a-half-cents' worth of bath, and make their exit. But they showed no signs of leaving. They sat there in the tub, still watching me, and I also sat there, watching them. Minutes passed. Half an hour passed. I now resembled a boiled lobster. Three quarters of an hour passed. No one made a move to get out. It was an endurance contest—America versus Japan—and Japan won the victory.

When, at the end of an hour and a half, I acknowledged defeat and finally crawled out of the tub, the Japanese, with loud sighs of relief, followed me.

"Good Heavens! Do your people stay in as long as that every day?" I asked Peter.

He grinned again, and placed both hands upon his round stomach. "Japanese man very polite. You no get out; he no get out."

And damning Oriental courtesy, I made my way back to the hotel.

VI

There followed a round of sightseeing.

Peter led the way out across the Kamo River, which flows through the city of Kyoto, and which is spanned by many arched bridges of stone. It was shallow and filthy, but Peter indicated it with pride. Peter was a home-booster unrivaled outside California, and he described the Kamo as the Number One river in all Japan. It was the Number One river because it flowed through Kyoto, which was the Number One city. So great was its fame that all the pretty girls bathed in it for beautifying effects. The girls of Kyoto, he added, were the Number One girls of Japan.

"How do you know so much about it?" I inquired.

Peter folded his hands over his stomach once more.

"Me savvy everything," he grinned. "Me Number One guide in Kyoto."

We started on the temples. Kyoto is the center of religion as well as art in Japan, and it contains 880 temples all told. Peter, for climatic effect, started on the 880th, and began to work backward. It was a rather tawdry place, its principal exhibit consisting of a gilded monstrosity of a Daibutsu or Great Buddha, standing twenty or thirty feet high, crudely carved of wood, from which the original gilding was rapidly peeling off. Behind the shed which guarded the abomination was a small museum laden with broken statuary and other worthless relics. More interesting was the adjoining beer garden, wherein was a huge bell weighing some sixty-three tons, a bell fourteen feet high and nine feet in diameter, which, when rung by a huge swinging log, gave forth the deepest and most beautiful toll I had ever heard, a sweet rumbling toll that reverberated for miles. Anyone desiring to pay Buddha the compliment was permitted to grasp a rope, start the log swinging, and ring the bell to his heart's content, and after I had refreshed Peter at the beer garden, he rang it for half an hour.

The Japanese seldom imbibe intoxicants, and as a result are surprisingly susceptible to their effects when they do break their abstinence, and having tolled the bell with great vigor and much silly giggling—and many repeated explanations that this was the Number One bell in Kyoto, and that he was the Number One bell ringer—Peter finally led the way unsteadily toward the 879th temple. It was reached by an ascending path through a park of reddening maples, which brought us finally to a cluster of pagoda-roofed structures where a dainty Japanese girl checked my shoes, and gave me a pair of slippers. Peter informed me that the lady was his wife, but he was inclined in his present condition to claim the same relationship with every pretty girl we passed.

This temple appeared to be a species of ecclesiastical museum, and was as stupid as any other formally arranged museum, where articles which might have been interesting in their original surroundings are grouped together in formal arrangement and scientifically tagged with labels. A shaven-headed priest led me from room to room and permitted me to gaze at earthenware jugs and brass candlesticks, pausing after each exhibit to stare inquiringly at me. As pennies and other coins, offered by previous visitors, were lying upon the matting before the exhibits I finally tried to hurry him along upon the tour by tossing a fifty-sen bill upon the floor, but thereafter he merely delayed longer at the other exhibits, staring at me even more inquiringly and hopefully.

But when I had finally impressed it upon Peter that I did not wish to see the temples which catered to American tourists, but the temples at which the Japanese themselves worshiped, our sightseeing journey improved. They were delightful little temples, perched usually upon a hillside among the maple trees, peaceful and restful, with doves cooing about the eaves, and Japanese worshipers who very sensibly performed no rites before the shrines but feasted their eyes upon the beauties of nature. Little women in graceful kimonos would stand in pairs, hand in hand, as one sees them so often in paintings, motionless and expressionless, absorbed in the charm of the temple gardens.

Having seen the material minded Chinese in Bangkok and Singapore, I was greatly impressed by the Japanese' appreciation for the beautiful in nature, and their capacity for the enjoyment of life. When they worked, and in the business streets they were working as industriously as the Chinese, they worked hard, but unlike the Chinese, whose only diversions consisted in gambling or gathering indoors to make the night hideous with the shriek of fiddles and the clash of gongs, these Japanese took delight in being outdoors. Many old-timers tell stories of Chinamen who, seeing Europeans play tennis, would inquire how much they were paid for such work, refusing to believe that anyone would jump around in such fashion for mere pleasure. But in Japan, every one seemed at least to ride the bicycle; boys on clogs, with blue and white checked kimonos flying in the breeze, were playing baseball in the temple grounds. And in one large park, an entire girls' school was at play under the supervision of teachers. Some of them were executing a military drill, marching in column by squads like so many old soldiers; others were having relay races. They were tiny little mites of girls, but they ran swiftly, their oval faces shining with excitement, their hair streaming behind them, their little legs twinkling. Anyone who believes the Oriental incapable of excitement should have seen them. Those who were watching leaped up and down, clapping their hands, and screeching; those who participated lost their heads so completely that they frequently cut short the corners and then, remembering the rules, would turn and race frantically back to go around the markers and continue on the proper course. It was an intriguing sight, save for the fact that many of the girls wore European clothing instead of their more attractive national costumes. In Japan's deplorable mania for the adoption of all things European, the Emperor has set the fashion of wearing European costume at court, and even the schools follow his example, although most of the children revert to the kimono after school hours.

Peter, having exhibited most of the 880 temples, led the way finally to a theater street resembling that of Yokohama. The playhouses as a rule were European buildings of stone, but the Japanese streamers and posters which covered their fronts, including an occasional placard which showed our own Charlie hitting another comedian with a custard pie, were all Japanese in style. I selected an average-looking theater, left my shoes in check among several huge piles of sandals and clogs at the entrance, and followed an usher upstairs to the balcony. It was partitioned into rows by low railings, and the patrons squatted upon pillows along the floor. Boxes of live coals were set beside each patron for his cigarette or pipe, and tea or fruit was served if desired. But as everywhere else in Japan, provision had been made for any stray European who might drift in, and the usher led me to a bench which quite evidently was kept for tourists, where one could sit in European fashion instead of squatting upon his heels.

The theater was square, and the stage was wide but not deep. From it, a runway like that at the Winter Garden led straight out through the orchestra, providing an additional exit for the actors. The scenery was realistic, for since a Japanese house is but a flimsy contraption of lattice and paper, there was no difficulty in duplicating it in actual size and composition upon the stage. The acting appeared stilted, yet the Japanese are stilted in their formal courtesy in real life, and the comedy consisted of horseplay which was devoid of subtlety, but which vastly amused the spectators. Actresses were impersonated well by boys, but there were no love scenes, the Japanese regarding any public manifestation of affection as extremely improper, and even censoring every kiss from the American moving pictures which they exhibit. But every one seemed to enjoy it, and when the curtain was finally dragged across the stage by a property man, the spectators in the orchestra rushed forward and lifted it up to peer beneath it with typical oriental curiosity at the changing of the scenery.

The sightseeing tour ended with another temple—the Higashi-Hongwonji. Peter called it the Number One Temple of Kyoto, and for once he did not exaggerate.

It defied description. A moat and wall surrounded it, and so huge and ornate were the doors that any one of them, with its high, curling roofs, might have been mistaken for a temple itself. The enclosure within was as large as a New York City block, and the Main Temple, surrounded by a dozen other huge structures, was larger than the New York Public Library. Throngs of Japanese pilgrims from all parts of the Empire, including schools under the guidance of spectacled male teachers, were pouring across the big stone bridges which spanned the moat, and up the great flight of wide steps which led to the temple.

Despite the immense size of the structure, not a square foot of it was without intricate carving, all so tiny and in such perfect harmony and taste that the entire effect was not one of over-embellishment but of perfect simplicity. It required seventeen years to build the Higashi-Hongwonji. The eight million dollars for its construction were provided in small sums by the comparatively poor, and in an outbuilding near the temple there is a rope of human hair three hundred feet long and three inches in diameter contributed from the heads of the faithful to be used in dragging the giant timbers into place.

The colossal proportions left me gasping. I followed the worshipers up the steps, checked my shoes—my entire visit to Japan seemed to be spent mostly lacing and unlacing my shoes—and walked into the central nave. This nave alone was immense, but through the rows of giant pillars which lined it on either side other immense naves could be seen; it was as though one looked through forests of pillars into other recesses that stretched away to infinity. For once I had discovered something in Japan that was not diminutive.

It was marvelous, yet the Oriental never seems devout in his worship, and the hundreds of Japanese who sat cross-legged upon the matting while shaven-headed priests in black and white robes conducted a meaningless service about half a mile distant, seemed unimpressed, eating oranges and leaving the peels upon the ground along with their offerings of pennies, and watching me with far more interest than they watched the service. Gradually I began to note details, but it would have taken weeks to note all of the details in that temple—the formally carved squares of dark hardwood overhead, the great wealth of brass ornamentation before the distant altar, the many statues of Buddha, and finally the principal Buddha itself. It was a kneeling Buddha, dimly lighted, seen through a recess like a long tunnel, appearing strangely alive. It was as simple as it could be, yet surrounded by so much wealth and the labor of years and the offerings of countless human beings, and worshiped—

although halfheartedly—by so many people, it was strangely impressive. To the imagination it became mysteriously alive, that shadowy figure in the distance, as though Buddha himself were squatting there, looking out at us, inscrutable yet infinitely wise, gazing into our souls.

Then the service ended. The priests swept up the orange peels, and pocketed the coins.

VII

Kyoto was so charming, and—despite the occasional visits of parties of tourists—so pleasantly devoid of western commercial influence, that my stay lengthened into a week.

My landlord, after our first conversation, did not call upon me again except to collect his daily rental, which he always collected in advance. Each evening, however, the old gentleman with the four goatlike hairs upon his chin, who seemed to be sort of a night clerk, would visit me, bow three or four times, and seat himself upon a pillow opposite me across the ash box where my teapot rattled. He spoke no English, but he would talk to me in Japanese, and listening intently I could catch the names of temples and other places of interest, and knew that he was inquiring where I had spent the day. It was a quaint visit, and I rather looked forward to it.

Peter guided me about town each day, exploiting me to the utmost, and extracting his "squeeze" or commission from every merchant, restaurant keeper, or shoe checker to whom he led me. When I venture out alone, however, I fared little better. For a while I thought that I had devised an excellent scheme to avoid being swindled by those with whom I dealt; when buying cigarettes, for instance, I would hand out a whole yen, and wait for my change with an expression of keen intelligence, trying to convince the merchant that I was an old-timer, familiar with the correct prices, and not to be short-changed; I observed that when I bought two packages and handed out a yen, I received four pennies in exchange; then one day, when I accidentally handed out only half a yen for the two packages, I received the same four pennies.

The Japanese, however, were all friendly, and if they possessed any anti-American feeling, they did not show it. They stared at me, of course, with the ill-mannered curiosity of all Asiatics, and if I turned quickly in the street I could always catch some of them grinning at me or mimicking me behind my back, but it was merely the grinning and mimicking with which they ridiculed all foreigners. The upper-class Japanese went out of their way to be courteous, and once when I had ventured to the other side of the city without Peter's guidance, had lost myself in a maze of winding streets, and was trying vainly to make inquiries of a rikisha man who lacked Peter's linguistic accomplishments, several passing college youths hastened to my rescue, and not merely gave me the proper directions, but walked several blocks to put me upon a trolley car. And once, when I had boarded another car to discover that it was taking me in the wrong direction, the conductor, since he spoke no English himself, stopped his car and left it standing for ten minutes while he searched the neighborhood for someone who could speak English. The other passengers made no objection, and showed no annoyance.

In all money transactions, however, I was considered fair game. For that matter, an ignorant foreigner was considered fair game anywhere else in the Orient. A tourist is cheated and short-changed so often in the East and usually for such trifling sums, that he longs for the day when he can again deal with a good, honest American, who won't steal from him unless he can steal an amount that makes it worthwhile. And among old travelers, the Japanese has the worst reputation of all the Orientals for his untrustworthiness.

"They'll use guile even when it isn't necessary," commented one salesman whom I had met upon the steamer. "Last time I was here, I had a line of hats, and I kept them in a cylindrical leather case. One day a Japanese hat merchant who had admired that case asked me to leave it in his office while he showed me around his plant. I just happened to step back to the office for a moment before they expected me, and I found two Japanese measuring that case and making a drawing of it. Now, if they'd asked me, I wouldn't have objected to their making a duplicate of it, but instead of asking me, they were trying to do it in secret. It's their nature."

"They can't invent anything themselves," said another traveling man, "but they'll steal everything that anyone else invents, and they won't pay for the patent or copyright if they can help it. I know lots of fellows who've sold them one shipment of goods, and then begin to wonder why they don't order a second shipment. And when those fellows come to Japan, they find the Japanese are making the same identical goods themselves, and even putting the foreign label or trademark on them.

The Japanese haven't learned yet that honesty is the best policy in the long run."

But even when the Japanese swindles you, he always does it so nicely and politely that you simply have to come back to be swindled again. That was my experience with Peter, who was quite the worst reprobate that I met in the East, but always so amusing and good natured about it that I enjoyed having him make a fool of me.

I had been eating at a small half-European establishment near the hotel, but since the proprietor could speak no English except "Ham and eggs," my fare had become rather monotonous, and one day I requested Peter to conduct me to a genuine Japanese restaurant.

At this request, he again placed both hands over his round stomach and grinned, a mannerism which had become decidedly ominous. We were on our way, at the moment, to the temple of Kiyomizu-dera, one of Kyoto's 880 temples, walking uphill through a street lined with porcelain shops, but there was a restaurant just ahead. At Peter's lusty summons, its proprietress met us on the way, a woman of indeterminable age, whose extreme joy upon seeing me was even more ominous than Peter's grin.

Laughing and chattering gaily, she led the way into a delightful garden with the gnarled and dwarfed matsu trees growing upon tiny islands of rock among waterless rivers. Here and there were frail houses of paper and lattice, and into one of these I was ushered, after I had removed my shoes for the seven though eight hundred and fifty-ninth time since my arrival in Japan.

Peter helped me plan the dinner. My funds had been disappearing at an alarming rate during my few days of life as a tourist, but we planned a feast, with geisha to sing and dance, for a price of only ten yen.

It was an elaborate sort of banquet, despite the fact that I was the only guest. In a Japanese restaurant each guest or party of guests is allotted a special room, with a special waitress to sit opposite him across the table and fill his glass with *sake*. The table was only one foot high, and I sat upon a pillow, clandestinely stretching my legs and changing my position whenever the waitress turned her back. She was not as attractive as she might have been, despite the elaborate arrangement of her black hair into a design which made it cover about two cubic feet of space, but she was very attentive.

Her first move was to feed me the tea, which seems to be the first rite of every Japanese host, hostess, hotel proprietor, or storekeeper. Then came four tiny plates upon a tray, which appeared to contain some species of fish. According to my guidebook—and incidentally *Terry's Guide* is so popular that some of the recent writers on Japan have contented themselves with merely paraphrasing it and reselling it as their own—the Japanese diet includes seaweed, whale meat, squid, sea slugs, and boiled octopus.

Surveying the viands before me, I judged that the waitress had supplied me with a sample of each. I had already learned to handle chopsticks, but to use them in splitting up a chunk of hard-boiled whale presented a new problem. The waitress, however, took the sticks and hacked the unsavory delicacy into small bits, and as a special courtesy, began to feed them to me, giggling until her hand became so unsteady that she was forced to cease operations.

Presently *sake* was served. *Sake* is the Japanese rice wine, pale yellow in color, and served warm. It is by no means unpalatable, and mildly exhilarating. It was served by the thimble-full, but as fast as I drained the thimble, the waitress promptly refilled it and offered it again. Since our enforced silence was becoming embarrassing, this operation was something of a relief, but after she had refilled the thimble for half an hour, I was more than mildly exhilarated. Peter, who had been dinning somewhere up a flight of stone steps in a place reserved for rikisha coolies, and who stumbled down from time to time to inquire about my welfare, was himself showing signs that his dinner also had been exhilarating, for he finally descended the steps by the simple process of sliding, his anatomy seeming to catch on each step and keep him suspended for a moment before he slid to the next.

He landed finally in the garden, grinning expansively.

"Geisha come," he announced. "Geisha upstairs. Nice geisha—number one geisha. Kyoto geisha number one geisha in all Japan."

The Japanese geisha represent a somewhat unique institution. Trained from childhood to sing, dance, play the *samisen*, and entertain by their clever conversation, they are a combination of cabaret performer and companion, a necessary adjunct to all Japanese dinners, and not necessarily immoral, although to the Occidental mind, just a trifle irregular. An American wife would not submit tamely to being left at home while her husband hired another lady at so much per hour for her clever conversation and entertaining company at luncheon, but the Japanese wife accepts the custom without protest, and no Japanese gentleman would think of giving a party without hiring geisha, whom he procures through a central geisha exchange or booking office.

My waitress led me up the stone steps to another room, and after a whispered consultation had been held outside, two young women crawled inn upon their hands and knees, bowing their heads to the floor several times in salutation. One, according to Peter, was a dancer; the other a musician. Instead of performing immediately, however, they began to eat a dinner similar to the one I had ordered, which evidently was to be charged to my account. In fact, they ate what appeared to be half a dozen dinners. Apparently they had not been fed for at least a week. I understood that I was hiring the geisha at three yen each per hour, and after they had devoted two hours and a half to eating, I tried to make inquiries about the agreement, but by this time Peter was stretched upon his back upon the floor, repeating, "Nice geisha. Number one geisha. Nice *sake*. Number one *sake*," and his utility as an interpreter was negligible.

I had my doubts about the quality of the geisha, especially when the performance finally began. The musician was rather elderly and overplump, and when she produced a samisen—a species of three-stringed guitar—she appeared to strike the stings at random, without much system. The dancer was younger, but her prime object seemed to be to make herself as awkward as possible while she performed her steps. Japanese music is weird and mournful, and is not music as we understand it; Japanese dancing is lacking in rhythm and grace, and is not dancing as we understand it. Pantomime would better describe it, for it consists in slow posturing that is symbolical. What this young lady tried to symbolize was not quite clear, but it seemed to be a poetic interpretation either of picking cherry blossoms, ascending a spiral staircase on stilts, or treading for oysters.

Peter, however, enjoyed it immensely, applauded vigorously, and finally joined in the dance, to the amusement of the assembling restaurant staff, informing me that he was the Number One Male Geisha in all Japan. The assembling restaurant staff joined the party, with the jovial proprietress supplementing the *sake* with Japanese beer, which she served fourteen bottles at a time, also charging it to my account, despite my meaningless protests in English which no one but Peter could understand. My bill had passed the ten yen mark, and was now about thirty yen, and still soaring.

I settled it, having finally shaken Peter into sensibility, and attempted a hurried escape. But when Peter and I started for Kiyomizu-dera, the geisha promptly joined us.

"Dance girl come, too," explained Peter.

I had not found her particularly entertaining or otherwise attractive and preferred to dispense with her services. From a remark which Peter had made, I understood that the dance girl, like many of the geisha, was somewhat lax in her mode of living, and a wild woman did not seem to be altogether an appropriate companion for a visit to a temple. Although I did not know it, the Japanese gentlemen when visiting a temple, frequently do take along a geisha to entertain them with the bright conversation of which regular wives are considered incapable, but I was not aware of the fact.

"Tell the dance girl to beat it," I directed Peter.

But Peter's mind was still hazy, and the dance girl, followed by the musician, and finally by several waitresses who also joined the procession in the hope of an additional tip, came clattering along behind us upon their wooden clogs.

I leaned forward from the carriage.

"Run!" I commanded Peter. "Run like the blazes! Run away from them!"

He caught the idea, and grinning all over his round face, he ran. Kiyomizu-dera is the most beautiful shrine in Kyoto, perched in a mountain gorge lined with maples, but its beauties passed in a blur as Peter, bobbing up and down between the shafts, dragged my rikisha up one path and down another, past toy gardens, past stands where knickknacks were sold, past curling temple roofs, and back again into the city. But we made our escape from the geisha.

VIII

A few days later, however, when Peter, threatened with physical violence if he allowed himself to become intoxicated, led me to a really good restaurant, I saw a really enjoyable performance by geisha.

The two musicians were homely, but the dancer—a child of twelve—was the cutest little dancer imaginable. Her face, in spite of a thick coat of kalsomine, was delicate and refined. She was arrayed like a little butterfly in elaborate silks, her hair was coiffeured to the Nth degree, and from either forehead dangled a jeweled ornament resembling the chandeliers in the White House ballroom. The music, as usual, impressed a westerner as mournful, and when the dancer sang in her weak, falsetto voice, one could imagine that she was suffering the agonies of appendicitis, but her dance, with all its awkward posturing, was pretty, and while a westerner could not catch the significance of the fan waving pantomime, one could at least appreciate that it was a dance and that there was symbolism to her gestures. At least, Japanese dancing is the most chaste dancing in the world; no dancing is so devoid of the sensuous.

In an adjoining room a large banquet was in progress. Two or three dozen geisha were playing the samisen and singing, while the male banqueters accentuated the rhythm by clapping the hands. The Japanese men, so practical in most things, find a surprising amount of enjoyment in sitting upon the floor and clapping their hands while children entertain them. This evidently was a college banquet of some kind, for when my own entertainment was concluded, I found the lower floor of the restaurant filled with young Japanese in blue-and-white wrappers and caps, sprawled out upon the matting, their faces red with *sake*, and wearing expression like that upon the face of a small boy who has just smoked his first cigar. Their usual temperance makes them extremely susceptible to the effects of wine. Yet it should be noted that none of them offered the least indignity to the geisha, for the Japanese, even when drunk, never so much as touches the arm of a woman in public.

Japanese morality is as puzzling and paradoxical to the western mind as is everything else in the Orient. The Japanese is practical and material-minded where the sexes are concerned. He allows his parents to select his wife, believing that love is undesirable in marriage, since too much affection for his wife may lessen his devotion to his family and to the state. If he wishes at any time to visit the Yoshiwara, or red light district, it is his privilege to do so, and he does so openly, making no attempt to conceal the fact, and seeing nothing wrong in it. He never insults a woman, and a woman is never guilty of flirtation upon the street. Men and women bathe together, use the same toilets, and sleep in the same hotel room, but neither molests or seeks to allure the other, or seems to notice the other person. Girls either retain their purity, or enter the Yoshiwara as a profession, a perfectly respected profession which does not deter a man from marrying them later. The only intermediate state seems to be that of the geisha, who sometimes behaves herself and sometimes does not.

I have heard some old-timers describe the Japanese as having a far higher sexual morality than Europeans, since they live up to their own conceptions of morality far more strictly than Europeans. As their conception of morality allows them to visit the Yoshiwara whenever they please, their code does not seem to be a very difficult code to conform to, but their indiscretions have the virtue of being always open and honest and never clandestine. And the well-known fact that when any fairly young foreigner climbs into a rikisha in a Japanese city without giving the collie any instructions as to destination, the coolie invariably takes him to the Yoshiwara, does not speak very highly of the habits of previous European visitors to Japan.

Peter had conscientiously urged me each day to visit the red-light district, urging it in a candid matter-of-fact manner, and returning from the restaurant we passed through it. The houses were larger than the average Japanese house, very ornate with a wealth of carved woodwork, and the streets were thronged with well-dressed gentlemen. Nothing could be more orderly and outwardly more correct than this district. Elderly ladies or gentlemen stood in the doorways to coax passers-by inside the establishment. In the Chinese brothels of Singapore the girls had stood on exhibition to be examined and criticized by prospective purchasers; in the Japanese houses of Kyoto, the picture bride system was in vogue, and the reception halls contained merely the photographs of the inmates. One's first impression was that the street was lined with photographers' shops. Everything about the district showed excellent taste and refinement. The only Japanese who were noisy were a party of the college banqueters, who rushed bumptiously into one house and out again into the next, giggling and attempting horseplay among themselves, like bad boys who wished to be mischievous but did not know just how.

CHAPTER THIRTEEN

SING-SONG AND OPERA IN SHANGHAI

I

I hunted the poet from city to city, throughout Japan, from Yokohama to Kobe, but he was not to be found.

Evidently he was somewhere in China, perhaps in his original stamping ground at Shanghai, and while my new funds held out—they had diminished considerably under the guidance of Peter—I caught a steamer westward.

On the steamer I met Tom Li.

Tom was a good-looking young Chinaman in a European suit which might have been copied from one of those Klassy Kollege Kut advertisements, and he introduced himself by hopping exuberantly through the smoking room door as though he were about to lead a cheer for the dear old Alma Mater, which, in his case, happened to be Cornell University.

"You American?" he inquired. "Good! At-a-boy! That's the spirit! Good for you!"

His welcome was almost bewildering. At the end of the first hour he shook hands six times in succession, and pronounced judgment that we were going to be friends. At the end of the second hour he shook hands all over again, and pronounced further judgment that we were going to be awfully good friends. As neither of us were drinking, his effusiveness was amazing.

"That's right, isn't it, doc?" he demanded, having already awarded me the new title. "We're good friends, aren't we?"

Somehow Tom reminded me slightly—I could not determine just how—of the Chinaman who had followed me through the Siamese jungle and had finally stolen my brown goggles. He was just a trifle too enthusiastic in his oft-repeated phrases about friendship to be convincing. Still, I was willing to concede that we were friends.

"Good! That's the spirit, doc! We're the best friends in the world. Maybe not the very best friends, but almost the best friends in the world. What do you say, doc? And when we get to Shanghai, you're going to be my guest. Wherever you want to go in China, you're my guest."

I could not quite determine whether he meant the invitation, or whether it was merely an expression of Oriental courtesy not intended to be taken literally.

II

For several reasons, I hesitated to accept such an offer.

In all my wanderings I had met just one race of people whom I did not like, and this race was the Chinese. I was willing to admit a ridiculous prejudice—being a vagabond myself I abominated any race as industrious as the Chinese—and being a vagabond, I had dealt mostly with coolies and not with educated gentlemen like Tom Li—but the prejudice existed, nevertheless, and I disliked them so profoundly that it seemed hypocrisy to accept anything from them.

Also, I had never met a Chinaman who offered kindness to another man without some hidden object of personal gain. All other natives throughout the Orient hated or despised them. White men of long experience in the East praised the Chinese, and those who dealt with the big merchants gave them an enviable reputation for sterling honesty, but with the exception of Kwong, I had not yet discovered an honest Chinaman. My experience, of course, had been that of a tourist, who is treated everywhere as an "easy mark."

For example, I had never yet asked a rikisha man whether he could take me to a certain place, but that he replied confidently in the affirmative, and then, having galloped two or three miles with me, paused to admit that he had no idea where the place was. If I climbed disgustedly out of his rikisha, he would demand payment for the two or three miles he had galloped, even though the ride had not served its purpose. If I started to argue, a crowd would collect, and the Chinaman, having the advantage of speaking the local jargon, would take much delight in amusing his audience by humorous remarks with which I could not compete. If I happened to get good service, and rewarded the rikisha man with an extra tip, he never could understand that this was a mark of appreciation, but regarded it as an indication that I was ignorant of the correct price, and would immediately begin to argue for more.

If I sent a hotel servant to purchase something for me, he invariably exacted his "squeeze" from the change. If I gave him thirty cents to pay to my rikisha man, he put a portion of the amount into his own pocket. This, of course, is Chinese custom, and is not recognized by the Chinese as dishonesty, any more than is the shopkeeper's custom of having several prices for each article, and charging whatever he thinks the customer will pay. Everyone squeezes in China, from the lowliest coolie up to the government officials, and everyone considers it his privilege to "squeeze."

I had never known a Chinaman to tell the truth when a lie could be invented. One day at a hotel, for instance, I had given my clothes to the boy to be sent to the laundry, but when, at nightfall, they were not returned as promised, the boy—although I recognized him well enough—denied having received them from me. As I had but one suit of clothes, my predicament was annoying, and I assembled the entire hotel staff in my room, including the manager, who made inquiries, and dispatched the boys to all the laundries in town. One of them presently returned to report that he had found the clothes at a certain establishment, but that they had not been ironed. I sent him away to bring them back unironed. He reappeared presently to deny his original story and to report that the clothes were not at the laundry. After two hours during which I shook my fists at the assembled Chinamen and failed to ruffle even their tempers, I did get the clothes back. They were completely washed and ironed. What the several boys hoped to gain by their evasion of the truth, I could not imagine.

A discussion of Chinese honesty is bound to be as paradoxical as a discussion of any other feature of Chinese character. From one source, we learn that Chinese merchants and bankers never go back on their word. From another source, we learn that when the first railroad started to operate from Shanghai to Woosung, the passengers were such thieves that they stole the window glass form the coaches; or that the Chinese are so untrustworthy that they can not be relied upon to run their own customs' service, which is run for the Chinese by foreigners, mostly Englishmen. No man has the same experience with the Chinese as has the next man; a writer can only tell what his own experience has been. My experience, limited mostly to dealings with the lower classes, was that the Chinese were liars and thieves.

"I couldn't think of accepting so much!" I told Li.

"So much? Why, doc, that's nothing. Do you know who I am? I'm nobody myself, but my brother's the Finance Minister in the Chinese government. We can do anything we like, and just sign a 'chit' for the bill. Chinese government officials make lots of graft, doc. We're both guests of the government! What do you say, doc?"

III

Our steamer's course led through the Inland Sea of Japan. It was three hundred miles in length, but its width varied from three to thirty miles, and since it is this sea which has been the inspiration of the Japanese gardeners, a voyage among its rocky islets was like a trip through a Japanese garden.

The setting sun was a ball of red, and outlined against the peak of a hilly island gave the effect of a volcano. Sea and sky became purple, outlining mountains of a darker purple, and the rising moon turned the brown sails of the drifting junks into sails of silver.

Then, in the morning, as though to warn us that we had left beautiful Japan behind and were approaching hideous China, the sea became besmirched with the flood of yellow-brown water from the Yangtse River, and the steamer crawled up a yellow-brown stream—the Whangpoo—between yellow-brown, marshy banks. Yet with all its ugliness, the scenery was fascinating. Chinese junks passed us—junks far more picturesque than the Japanese—clumsy lumbering vessels, with high, ungainly poops, with sails patched and reinforced by numerous ribs of bamboo, with three or four masts tilting at absurd angles, and with bulging eyes upon the bow—uncanny eyes that gave the junks the appearance of a huge fish in order to fool the devils in the water, or according to another explanation, to enable ships to see their way across the shoals. Crude, medieval relics were these junks, yet their Chinese crews who chanted weird heathen chanteys as they marched about the primitive capstan, navigated them to the farthest shores of the Orient, to Malaya and Borneo and Siam, exactly as their forefathers had navigated the same vessels in the days when the white race hesitated to venture beyond the confines of the Mediterranean.

The usual pall of smoke appeared ahead; factories, mills, and refineries began to mar the landscape, scores of other steamers churned past us, and presently Shanghai appeared—a big city of stone buildings which might have been any large European city. Fresh-faced young Englishmen of the customs' service examined our luggage, and Tom—who could not be denied—bundled me into a trolley car. We clanged through Europeanized streets of the most modern metropolis in the East, turned a corner, and—

If Japan had been confusing at first sight, China was more so. Once we had turned the corner beyond the European district, we entered the land of the Arabian Nights—a land of Chinese shops covered with golden dragons, of huge advertising placards that looked like overgrown laundry tickets, of streets filled with clatter and movement, where pedestrians threaded their way precariously among dashing rikishas, where burden-bearers with cargoes twice as large as themselves rushed hither and thither, shouting in sing-song cadence to warn others from their paths—an incongruously over-colored ant hill that swarmed with human ants. Shanghai is an independent republic in itself, its international settlement governed by a Municipal Council elected by the taxpayers, but the Chinese crowd eagerly into the European district, partly for the opportunity to do business, and partly for the better protection offered by the international authorities.

We alighted finally at a Chinese hotel, a large hotel modeled after European hostelries but owned and operated by Chinese. The lobby, although resembling any American or European lobby, was thronged with upper-class Chinese in long mandarin robes, and behind the desk sat several clerks in black silk skull caps, one of whom seized a paint brush and drew upon the ledger a series of figures which looked as though they might mean "Two collars, four shirts," but which Li informed me meant "Harry L. Foster."

Li presented me with an air of prideful ownership which was decidedly flattering, and after he had exchanged whines and grunts with the clerk, that personage surveyed me with increased respect, and jotted several additional figures after my name.

"I told him, doc, that you were the Dean of Cornell University," explained Li.

I began to understand his eagerness in urging me to become his guest. It is another paradox in the Chinese character, that despite the humility which the well-bred Chinaman assumes, he is vastly concerned about the opinion of those he meets, and wishes at all times to make an impressive appearance—in the local vernacular, he is vastly concerned about "face." Li was giving himself "face" by proving to his countrymen that his importance in his American university was such that the Dean was escorting him home.

IV

Li was a puzzling character. He combined the ebullient, bubbling enthusiasm of an American college boy with the formal politeness of the Chinese aristocrat.

At one moment he bragged and boasted with undergraduate self-assurance; at the next moment he belittled himself and flattered me with the Oriental humility.

"You see, doc, the Chinese have very good hotel. The Chinese are great people, doc. We invented gunpowder. We—" and two minutes later—"You are a great man, doc, and I'm a nobody. It's a shame that I ask such a fine fellow to be the friend of such a worthless person as myself."

Secretly, Li was extremely vain. He would examine his features at great length in the looking glass, and he made a practice of painting dark circles under his eyes with a pinkish-yellow paint specially designed for the Chinese complexion. Still, he liked to talk about how homely he was.

"It's a shame, doc, that a good-looking fellow like you has to associate with an ugly fellow like me."

As I had never prided myself upon beauty, this comment was almost offensive. Equally annoying was his constant repetition of phrases about our friendship. Friendship, to the Occidental, is something understood, and requires little discussion, but Li discussed it for hours at a time.

We occupied a double room, European in its furnishings, but Chinese in the excellence of its service. As I had discovered on my wanderings, no servant can equal the Chinese for attentiveness. He studies his master until he knows him better than the master knows himself. Not an idiosyncrasy of taste escapes his eye. He is inclined to believe his master a creature of habit, and if one happens to praise the roast beef at the first dinner, the Chinese servant will serve roast beef at all succeeding meals until the master specifically demands a change. He will make his "squeeze" on every sum of money that the master may entrust him wherewith to make purchases. But he is tirelessly attentive. Ten servants were regularly on duty outside the door of the hotel room, ready at our slightest move to bring us green tea to drink, to open the door for us, or to close and lock it behind us.

There appeared, however, to be some slight misunderstanding about Li's promise that all we would have to do would be to name our wants, sign a chit, and let the government pay our bills. It appeared that we were paying for everything we bought, and that I was doing most of the paying.

"No," explained Li with his usual bland nonchalance, when I delicately brought up the subject. "We can sign no chits here because they do not know my brother. But I'm going to take you to Hangkow, where I have my home. I have lots of homes in Hangkow—fine big homes. We can have automobiles, and a yacht on the Yangtse—everything, doc, and the government pays for everything. You're my guest, doc, when we get to Hangkow."

Li, although his manners were the unmistakable manners of a gentleman, and although his education was both Oriental and Occidental, seemed to have as little conception of accuracy as the lowliest rikisha coolie. When I first met him, he professed to be on his way home to Hangkow because his mother was dying. He talked much about the virtues of his mother and about his devotion to her, but once landed in Shanghai he settled down at the hotel as though preparing for a lengthy sojourn, and when asked whether he was not in a hurry to proceed home before she died, he responded blandly by saying that his mother, who was in Peking, was enjoying excellent health.

I had about concluded that my original suspicions of Tom were correct, and that he did have an ulterior purpose in inviting me to become his guest, for it appeared to be the first duty of Tom's guest to defray the expenses for the two of us. Then, just as something had invariably happened to upset every generalization that I had made about the Asiatics, young Mr. Sun appeared upon the scene.

Sun was another nice-looking Chinese youth, a boyhood friend of Li's who came to call upon us. Sun had never been educated abroad, and he possessed a charming Oriental dignity quite devoid of the ebullient breeziness and affectation of Li. He wore Chinese costume, consisting of a black silk coat which buttoned on the side, and a flowing skirt of silvered cloth; Li described him as the classiest dresser in Chinese Shanghai.

And Sun commanded one's respect, as does any man who observes with pride the customs and traditions of his own people.

Just as the natives back on the Battambang-Chantaboun trail, who had met but few white men, proved more kindly, and honest, and genuine than those of the seaports who had had intercourse with foreigners, so did Sun, who spoke but a few English phrases learned in a Chinese school, prove himself an unaffectedly cordial host.

His first invitation was to a Chinese dinner.

The restaurant was an ornate structure on a back street, a structure emblazoned externally with dragon designs in gold and black. A waiter escorted us inside and led us down a long, dark hallway past individual rooms in which sleek-looking Chinese of wealth were seated about tables, each gentleman still wearing his black skull-cap.

Our own room was drab, and devoid of furnishings save for the table and chairs without backrests, and numerous crumbs upon table and floor testified to the menus of previous diners, but this was one of the leading restaurants of China according to Li. A second waiter brought us the bill of fare, consisting of a board six feet square covered with Chinese lettering, and Sun, after studying it carefully, took a paint brush and wrote a long order in Chinese upon a strip of paper provided for the purpose. Li explained for my benefit that Sun was a beautiful penman.

The dinner, like everything else in China, ran in courses in exactly the opposite order of any Western dinner. First came tea. Then came finger bowls, or in this case, damp towels upon which we washed our hands. Then came meat, followed by fish, and finally the soup. Sun evidently was making a splurge. There were several kinds of meat, ham, beef, duck, and chicken, all cut into pieces small enough to be picked up with chopsticks, and served upon platters into which we all dug and picked at the same time. Individual plates were not provided, and it was Chinese courtesy for each of us to pick out the nicest portion and feed it with our chopsticks to one of the others.

Li, who presumably was aggrandizing himself by presenting me to Sun as the Dean of Cornell University, was very anxious that I should make no social errors. He coached me from time to time in an undertone.

"Keep your elbows on the table, doc. We always keep the elbows on the table in China. At-a-boy, doc. Now pick out the best part of that crab—see that gooey part there—and give it to Sun. At-a-boy, doc. And when the soup comes, please to make lots of noise. Chinese always make noise when they eat soup, doc. That will show Sun we're enjoying it. At-a-boy, doc. Only, make more noise. That's the spirit. You've got the idea. At-a-boy. That's the stuff. Lots of pep!"

Noise in a Chinese restaurant was by no means limited to the drinking of soup. In the neighboring room several banquets were in progress, accompanied by the clashing of gongs and the shrieking of fiddles, until the resort resembled nothing so much as a madhouse. Above the clashing and the shrieking arose the shrill, almost wailing voices of the sing-song girls, the Chinese equivalent of the Japanese geisha, many of whom—tiny almond-eyed creatures in pink or blue pajamas—could be seen paddling past our door from room to room. Chinese business men habitually meet at dinner to talk business, or entertain their best customers with sixty-plate banquets, and like the Japanese, they must have professional entertainers.

It is another paradox of the Chinese character that although the Chinaman in business will pinch a cent ten times harder than any Hebrew that every lived, when he becomes wealthy and plays the part of host he becomes the most lavish host in the world. Course followed course—more meats, more duck, more fish, strange conglomerations of vegetables, roots, rice, fruit, and much rice wine which resembled *sake*—while Sun, in accordance with the Chinese ceremonial code, urged us to eat.

"He says, doc, that you're not touching a thing. Eat hearty, doc, or he'll think you don't like it. That's better. At-a-boy. Have a shrimp, doc. Have some of that stuff. That's a Chinese dish. That's a bird's nest, doc. At-a-boy. Keep it up. Only, make more noise, doc. That's the spirit!"

It was several hours before we waddled out into the crowded street.

The dinner, it seemed, was but a preliminary. The second item on the evening's program was a Chinese Coney Island.

It was housed in two several-storied buildings on opposite sides of Nanking Road, the leading thoroughfare of Shanghai, which were labeled respectively in English electric-lighted titles, "The New World," and "The Great World." An underground passageway joined them. We went to the roof of one, by elevator, and worked down, floor by floor. The amusements presented a curious mixture of the Chinese and the western. In one room a Chinese storyteller was holding forth with the usual grunts and wheezes, to the huge enjoyment of his audience. In other rooms, Chinese orchestras were making the night hideous; a man and a girl were singing, the man banging so loudly upon cymbals that the voices were scarcely audible. In another room moving pictures of the wild and woolly west were being exhibited, and Bill Hart was showing Shanghai how to hold up a stagecoach single-handed. There were rooms filled with curved looking glasses which made fat men out of thin Chinamen; there were slot machines of the penny arcade type, wherein Chinese were peering to see such dramas as "Adam and Eve," or "The Adventure of the Female Drummer," or "What Happened at the Moulin Rouge."

Scattered among the shows were booths where refreshments were sold—mysterious Chinese delicacies—and at every booth, Sun, despite my protests that I couldn't eat another thing, insisted upon regaling me with uncured olives, watermelon seeds, lollypops, rice cakes, and Heaven knows what. "Eat them, doc," Li would urge. "You're not touching a thing. Sun's taking us out, you know, and we have to eat them to be polite. Go to it, doc. At-a-boy. Have another horse chestnut, doc. He'll think we don't like them if we don't eat."

All Shanghai seemed to resound to the clashing of gongs and the shriek of fiddles, and when, sometime after midnight, we waddled back to our hotel, still under the guidance of Sun, it was only to discover that the two upper floors here were also amusement places like the other Coney Island, and that the same bedlam reigned. The elevator which took us to our rooms was filled with pajama-clad sing-song girls bound for midnight suppers. Upon our table were several forms on red paper printed in Chinese, upon which anyone desiring entertainment might inscribe the names of his favorite entertainers, much as one might order a dinner.

Sun, who was a man-about-town, called for a paint brush, filled out one of the blanks, and dispatched it by the room boy, and presently four dainty little Oriental creatures in black silk pajamas were ushered into the apartment, and joined us at the table.

"Why the wild women?" I inquired.

"They're not wild women," explained Tom. "They're sing-song girls."

"Oh, they're going to sing, are they?"

"No. It's too late to sing. They just sit and talk while we have supper. Sun's going to give us a supper."

And Sun did give us a supper. I already was suffering from a bursting sensation where Sun's elaborate dinner had lodged, but sun was not to be denied. He protested that I had not eaten a thing. He assured me that his offerings had been trifling; that the mean and contemptible dinner had been but a mere appetizer. He regretted that he could offer so little. Would I not honor him by accepting and eating this equally mean and contemptible supper? And then six waiters came in laden with armfuls of platters.

And when the sing-song girls had finally gone—they remained but a half-hour to supply the proper atmosphere for a Chinese banquet—and I was free to retire, it was with the finest case of indigestion I had ever experienced. And to think that I had believed the Chinese to be selfish and stingy and niggardly and parsimonious!

V

The first night was merely a beginning.

Every afternoon Sun appeared, always in some new Chinese garment, of which the most ravishing was a cerise-colored robe which began in a snug-fitting military collar and ended by sweeping in graceful folds to the ground.

Sun never appeared without extending an invitation of some sort. He rushed us out to dinners, to the Chinese opera, to every conceivable form of entertainment, and always insisted upon paying. When I attempted to do my share, Li would protest vigorously.

"No, no, no, doc. This is our party. You're our guest."

It was observable, however, that although Li called it "our" party, he did not share in the expenses. When I protested against allowing

Sun to pay for everything, Li merely stated in his bland manner:

"That's all right, doc. I lent him all the money he has."

Ten minutes later, he explained just as blandly:

"Sun's brother is very rich, doc. Sun gets all his money from his brother. Sun keeps several boxes all the time reserved at all the theaters. Sun has six mistresses. Sun has a private room in every restaurant. You think maybe all Chinese are poor like the coolies, doc, but the Chinese have lots of money. My brothers have more money than Sun's brother, and when we get to Hangkow—"

Li's gift of gab was another thing which reminded me of that Chinaman on the trail through Siam. While I tried vainly to write my notes, he would hop up and down the room to show me how the cheerleaders worked at Cornell. Or else he discussed our friendship, repeating endlessly:

"I'm not worthy to be your friend, doc, but I want to be your friend. If there is anything I do which you do not like, please tell me, and I shall try to do better."

One day I surprised him by taking him at his word.

"All right. You might shut up for half an hour until I've finished writing."

"Is that so, doc? You do not like that I talk so much? I'm sorry, doc. I'm a bad fellow to talk so much. I'm sorry. I say, I'm sorry. If there is anything else I do that you do not like—"

"I wish you wouldn't apologize for yourself all the time."

"Is that so, doc? You do not like that I say 'I'm sorry.' All right, doc. I'm sorry. I mean I'm sorry that I keep saying 'I'm sorry.' I say, I'm sorry, doc, that I can't tell you how sorry I am that I say 'I'm sorry' without saying 'I'm sorry.'"

He was not trying to be funny. He meant it all very seriously. It was a part of Oriental etiquette to be apologetic. Sun constantly belittled himself, and apologized for his most lavish entertainment with a patient repetition of excuses of which no one but an Oriental would be capable.

He took us one day to visit his wealthy brother, who lived in a magnificent European mansion out on bubbling Well Road, in the residential district of the elite. Sun's brother had been educated in the United States, and was very proud of the European furnishings, which included piano and victrola, the latter being equipped with records which consisted entirely of gospel hymns recommended by missionaries. Wishing to observe American customs, Sun instructed a nurse to show me his brother's baby, and the nurse, with typical Chinese observance of a master's orders, stayed behind my left shoulder throughout the call, holding up the baby whenever I glanced in her direction. As usual, Sun's hospitality included stuffing his guests with food; having observed that I ate chestnuts with relish the first night, he had pressed chestnuts upon me wherever we went, and had prepared for my visit by laying out platters of them on every article of furniture from the table to the piano. Also he served hot crabs, for which—and this was the only touch of Chinese custom to be seen—he provided silver chopsticks. Still he offered the usual apologies for the fact that he had no refreshments.

When Sun's brother appeared—a charming young man who had completed his American education without acquiring any of Li's undergraduate mannerisms—it became good form for Li to apologize for intruding upon the household.

"We have made you much trouble," he said. "We have brought dirt into your house upon our contemptible feet."

"You have honored my humble house," protested the host.

"It is we who are honored," insisted Li. "We have intruded very much. We have spilled crab meat upon your floor. I am very sorry."

The argument seemed still undecided when young Sun led us to another restaurant for another elaborate banquet. Afterwards, as usual, he produced tickets for the theater, and led the way to a playhouse built not unlike an American playhouse, but resounding to the clash of gongs and the shouted dialogue of actors who strutted across a scene-less stage.

The drama commenced at 6 p.m., and lasted through without intermission until 2 a.m., for the Chinese, who work long hours, demand equally long hours of entertainment, economizing apparently upon sleep. The story, as Li explained it, was of ancient times when three jealous Chinese kings fought for supremacy in the Empire, and in its rendition not an element of theatrical entertainment was lacking.

To a foreigner, the long periods of meaningless dialogue were tedious, but the pageantry was always fascinating. Kings and generals in elaborate silks and helmets and crowns and plumes—costumes which would have blinded Flo Ziegfield with their magnificence—were constantly strutting about, trying to make themselves heard above the clashing and shrieking of the orchestra which sat to one side of the stage. Warriors in devil masks, or with their faces painted with gaudy red and blue stripes, were constantly arousing expectations by preparing for combat, and defying one another.

One thing followed another with endless variety. There was slapstick comedy. There was dancing by the various warriors, accompanied by much brandishing of weapons, and marked principally by much pirouetting upon one foot with the other foot raised stiffly in the air. There was military drill by a male chorus armed with spears and battle axes. There was one amusing scene in which men dressed as dragons bounced upon the stage and cavorted about on all fours until slain by the chorus. There were mystifying spectacles; in one, an actress, impersonated by a pretty boy, was transformed into a dragon—a truly mystifying spectacle upon a darkened stage, wherein the actress faded from view as dream characters fade from the movie screen, to be replaced by a hideous statue; and another, wherein a man was supposed to be burned alive, a sulphur-soaked screen being lowered over him, and lighted, its sparks soaring dangerously among the curtains overhead, until, the screen having been burned away, a skeleton appeared in its place. There was much Chinese music, hideous to western ears, but always more sprightly than the Japanese music, and in excellent rhythm. There were numerous songs, all rendered in the shrill falsetto in which the Asiatics sing. Particularly horrible were the squealing voices of the actresses—always boys dressed and painted to represent women, since the Chinese have devised this method of avoiding the nuisance of the stage-door Johnie—and most horrible of all, to my ears, was the screeching of an actor whom Li pointed out as the Chinese Caruso.

Through it all, from 6 p.m. until 2 a.m., the orchestra pounded upon gongs with deafening effect, to the evident enjoyment of the audience, which filled every seat, and remained throughout.

The whole performance was a mixture of realism and absurdity. The costumes could not have been surpassed, but the scenery, such as it was, was merely a stimulant to the imagination. A hill was represented by a small triangular piece of cardboard held in the hands of a property man while the actor stood on a chair behind it. The property man was theoretically invisible, but always in evidence, strolling about in blue pajamas, looking exceedingly bored, but always ready to drop a pillow upon the floor when some courtier was about to kneel before the king, or to hand the warrior a sword when a battle was next on the program. When an army marched through the gate of a city, two waiting property men stepped out and held a cardboard arch, carelessly folding it up and tossing it aside as soon as the last straggler had passed beneath it. Now and then, for variety, they scattered fire in the path of an entering ghost, or dragged across the scene a bedraggled curtain covered with the advertisement of an English-made cigarette, before which the King was quite likely to convene his court, no one seeming to be aware of any incongruity in such a background. And actors to suggest a journey of several days, would follow one another in procession several times around the stage. But never for a single instant did the spectacle cease, the actors continuing with a freedom from fatigue which could be found nowhere except in the Orient.

From time to time an usher brought us wet towels upon which we wiped our hands. From the back of the seats ahead protruded a shelf, upon which a repast of oranges, bananas, chestnuts, sugar cane, and watermelon seeds was served, and from time to time a second usher filled our tea cups from a pot which resembled a sprinkling can. I seemed to attract as much attention from the Chinese spectators as did the actors, those in front of me craning their necks about to see what the foreign devil was doing in such a place. They laughed and talked among themselves during the uninteresting scenes, but when the pretty boy changed into a dragon—an effect which was visible only from the center aisles—the entire audience rushed excitedly to the point of vantage, climbing over one another's shoulders, while the ushers opened a free-for-all fight by attempting to stem the tide.

And when the play reached its climax in a battle scene, any one who believed the Chinaman to be an impassive, unemotional creature was forced to revise his opinion, for everyone screamed applause.

The battle surpassed in realism anything to be seen upon a western stage. It began with a single combat, two actors with swords—real swords—rushing at one another, swinging their weapons in the air, chopping at one another with strokes which missed the adversary by a fraction of an inch, until I expected that the next stroke would surely send a severed head sailing over the footlights. If one swung low, the other leaped over his blade; if he swung high, the other ducked beneath it, avoiding it by the narrowest margin. It was all done so swiftly that the swords became streaks of light, and I sat like the Chinese spectators upon the edge of my seat, breathless.

Then two men with spears dashed at each other to five a similar performance. Then one man fought half a dozen, darting about among swinging blades and thrusting lances. And finally the entire chorus of forty men was fighting and continued to fight for an hour, one army driving the other through the ludicrous city gate, to be in turn driven out. Back and forth they surged, warriors crossing and crisscrossing among the blades which flashed like so many streaks of light. Yet even this spectacle, which surpassed anything to be seen upon any western stage, had its absurd phase, for the supposedly wounded flopped into the air, turning handsprings and somersaults until at length two-thirds of the combatants were flopping and cavorting in all directions.

VI

Since we retired in the early morning, Sun and Li slept until it was time for the next evening's entertainment, and I saw little of the great cosmopolis of Shanghai except the night life of the fast young Chinese set.

To escape from Sun's hospitality long enough to carry out my prime object in hunting the poet, I was forced to rise before my hosts and wander off by myself. There was still no trace of his having arrived, but intuition told me that he would presently return to his former stamping-ground, and I hung about the waterfront, among the bales and bundles, and the straining coolies who replaced horses as beasts of burden, watching the little sampans of red, yellow, or blue, which zigzagged across the yellow-brown water like so many gaily colored bugs, or the unwieldy junks with prows like the mouths of giant fish, and the glassy eyes protruding from their forward hulks, or the rusty freighters which churned up the river from all the strange ports of the China Sea.

But the poet never appeared, and I would walk back through the streets swarming with Chinese humanity, with the ever-active humanity that swirled and eddied about the only stationary persons in sight, which were the policemen. In the French section—Shanghai is divided into the old Chinese city, the French concession, and the International Settlement—the gendarmes were Chinese clad in long green cloaks, with carbines slung over their shoulders. In the International Settlement, there were Chinese in costumes resembling those of London bobbies, and Sikhs imported by the British from India—the imposing chaps I had seen in Singapore, who towered above the swirling Chinamen, looking down upon pedestrians with a serene air of majesty, their penetrating brown eyes peering from between a multi-colored turban and a crinkly black beard.

It was for the Sikh that the Chinese had the most respect. When I stepped from the hotel, a dozen or more rikisha men would dash toward me with their carriages, and when the Chinese policeman on duty tried to drive them away by striking at them with his club or carbine, they would merely dodge and try to duck in behind him, but when a Sikh appeared around the corner they scattered hurriedly.

Among the Chinese in Shanghai there was a mixture of types. The Chinese vary as one proceeds from north to south. In the north, they are tall, stolid, and generally dull, as one proceeds toward Hong Kong and Canton, they are shorter, more intelligent and more mobile in their features. To venture a rash generalization, the Chinese of the north are more stupid and more inclined to be honest, while the Chinese in the south are more alert and more inclined to be wily. It is the southern Cantonese who emigrates to the Chinatowns of foreign cities to indulge in gang feuds and to give the Chinese an evil reputation in the minds of other nationals.

On rare occasions Li rose early enough to be my guide, but his information was casual. He pointed out the returned students, usually in western dress, and the upper-class merchants who wore long robes, and the middle-class artisans who wore separate jacket and skirt, and the lower-class coolies in the drab blue trousers that bulged around the hips and narrowed at the ankle. Autumn was approaching, and instead of donning overcoats, the Chinese were padding their other garments until they bulged like animated round balls. Women of the better families wore skirts. Working girls, sing-song girls, and servants wore pajamas. Sing-song girls were distinguishable by their shorter sleeves and shorter trousers. Unmarried girls, as a rule, wore their hair down the back; married women put it up in a knot. Women students wore skirts, eyeglasses, and a coldly intellectual expression. Broken feet were seldom to be seen, except upon older women, whose "golden lilies" had been broken before the western missionaries prevailed against the custom, or upon young women from remote rural districts. The younger girls were slim and shapely, but unlike the Japanese, who may become plump but seldom fat, the Chinese ladies showed a tendency in their riper years to become monstrously fat. The Chinese, according to Li, frequently compared women to flowers—beautiful immediately after budding, but destined soon to wither.

In my own opinion, the younger Chinese girls were prettier than the Japanese. Their faces were not so broad and flat; their hair, fastened more simply in a knot or pigtail instead of a fantastic coiffeur, gave their faces a more human contour; their expressions contained more individuality and personality, appearing less like graven images; in their pajamas they walked with more freedom and grace, instead of appearing to bounce along like animated dolls in the manner of the kimono-clad Japanese maidens.

Sun, who was a most well informed man-about-town, always sent out for the most beautiful of the sing-song girls to grace our board at the nightly supper. Just what pleasure Li and Sun found in the hired company of these entertainers, who never entertained, was a mystery. The girls always entered with ladylike bows, accepted the proffered seats at the table, smoked a cigarette—all Oriental women smoke—but declined other refreshment, and talked but little. Presumably they were present mainly to embellish the room. Li did most of the talking, apparently talking about himself with a male vanity which seems to be international, and occasionally pointing me out as the Dean who was personally escorting him home from college wherein he had so distinguished himself. The young ladies never seemed much impressed with me; the Chinese who have had little experience with the White Man have a feeling of contempt and loathing for the strange specimen of a strange race. Toward Sun and Li they were strictly formal, and although one of the girls was said to be Sun's mistress, neither she nor Sun gave the least sign of familiarity during these suppers. It is bad form in China even for husband and wife to show any affection in public, and in the conservative Chinese circles, men treat their wives like total strangers when in the presence of others. These unchaperoned suppers might have been regarded as a bit unconventional by western puritans; in reality, nothing—not even a funeral—could have been less conventional and proper, or less thrilling.

Custom, it seemed, prescribed that such functions as a supper should be accompanied by sing-song entertainers, and Sun was proving to me that he could play the host in correct style. No host could have been more attentive. On our first visit to the opera, although the Chinese consider the balcony to be the choicest part of the theater, Sun tried to show his knowledge of American custom by taking me to an orchestra seat. The Chinese keep their hats on at the theater, but when I absent-mindedly removed mine, both Sun and Li removed theirs. If I expressed the least wish for anything, it was supplied in ridiculous over-abundance. One night, as autumn approached, and the temperature in the unheated playhouse dropped until I shivered, Li suggested that a glass of whiskey might warm me up, and Sun promptly rushed out to return with the hugest bottle I had ever seen—a bottle of Chinese manufacture which contained some four quarts of vile liquor.

The Chinese proved as susceptible to its magic as had the Japanese. My companions seldom touched anything but light rice wine, but joined me this evening.

"Drink it, doc. At-a-boy. Maybe you do not like, but we must be polite to Sun."

Li walked home through the crowded streets, with one arm around my neck, and one around Sun's, kicking his feet into the air and shouting "Hi! Hi! Hi!" at the other pedestrians, after the manner of the rikisha man who warns other rikishas from his path. He said that the other two of us were disgustingly intoxicated, that it was his own fault for letting us get so drunk, but that if we would both hang onto him, he would get us home without mishap.

When we finally carried Li to the room, he lay upon the bed and waved both feet in the air, giving his college yell, and still apologizing for having allowed us to get into such a condition. Then, for half an hour, he gave us his favorite dissertation upon friendship, repeating his ceaseless phrase about our being the best friends in the world. Sun was less demonstrative. He sat at the table, his head nodding sleepily, but summoning his last remaining strength, he took a paint brush and filled out an order for ten sing-song girls and for a supper large enough to feed an army.

VII

Chinese hospitality was more than I could stand.

I had to escape before my digestion was completely ruined, and although I had intended to wait in Shanghai for the poet, I finally was forced to hasten to the river and arrange with the captain of a British freighter to take me to Canton.

Li, when he learned what I had done, was both surprised and shocked.

"But I have told everybody, doc, that you are coming to Hangkow to escort me home! What will they think? I have told them that you are the Dean, and that you are my best friend! What will Sun think? What will my people think? What will the servants in the hotel think? I have told everybody—even the room boy. And when we get to Hangkow, doc, you will be my guest—you will have automobiles and a yacht—everything you want. Why don't you come? You do not like me?"

Frankly, I did not. His affected mannerisms, amusing for a time, had become irritating and his constant companionship had become boresome. But I tried to be polite. I explained that I was going southward to avoid the coming winter, which is severe in Shanghai. Thereupon he insisted that Hangkow was warm. I pointed out that it was in approximately the same latitude as Shanghai. Thereupon Li, with his usual disregard of accuracy, drew a picture of the globe, showing that the equator, instead of running around the earth in a perfect circle, bulged up toward Hangkow and gave it a deliciously warm winter.

"And if you want an overcoat, doc, just go to the tailor here and order one. Order a fur-lined overcoat, doc. Just sign a chit for it. My brother's Finance Minister in the government, doc."

And just as Li was bragging about the importance and wealth of his other relatives, a knock sounded at our door, and one of his uncles came to call. He was an extremely "seedy" appearing individual, and Li hastily explained that he came from one of the distant branches of the family. The visitor brought news that Li's "eldest mother" had died. I began to understand why Li referred so disconnectedly to his mother in Peking or to his mother in Hangkow. It seems that Li's father had had several wives, and Li described each as his mother, and venerated each of them in proportion to her age, as prescribed by the formal Chinese Classics. Since he was required by custom to love his eldest mother best after his own actual mother, he became dutifully overwhelmed with grief, and when the seedy uncle—after two hours of beating about the bush, and breaking the news gently—conveyed the additional information that during Li's absence in America, death had also claimed eight nephews, six nieces, four aunts, two brothers, and fourteen cousins, Li's grief knew no bounds, although it impressed me as a purely conventional grief simulated in accordance with the dictates of Confucius—a formal, correct grief simulated merely to show others that Li knew what was required in the line of filial piety and family loyalty.

For in Li's Chinese manner of speech, a cousin might mean a relative so distant that he scarcely knew of his existence, while a brother might mean a forty-second cousin. The so-called brother who was Finance Minister probably did not know of Li's existence. Li's mind worked in Chinese grooves; he spoke of himself as having come from Canton six hundred years ago, meaning that his ancestors had come from Canton at that time. And when he spoke of the vast wealth of his relatives in Hangkow, he probably referred to the combined wealth of some several hundred distantly related families, with two-thirds of which he had not even a speaking acquaintance.

He was not lying with the deliberate intention to deceive. His promises were prompted by the oriental desire to say something pleasant, and he seemed to deceive himself into believing that they could be fulfilled. The Chinese have no conception of accuracy as we understand it. Because of the Chinese artisans' reputation for copying with exactness a model set before them, we are inclined to suppose them an accurately thinking race, but the contrary is true. A pound at one Chinese store is not the accepted pound at another. A mile in one part of China is not the mile used in another district. A mile uphill is shorter in length than a mile downhill. In Shanghai a dollar is theoretically one hundred cents, but if you pay for a dollar's worth of goods in twenty cent pieces, the merchant may require six of them instead of five; if you buy twenty cents' worth of goods and pay for it in pennies, the merchant may require twenty-three or twenty-four pennies. A merchant names the price of an article as "eighty cents, big money," by which he probably means ninety cents. And the Chinese mind sees nothing absurd in such irregularity. Practices which we consider dishonest—such as having several prices for one article, or making the customary "squeeze"—are accepted by custom, and regarded as honest. And in conversation, the same sliding scale of accuracy or truth is acceptable to the Chinaman. In the Chinese language there is no case or gender or voice or mode or tense or number or person. The Chinaman in his native tongue does not distinguish between what happened in the past, what is happening today, or what may happen in the future. The pigeon-English which coolies and servants speak is but English devoid of grammar, with sentences built in Chinese fashion. And although Li had learned to speak correct English, his mind was still Chinese.

Li's every act was prompted by the upperclass Chinaman's love of "face." Whether he spoke the truth or not, he must always make an impression upon those about him. Penniless aristocrat, as he proved to be, he must boast of the wealth of his relatives—one of whom had sent him to college—and must describe that wealth as his own. He still urged me to come to Hangkow as his guest, but when I firmly refused, he made the final effort at "face-saving" by withdrawing the invitation himself.

"I'm sorry, doc. I'm very sorry. I want very much to take you to Hangkow, but so many relatives are dead that all my family will be in mourning, and we could not entertain a guest."

Some old-timers question the genuineness of Chinese hospitality. According to one that I met, the Chinaman has no real consideration for others, but has developed his cumbrous set of ceremonials to take its place in oiling with politeness the wheels of social intercourse. He has an elaborate ritual which he follows not so much from kindness towards others as to show that he himself knows the proper thing to do. Wherefore, like Sun, hi piles more food upon the plate of his protesting guest, not because he wishes to feed the guest, but because he gives himself face by showing the guest his generosity.

But I can not quite accept the old-timer's verdict in regard to Sun. Foolish little spendthrift and waster though he was, he possessed a dignity and charm of manner, a modesty and sweetness of disposition which no Occidental could surpass. And he had urged his hospitality upon me with a kindliness which I could not question, and so lavishly that I was forced to run away from him.

In a final effort to make some slight repayment, I invited him and Li to dinner at the best European hotel upon my last night, urging upon them the choicest dishes in a manner as Chinese as their own, apologizing for my poor offerings and begging them to eat. But when I called for the check, it was only to discover that Sun had quietly paid it. And Sun again produced tickets for the theater. As my steamer was to sail at daybreak, I excused myself early, and went to bed, but some time during the night I was awakened by the sound of voices, and peering from the curtains which hid my bed, I could see Li and Sun indulging in the usual midnight supper, with four sing-song girls seated at the table.

They had both announced an intention of accompanying me on board the ship, but in the morning, Li was apologetic. He was sorry, very sorry to have a headache. He was a very bad fellow, he said, to have a headache when his best friend was leaving. And Sun reached up a feeble hand from the lounge upon which he slept. They were both of them fine little gentlemen, but the East was East and the West was West, and our habits could not be made to meet.

CHAPTER FOURTEEN

THE NIGHTMARE CITY OF CANTON

THE British freighter carried me southward toward Canton.

I had quite given up hope of finding the poet, but I had a little money; I intended to see something of the great swarming cities of South China while it lasted; then I would return to Hong Kong, and try to ship home as a seaman.

Four days we plowed southward, the British officers dining with me silently in the tiny cabin for three of those days, and then, having overcome their British reticence, proving perfectly sociable on the fourth.

We passed the entrance to Hong Kong, and turning westward, threaded our way through a maze of brown hilly islands, upon which not a single tree was to be seen, the Chinese in their struggle for an over-crowded existence having long ago deforested their land. A local steamer which passed us resembled the Hudson River Day Boat, but it was equipped with iron gratings to separate the First Class deck from the steerage, and an iron door, pierced for rifles, protected its bridge, while two Hindu guards patrolled the deck with carbines.

The precautions were being taken against an attack by Chinese pirates. The waters of South China are infested with robbers, and at times they are so numerous that foreigners, with the exception of missionaries, are not allowed to ascend the West River above Canton. The missionaries apparently have so little worldly wealth that they are considered immune from robbery. At the time of my visit, a Standard Oil man was being held for ransom by the pirates, and a daily Hong Kong paper contained the story of the capture of a whole fleet of merchant junks by the desperadoes, who had attacked the fleet in numbers estimated at over a thousand.

One finds it extremely difficult to reconcile all the conflicting statements he reads or hears about the Chinese. I had always heard that Chinamen were the most peaceable, law-abiding people oil earth; then I heard these stories. But the barren, deforested islands we passed, and the crowded, poverty stricken city of Canton at which we landed, testified to the unbelievably hard struggle for existence that prevails in South China—a struggle for existence which explains many seemingly contradictory traits in the Chinese character—and I understood why this naturally peaceable race takes so frequently to revolution and wholesale piracy.

II

I was awakened in the morning by what sounded like an attack. It was not. We were merely tying up to a wharf, and the frightful racket was but the normal quantity of noise which characterizes any Chinese city. The dock hands, straining at the ropes, were shouting and screeching in unison with every heave. Others were rushing up and down the quay and scrambling across the gangplank with bales and bundles of cargo, each carrier singing or gasping or howling or screaming to warn other carriers out of his way. The Chinese method of checking up on goods sent ashore consisted in sending with each bundle a small stick to be collected by the freight clerks, and the clerks, with Chinese love of noise, would sit and drum with these sticks upon the head of a hollow barrel. There were fully two dozen of them, and each seemed trying to out-drum his fellows, accompanying his drumming by singing at the top of his lungs in a shrill, wailing, unmelodious voice.

Not a few of the stevedores were women. When I hailed a sampan to carry me to the Shameen, where the English hotel was situated, the rowers proved to be two wrinkled old ladies and a child of undetermined sex with a face deeply pitted from smallpox. I hesitated, looking about for another sampan, but every craft in sight, and there were hundreds of them swarming about the wharves, was similarly manned—or rather, womanned. When the two aged females had landed me at the

Shameen, one of them informed me in broken English that her "son" would carry my pack to the hotel for ten cents, but when I had agreed, her "son"—owing perhaps to the mother's misunderstanding of English—proved to be a middle-aged woman who shouldered my belongings before I could protest, and left me to follow her, feeling decidedly ungallant as I listened to her puffing and grunting. She led the way at a rapid trot, and in order to keep her in sight, I was forced also to a rapid trot, thanking Dame Fortune that no moving-picture operator was on hand to immortalize the ridiculous scene.

Thus we entered the European district, situated upon an island beside Canton, an island to which the Chinese, except on special business, are denied admittance. For Canton, of all the large Chinese cities, is the center of the anti-foreign feeling. Upon the bridges that spanned a canal to the main city were Chinese sentries, and at night the barred gates were closed and locked.

II

I stopped at the European hotel, and hired a professional guide.

He was an elderly, dignified, scholarly Chinaman in a black robe and skull cap, of such aristocratic habits that he came to the hotel in a sedan chair carried by four coolies, and seemed vastly insulted when I informed him that we would walk on foot. Although he consented to this bourgeois plan of locomotion, it was with evident disdain.

A guide, however, was an absolute necessity in Canton. Once we had crossed the bridge from the Shameen, the streets became a perfect labyrinth of narrow alleys, seldom more than six feet in width, and frequently covered overhead so that only a gloomy apology for light penetrated to their uneven cobbles.

Canton has well been described as a "City of Nightmares." It is New York's Chinatown with the unpleasant features multiplied a thousand-fold. Its narrow, overcrowded alleys never continue in a straight line for more than a hundred yards; then one must zigzag at right-angles through a still narrower alley to a third alley which is even narrower and darker and more crowded. Two million Chinese are packed into the smelly hovels that border these gloomy thoroughfares, tunnel-like caverns that reek of joss and filth and human stench. Walking, in these crowded lanes, is nerve-wracking to any one but the nerveless Chinaman.

When a sedan chair comes along, pedestrians must step inside a house to let it pass. Runners dash upon you around corners, each runner carrying burden twice as large as himself. The more unwieldy the burden, the faster he runs. He shouts his warning to you, but since every one else is shouting and moving about, you never hear him until his bundle lands upon your head.

Canton is a city of human animals. Scarcely a machine and not a beast of burden is to be seen, for life is cheap, and men serve both as machines and beasts. One sees the burden bearer straining with his bulky cargo, his teeth clenched, his neck and shoulders calloused, his face contorted with effort. Yet he never ceases his racket. Despite his panting for breath, he keeps up his warning song, and two of them together on the same burden keep up a never-ending duet, one singing "Hi! Hi! Hi!" and the second chorusing with "Wong! Wong! Wong!" or something that sounds like it to the unpracticed ear, the two of them galloping around corners, crashing into other carriers, recovering their balance, and galloping onward through the mass of humanity with that never-ceasing chorus of "Hi! Hi! Hi! Wong! Wong! Wong! Hi! Hi! Hi! Wong! Wong! Wong!"

No one seems to worry about his neighbor's comfort. Boys amusing themselves by kicking a feathered ball into the air and keeping it from touching the ground, continually kick their fellows in the eye. Sweepers sweep the dust into the air until no one can see. A merchant scattering a bucket of water from his shop doorway to settle the dust scatters the water over the pedestrians. And no one objects, but takes it as a matter of course, in the even-tempered, fatalistic manner of the Celestial.

If the streets are dark, the narrow booths and shops are still darker. Usually goods of one kind are to be found in a certain district. On one street were the banks, where thousands of brass cash rattled from the deft fingers of the cashiers and money-changers. On another street the always terrific din was increased by the pounding of hammers from hundreds of shoemakers' establishments. On another street brass utensils were being made, and the crash was comparable only to that of a boiler factory.

On other streets food-stuffs were being sold—all the loathsome food stuffs of the Chinese market—sharks, fins, entrails, bloody fish, the varnished backs of ducks, dead rats, chunks of vermicelli in brilliantly colored liquids, a black jelly which resembled axle-grease, cats, dogs, pickled eggs of purple hue. Nothing goes to waste in China, and no animal dies, no matter of what malady, but its remains find their way to the larder. In the colossal struggle for existence, the Chinaman has learned to eat anything and to thrive upon it; those who couldn't were long ago weeded out of the race; only the fittest have survived, and the Chinese coolie of to-day can live upon a diet that would kill any other human being.

But among these squalid lanes were also shops with the richest of stocks and the finest of wares, where heavy wooden bars protected the doorway against robbers. When the guide knocked, the merchants would peer out at us and then remove the bars, hastily replacing them after we had entered. Then from their shelves they brought out carved ivory, kingfishers' tails inlaid in gold, silks and laces and jewelry, all the priceless things that only Chinese patience and Chinese labor could have made. And in their back rooms other Chinamen were at work, straining their eyes over the delicate jewelry, or manipulating a primitive mechanism with their feet while their tireless hands wove thread after thread into silken cloth, haggard, harassed-looking slaves of toil, who labored sixteen and eighteen hours a day for a mere pittance wherewith to buy themselves a diet of rice, entrails, and boiled rats.

My guide, disappointed at his discovery that I was not investing in silks and jewelry, for which he would have received a "squeeze" or commission from the merchants, finally began to lead me to Chinese temples. They were tawdry, dismal places, unlike the artistically barbaric temples of Buddhist Siam. Some were of the Buddhist religion, some of the Confucianist, but all were ornamented by ugly knick-knacks of carved glass and porcelain, all were dark and forbidding, and all reeked with joss.

The temples to which he led me were those accustomed to tourists. As we approached the altars through the smoke and darkness, a priest would bang upon a gong to awaken the gods, but the gods, crudely carved wooden figures, if awakened, showed no evidence of life. A second priest—all the priests were slovenly, unpriestly Chinamen—handed me a bucket containing thirty-six sticks of wood, with a message written on each. I was to shake the bucket until a stick fell out; then I was to consult the message to learn what ailed me. According to the guide's interpretation, it seems that I was suffering from cholera, and could be cured only by purchasing from the priest a certain amount of joss to burn at the altar. In a second temple we found sixty wooden gods, and the guide, inquiring my age, pointed out god No.27 as my special deity. Some of the gods sat upon the shelf, but a few were raised above the others with one or two bricks; if I wanted good-luck, the guide explained, I should purchase a few bricks to raise No.27 above his fellows, which would tickle the vanity of the deity and make me his special protégé. At every temple doorway there was a screen set back a few feet, but overlapping the opening; it seems that the spirits, who are everywhere in China, can fly only in a straight line, and therefore can not enter such a doorway. All of this was explained very seriously by the guide. The Chinaman's belief in the supernatural is most incomprehensible to an Occidental. The Chinaman seems surrounded by evil spirits whom he fears and constantly tries to placate, yet they are such silly, stupid spirits that they can be frightened by firecrackers and fooled or cajoled at will-such absolutely ridiculous spirits that one can not understand why the Chinaman fears them.

We went through temple after temple, all dark and tawdry and over-embellished with carving and statuary of great quantity but little artistry, among them the Genii temple, with four big hideous idols representing North, South, East, and West, and with an inner room that contained five hundred Buddhas in brass, no two of which were alike, and of which the most popular seemed to be the large, pot-bellied Buddha with carved children climbing all over him, who was reputed to help those who wished progeny. Many women were reverently placing joss-sticks before him, and the guide, pointing to them, informed me that these were the most unhappy women in Canton—the wives who were sterile.

But such wives were evidently few in China, for children swarmed about the streets, following me with outstretched hands and pleas for "cumsha." So did numerous grown-up beggars, men with enormous goiters, men with features eaten away by disease, men with shriveled limbs.

Canton was a city of horrors, and it was with relief that I turned back to the European Shameen, with its wide streets and its pleasant gardens. But the crowded humanity of the Chinese city had even overflowed to the canal, and beneath the guarded bridges the waterway was filled with houseboats, some with rounded roofs, some with peaked roofs, beneath which hordes of Chinamen lived, scarcely setting foot to land from childhood to old age, but eating, sleeping, working, and propagating in their crowded floating homes. At night more pretentious boats would join the fleet, poled slowly along by boatmen who scanned the shore and beckoned to me, and through their silken draperies I caught glimpses of tiny, painted-faced girls who awaited customers, and of fat, dissipated-looking Chinamen who smoked fat, bloated-looking pipes.

IV

There was no trace of the poet in Canton, but I spent another day of sightseeing with the guide.

He wanted to take me to see the "City of the Dead," the Chinese burial ground, and since it was a long journey, I succumbed to the lure of a sedan chair. There were three bearers to each chair, and the six of them kept up a sing-song chorus that was ear-splitting. Through the winding alleys they bore us at a swift trot, running full-tilt into other chairs and into burden-bearers, usually getting the victory in collisions, save when a huge packing-case on the shoulders of eight coolies came suddenly around a corner and upset both of our chairs.

It happened to be a Chinese "good luck" day, considered propitious for funerals. We passed many processions. A Chinese funeral, like every other ceremony in China, is an occasion for noise. The more prosperous processions were led by several bands, usually native bands with flutes, gongs, fiddles, and cymbals, but occasionally by bands with European horns, which are popular because of their greater volume of noise. Lively airs, such as "Yankee Doodle" or "There'll Be a Hot Time in the Old Town To-night," were not recognized as inappropriate, since everything in China is the exact opposite of everything in Europe or America, even to the costume of the mourners, who were dressed in white. Behind the music came long files of boys carrying banners printed in Chinese, men Carrying altars laden with fruit for the deceased, then the coffin with its elaborate silken canopy, and finally the mourners, some of whom were weeping, but most of whom appeared to be enjoying it hugely.

At length, however, I observed a procession which seemed to be conducting itself with proper solemnity. One young woman, although dressed in gay colors, was not only weeping and wailing with grief but had to be supported and dragged by several older women.

"That," I said to the guide, "is what I'd call a real funeral."

"That," said he, "is a wedding."

The young woman who wept and wailed, it seems, was the bride, who might really have been charmed with the prospect of matrimony, but who was required by custom to make a pretense of grief in order to show her sorrow at leaving the home of her beloved parents.

Our carriers took us out into the suburbs. Some children still pursued me with requests for "Cumsha!" but most of them stood in the doorway, as did their parents, staring at me with hostility and contempt, and muttering remarks which, had I understood, would probably have contained revilement of my ancestors to the Nth generation. While the cultivated Chinaman treats the foreigner with extreme politeness, the ignorant coolie regards him with supreme contempt. For years before the coming of the White Man, China dominated the East, and the Chinese regarded all their neighbors as barbarians; among the ignorant, the same attitude—astonishing as it sounds to us White Men, who believe that our superiority must be instantly recognized anywhere—still prevails to-day. The coolie may marvel at our cameras and automobiles and steam-engines, but instead of crediting us with cleverness, he is inclined to think—if lie thinks about them at all—that these contrivances were given to us by the gods, or rather, by the evil spirits. He judges us by his own standards and finds us inferior to himself. We dress strangely; we can not speak his language; we are ignorant of his customs; we can not live as he lives or eat what he eats. Altogether we are pretty poor specimens in his estimation.

A few months earlier I might have wanted to leap from my sedan chair and thrash every Chinaman who insulted me, but I had become accustomed to his attitude. It seemed, however, that every one I passed was either spitting or clearing his throat preparatory to spitting, and since I constantly had the feeling that I would be the recipient of the demonstration, I rode through the suburbs with a figurative chip on my shoulder, turning quickly about at every sound of another throat being cleared.

The guide stopped first at the Chan Temple. The Chan family, he explained, was the Number One Family of South China. He himself belonged to it. This temple, in which they worshiped all the dead Chans, was a forbidding, weather-beaten structure of stone, but its roof was decorated with thousands of carvings. Dragons writhed about the eaves, and gargoyles snarled from over the doorway. Inside were thousands of wooden tablets, enumerating the virtues of the Chans, set in different groups according to the rentals paid, which varied from $300 to one dollar for each tablet. Each member of the family buys a tablet according to his means, has his virtues inscribed thereon, and then plasters a strip of red paper over them; when he dies, his relatives remove the paper and every one who reads the list of his virtues will learn what a fine man he was. Once each year, my guide said, the entire family assembles here to worship the dead. The family numbers something over seven thousand, and according to the guide, it is a wonderful treat to hear them all drinking tea and shooting off firecrackers.

From the temple we proceeded to a group of buildings where the dead are left until the family sorcerers and diviners have selected a suitable time and place for the final burial. The time and place are considered of tremendous importance since the corpse, if it does not rest contentedly, may visit its descendants with indescribable bad fortune. A gatekeeper admitted us into a long corridor bordered by a row of booths containing coffins. It was a Number One place, and the coffins were magnificent boxes of carved ebony, sandalwood, and other valuable woods. Some had been there for over a year, awaiting the verdict of the diviners. Everywhere was evidence of superstition. Some of the coffins were guarded by statues of warriors. Garments and imitation jewelry, made of paper, surrounded the corpse. Joss was burning before the deceased, and some had statues of servants to wait upon them. A real, live attendant, however, served fresh tea to the corpse every morning.

From this temporary resting place, the guide led me out into the open country. The land was cut up into rice paddies, and both men and women were laboring waist-deep in scummy pools. Not an inch of land was wasted, the cultivated fields coming right up to the edge of the uneven trail that zigzagged up and down the rolling hills. In the absence of woods, the natives were gathering every twig and bush and blade of grass for fuel.

But having passed over a rough and narrow trail through a dirty little stone village, we came at length to a dilapidated pile of masonry that once had been the city gate, and from this point I could look out across the one species of land in China that is not utilized for material purposes It was an ugly vista of brown hills dotted with slabs of gray rock—the final resting-place of millions of venerated ancestors. So much land had been consecrated to the dead that comparatively little farm land remained to support the hordes of those still living.

V

And still the population increases!

China's greatest need is birth control, but the Chinese philosophy forbids. In a country where ancestors are worshiped, every man wants sons to burn joss for him when he becomes an ancestor. Otherwise he may not rest easy in the Hereafter.

The philosophy has one pleasant feature. A man, and even a woman, gains in importance and respect as he or she grows older. One always has something to which he may look forward. The longer one lives, the more important he becomes among his fellows, and when he reaches his death-bed he can reflect joyously that by becoming a corpse he will increase his importance still more.

The mania for sons, and its resultant overcrowding, has molded the Chinese character. The Chinaman is industrious, as any one else would be who was forced to toil ceaselessly for an existence. He is indifferent to comfort and convenience. He is absolutely lacking in nerves, can sleep anywhere, eat anything, and endure noise or stench with apparent enjoyment. He has remarkable vitality; he is patient and persevering. Naturally, from his struggle, he is cold-blooded, cruel, self-seeking, unsentimental, and unsympathetic towards others. He is wily and shrewd where money is concerned. He is frugal, parsimonious, saving, careful, and conservative in business. He is contented and cheerful under adversity.

The Chinaman does not realize that his hardships are due to his philosophy, or to the philosophy of the ancestors whom he venerates. Sons are an insurance against Hell in the Hereafter. Also, sons help the family in the struggle for existence against the other families. As the population increases and the struggle becomes harder, he propagates with increased enthusiasm. So do the neighboring families. Thus the struggle continues.

Gradually the Chinese are being crowded out of China. No one is more of a home-loving creature than John J. Chinaman; no one is more firmly rooted by conservatism to the spot in which he was born and where his relatives live; yet, according to the estimate of Prof. Edward

Alsworth Ross, there are to-day some ten millions of Chinese living outside China.

The Chinaman, trained in a hard school, can live anywhere, and thrives equally well from the Equator to the Pole. I have run across him in all sorts of strange places; along the Andes or down the Amazon, no cluster of thatched huts was complete without at least one Chinese merchant. In Mexico, where the peons hate old John, and where the slaying of a "Chino" is considered diversion rather than murder, old John was to be found in every town and hamlet. He is irrepressible. You can't get away from him. In the Orient, you may penetrate the jungles of Indo-China or Siam beyond the haunt of the European, and just as you begin to feel that you are an intrepid adventurer and explorer, you will find some Chinaman there before you.

Wherever he finds a few other natives, John stops and builds a shop or a laundry or a restaurant or something. If the natives burn it down, he builds another one. John is a shrewd businessman. Given the broader opportunities of an undeveloped country, he soon rises above the coolie class. He takes insult with humility, rakes in the cash, and drives all other natives out of business. In Indo-China, the authorities admitted him freely enough but taxed him more heavily than they taxed any other nationalities, but he was landing there in droves and displacing the Annamites. In Siam, he already comprised half the population of the capital, and was slowly driving the Siamese out of their own land. In the Straits Settlements, where he was imported for his labor by the British, he had driven out the Malays and had given Penang and Singapore the complexion of Chinese cities. In the Philippines, although in the earlier days the Filipinos had mobbed him and persecuted him, although the Spaniards had taxed him and the Americans had restricted him, he was present in large numbers, as bland and cheerful as ever, defying extermination, and prospering.

I do not like John. In all my ramblings, he is the first foreigner I've met to whom I have a profound-and probably a prejudiced-aversion. But, to use the vernacular, you have to hand it to him.

VI

Setting out for Hong Kong, I stopped at the Portuguese colony of Macao—one of the few reminders that the Portuguese were the first

Europeans to invade the East.

A river-boat with iron gratings and Hindu guards took me through another maze of barren islands, past aged junks equipped with still more aged muzzle-loading cannon—cannon which probably did not work, but which were expected to frighten the pirates—and landed me finally upon a beautiful island whose many trees and parks testified to its European occupancy. Macao was a quaint city of stucco houses-houses of blue, pink, yellow, and brown, their colors softened with age into tints like those of the "old masters"—and it perched upon a hillside overlooking a delightful crescent-shaped bay.

The Portuguese first established themselves here in 1557, and Macao was Europe's first outpost in the Orient, but when the British came to Hong Kong, the Portuguese city lost its commercial importance. The Europeans, after the manner of Latin colonists, intermarried with the Chinese, and the latter absorbed them as they have absorbed all other races with whom they have intermarried, and the only remaining Portuguese are a few officials and the garrison, numbering altogether but a few hundred. It seemed odd to walk the streets that bore Portuguese names, among houses of Latin architecture, past old medieval castles, and to see nothing but Chinese.

Macao now survives only as a pleasure resort—a den of vice and iniquity, to which the wealthy Chinese come from Hong Kong and Canton for purposes of gambling and dissipation. The Portuguese derive their revenue from the sale of lottery tickets, and from the licenses which they seem to grant readily to any species of evil resort which chooses to do business. It is the Monte Carlo of the East with its many gambling farms, where Chinese of all descriptions crowd eagerly about the fan-tan tables, and a stranger may land in Macao without any of the immigration and customs formalities which annoy him in all other ports, for the authorities welcome visitors. By day the city is but a lazy, quaint old-world city basking peacefully in the semi-tropic sunshine, but with the coming of night the lanterns advertising "First-Class Gambling House" begin to illumine the town, and in the blaze of light from every other doorway may be seen a troupe of almond-eyed girls with heavily rouged lips. The steamer which took me onward to Hong Kong was fitted with sodden, opulent-looking Chinese, whose eyes were bloodshot and whose brains were befogged with opium.

I have heard it stated by sentimental friends of the Chinese that all evil, vice, dishonesty, and wickedness in China dates from the coming of the White Man. Either this statement is an exaggeration, or else the Chinese have proved remarkably apt pupils. Yet the policy of the Portuguese in Macao is but the policy, to a lesser degree, of the French in Indo-China and the British in Borneo, who grant licenses to opium resorts on the theory that the Chinese are bound to obtain opium in some fashion and might as well buy it from the government. Still, one might bring up the old, much-quoted charge that Great Britain once fought a war to force opium upon the protesting Empire of China.

VII

No author would think of concluding a book on the Orient to-day without discussing the "Rising tide of color," dismissing with a stroke of his pen the conclusions of all other authors, and expressing his own personal opinion in the third person as though it were the word of God instead of the haphazard conviction of one small specimen of the human race.

The Yellow Peril, as seen by most authorities, is three-fold in its possibilities.

One alarmist warns us against a militant Orient of the future, united in arms under the leadership of Japan, sweeping westward with sword and fire, and resting only when it has overthrown the entire White Race.

Another warns us against a commercially awakened Orient, educated in European business methods but still blessed with its abundance of cheap labor, underworking and underselling the Western manufacturers and merchants.

Another warns us against a numerically growing Orient, imbued with ancestor worship and the resultant fondness for progeny, propagating and propagating with the virility and persistence wherein no race can equal the Yellow, until the hordes of slant-eyed Asiatic babies crowd our own white grandchildren to the edge of their constantly diminishing territory and finally shove them into the Atlantic Ocean.

All of these catastrophes are possible, but none is so immediately probable that we of the White Race need worry about it at present.

Of the three, the least troublesome is the first. An Orient united in arms is an absurdity. If the Asiatic cherishes an antipathy toward the White Race, he cherishes an equal antipathy toward his immediate neighbors. The Chinese, for instance, can not stop quarreling among themselves, or cease their annual civil wars, long enough to present a united front to any one else. The same Chinese, furthermore, despite their traditional hostility to the "foreign devils" from Europe and America, have an equally deep hatred, and in some parts a deeper hatred, for the Japanese. Simultaneous uprisings throughout the European possessions in the East might accompany a war between Japan and a nation or group of nations from the Occident, but the East, for some hundreds of years at least, will never be allied in a systematically organized Race-War.

The Japanese alone, of all the potentially powerful peoples in Asia, possess the national unity essential to a warlike country. The Japanese are not only loyal to their Empire, but their devotion possesses an active, energetic quality seldom found either in the East or in the West. To illustrate with one of my own experiences, when my steamer from Kobe to Shanghai was passing through the Inland Sea of Japan, the stewards posted maps upon the deck to indicate the various fortified zones in which passengers were forbidden to take photographs; having been below, I had not observed them, and when I appeared upon deck with my camera, the first Japanese who saw me—he happened to be a seaman from the forecastle—immediately shouted for a ship's officer. The rule against carrying a camera in the vicinity of fortifications—although the fortifications were so far distant that they could not be discerned through a telescope—is typical of Japan, and the seaman's prompt action in enforcing the rule is typical of the Japanese. Although the Japs are individually a peaceable, quarrel-avoiding people, one can not observe them at home without making the mental note that they are preeminently fitted to make wonderful soldiers. Their carefully restrained aggressiveness is accompanied with a keen respect for order and authority, which lends itself far better to discipline than does our western independence. The training which we western nations must inculcate in our soldiers to inure them to a frugal diet, to ceaseless physical labor, to long hours and little sleep, is but the daily life of the average Japanese. In a man-to-man bayonet duel, I would bet on a White Man; in a long grueling campaign with little fighting but tremendous hardship, I would bet on the Japanese. But although the Japanese are reputed to dream secretly of a future Race-War in which they will lead the rest of the Yellow World, and although they have already posed on every possible occasion—in the Russo-Japanese War and at the Versailles Conference—as the standard bearers of the Yellow Race, the comforting fact remains that Japan has few, if any, friends among her Asiatic neighbors. If Japan fights the White Race, or any part of it, she must fight more or less alone.

A more probable Yellow Peril is the second—that of a commercial conquest. The Asiatic laborer or artisan, of course, is not capable of the intensive industry which marks the Occidental workman, but he works longer hours, and lives upon a fourth of the wages required to keep an Occidental from starvation. The Asiatic business man is shrewd; he is aggressive and persistent in going after business, and although he hides his aggressiveness under the cloak of Oriental humility, he usually gets what he goes after; like Kwong Bee in Singapore, he lets his patrons call him a "Bloody Chink," but penny by penny, he takes away their money; like the "Christian" on the trail to Siam, he accepts a blow and turns the other cheek, but in the end he brings home the brown goggles.

Yet conditions are changing, even in the East. On the Malay Peninsula, as the reader will recall, the Chinese coolies were forming labor unions, and demanding higher wages. In Hong Kong, during my wanderings, there had been a colossal strike which had entirely paralyzed the harbor, and which rested in the steamship companies raising the pay of the Chinese seamen. Wages are still low in the East, but they are going higher. Before Asiatic labor drives our western products from the market, labor will not be so cheap in Asia.

The most probable phase of the Yellow Peril is the third—the peril of a rapid increase in the Yellow Race—yet its results will be sufficiently remote to give us a pleasant breathing spell. At present, the White Race is still numerically superior. I haven't counted them myself, but according to figures which I have stolen from Dr. Lathrop Stoddard's "The Rising Tide of Color," there are 550,000,000 white people to 500,000,000 yellow. The Chinese lead the yellow race with 400,000,000; the Japanese follow with 60,000,000. The peril lies in the ratio of increase, the Chinese breeding at the rate of 6,000,000 a year, and the Japanese at 800,000 which means—at a rough estimate—that two yellow children are born to every white child. Furthermore, the yellow children will marry before they reach the twenties—no one remains unmarried in Asia—and will be raising families of their own long before the white child will think of marrying. Thus, the problem works with compound interest, and the ratio presently will be three to one, and then four to one. There are still tremendous tracts of uncultivated and sparsely populated territory in Asia—in Borneo, in Siam, in Cambodia, in Malaya—into which these offspring can overflow without disturbing the White Race, and where they may propagate for many years to their hearts' content, but some day the world will have to expand, or something is going to break.

China, where the increase has been greatest, has had a system of safety valves in its infant mortality, its floods, and its famines, which—to speak of the question from a cold-blooded Occidental viewpoint—have settled from time to time the problem of its superfluous population. We of the West, however, guided by our hearts rather than by our reason or our consideration for our own progeny, are now doing all that we can to stop and seal these safety valves by contributing to famine relief and flood prevention. I once heard an old-timer in the East, during an argument with a missionary, express the rather startling opinion:

"You're doing what you believe to be right, but in teaching hygiene to these Chinks, you're helping to keep the Yellow Race on the increase. Those people in the missionary societies at home don't realize that every cent they send to you is a cent devoted toward the eventual extermination of our own great-grandchildren."

And still, having seen the poverty-stricken Chinese in China, it is difficult to preach such a cold-blooded doctrine against charity. For as I sailed away from Macao, the Chinese followed us in sampans, fishing from the brine such scraps of food as the ship's cook dumped from the galley. At least, it will be some hundreds of years before the hordes of Chinese progeny shove ours into the Atlantic Ocean, and that's long enough for any race to get some pleasure out of life.

Furthermore, if any of the three Yellow Perils overtake us, we shall get just exactly what we deserve. In the beginning, the Yellow Race wished to stay at home and mind its own business, but we, in our lust for conquest and commercial gain, knocked at their doors with fleets of gunboats, and demanded that they open their gates to us. We taught them to use modern weapons and modern machinery. We took swarms of their people to foreign lands to exploit their cheap labor. And now, if they beat us at any of the games we taught them to play, we have no sportsmanlike ground for complaint.

Finally, this is just one man's opinion, and frankly, the more I saw of the Orient, the less I knew about it. To understand it, one should live there for at least a hundred and fifty years, and I couldn't spare the time. I had to pursue the poet.

CHAPTER FIFTEEN

BACK TO HONG KONG

I

IT was almost a year since a tramp freighter had dropped me at the waterfront of Hong Kong, where the Prophet had warned me.

I wondered whether the same hobo would still be sitting upon the same cotton bale, among the same Chinese coolies. And since my funds had dwindled considerably, I also wondered whether there would be room upon the cotton bale for one more hobo.

But it was night when another tramp freighter brought me through a winding channel among hilly islands into the harbor. A circle of lights appeared ahead, trailing out around the waterfront, but rising skyward in the center toward the famous "Peak," until one could not be certain where the lights ended and the stars began. Then day broke, revealing the most beautiful metropolis in the East, the ugliness of its Chinese section eclipsed by its handsome stone business district and by its many charming English bungalows perched among the towering, palm-clad hills.

The only thing missing was the Prophet, and I had a feeling of relief. At least, there was no one present to say, "I told you so." For although I spent another day in examining hotel registers, steamship lists, newspaper files, and police records, I found no trace of Signor Enrico ———, poet and absconder. And since I had hunted him at all the principal steamship ports of the Orient, the last hope of finding him had vanished.

II

Hong Kong reminded me—rather appropriately—of Singapore.

The topography was different, but the buildings and the people and the harbor full of shipping were all much the same.

In the Anglicized business district were the same solid structures of stone, built with the second and succeeding stories projecting over the sidewalk and supported by heavy square pillars. Lean-faced superior-looking English civilians swung along with jaunty canes, their white linen contrasting with the uniforms of the khaki-clad British Tommies. The climate was warmer than that of Shanghai, and the Chinese rikisha coolies were clad, like those of Singapore, in dirty white drawers and wide-brimmed hats of straw. As in Singapore, the streets were thronged with Sikhs and Tamils and Japanese and all the other races of the Orient.

On either side of the Anglicized section were the Chinese districts. The houses were narrow and overcrowded. The streets were narrow and overcrowded and noisy. Women pushed their way about with children strapped to their backs. In one street people were eating; from a jumble of cook-stoves which covered both roadway and sidewalk arose a cloud of stifling smoke, and with it the odors of grease and general nastiness. Throngs of coolies were gobbling their rice, some standing, some sitting upon the curb, some squatted upon their haunches in the middle of the street. The Chinese being overcrowded in their homes, did everything upon the sidewalk. Vegetables were spread out to dry. Merchants and peddlers exhibited their wares. Everybody was buying something or selling something or carrying something. Rikisha men forced their way through swarms of pedestrians, double-decked trolley cars clanged their warnings—

Hoping to escape from the Chinese bedlam, I climbed laboriously to the Peak, ascending one of the numerous curving roadways of cement that twisted steeply uphill through groves of palms and past the pleasant tropical gardens of the wealthy and the homes of British officialdom. The view from the Peak was magnificent. One could look down upon a great expanse of inland sea wherein the big ocean liners resembled toys. I could scarcely make out the flags at their mastheads, but I could distinguish the green hulk that proclaimed one steamer to be a Shipping Board vessel.

That settled it! If possible, I was going home. I would call upon the American Consul, tell him my story, and ask him to help sign me on that ship as a deckhand, stoker, steward—anything at all, if I could work my way home. Then I recalled that it was Sunday, and that the Consulate would be closed.

III

I said that my funds had dwindled considerably. To be exact, they had dwindled to forty-three cents. This fact also reminded me of Singapore.

I would spend it for supper; then I would haunt the dock in search of an officer from that Shipping Board steamer, praying that the captain himself might come ashore.

It must be a light supper in some chop-suey house, and I walked through the Chinese section again, turning at length into a narrow place whose front bore a misspelled English name. It was almost as though I had walked into Kwong Bee's grog-shop. The same narrow room; the same narrow bar; the same rough table; the same battered piano; the same sort of Chinese waiters; and the same sort of patrons. One beachcomber—a rather slight, timid-looking chap—completed the picture by approaching me for a "hand-out."

"I say, could you spare a few cents, mate, for a cup o' coffee?"

It was so much like old times that I grinned at him.

"You're new, aren't you?" I asked.

"Yes," he admitted.

And almost to my own surprise, I found myself talking to him as the Kid had once talked to me:

"Then, let me give you some advice. When you ask a guy for a hand-out, don't do it as if you were afraid of him. Walk right up as if you'd bash his bleeding face in if he didn't come across."

But it reminded me of the pawning of the camera. It was a long time since my camera had rested at a pawnshop. And there was the piano, the chance of passing the hat. Those old days did not linger pleasantly in the memory, but if worst came to worst, and the captain of the steamer refused to sign me on—

Then the voice of another bum, lounging at the bar, caught my attention. The man was not familiar, although his was the type of the Gorilla. He was talking to the Chinese bartender:

"That's the kind of a man I am, d'ye see? D 'y 'understand? I don't tike no impudence from nobody, I don't. An' I asked this blighter for a few pennies— 'e was a funny little blighter, pretty swank in 'is little white suit—an' what does 'e do but 'e gives me one penny. 'Tike!' says 'e, just like that—'Tike!' And I sez, 'Look 'ere, I can't buy nawthink for a penny!' An' what does 'e do, but 'e tikes the penny, an' sez 'Give!'—just one word like that. An' 'e starts to walk away, an' I up an' 'its 'im in the nose."

My mind raced back to another funny little fellow, back in Saigon, who poured the dregs of our beer into my glass with an exclamation of "Take!" and reached for my cigarettes with an exclamation of "Give!"

Forgetting everything else, I seized the bum by the shoulder.

"Say, was this bird an Italian?"

A pair of bleery eyes examined me suspiciously.

"'E was Italian or French or something. D 'ye thing I'm lyin' to ye? Look 'ere, 'oo in 'ell are you, anyway? I don't tike no impudence from—"

He was rolling up his sleeves.

"I'm not calling you a liar. I'm looking for that fellow myself. Do you know where he went?"

"'E went into the Prince Albert 'otel, I'm tellin' ye, an' if ye call me a liar agin—"

But I was already hurrying through the crowded streets toward the Prince Albert. So the poet *was* in town! His name had not been upon any of the records. Had he changed his name? But upon the hotel register it appeared, in ink that was scarcely dry—Signor Enrico —— with several degrees after it—degrees which he had conferred upon himself. Here he was staying at another big hotel, living in comfort upon my money, while I sought a low-class beachcombers' dive for supper! I had roamed all over the Orient to catch him, and at last I had him! Just what I was going to do to him, I had not determined, but—

A Chinese hotel boy led the way upstairs, and knocked upon the door. A familiar voice said, "Come!"

I pushed open the door, and the next minute the poet had both arms around me. But he was not trying to fight. That idiot was hugging me with glee!

"Fostair! Fostair! Fostair! So glad I am to see you! Kiss me upon the cheek, Fostair!"

"Kiss you?" I growled. "I'll smash you! Why didn't you come to Bangkok?"

"Come to Bangkok? Why, Fostair, right away after the honeymoon I have come to Bangkok."

"But the newspapers said you had gone to Manila."

"No, Fostair. See the ticket, Fostair."

And he showed me a handful of ticket stubs. The newspaper account in Singapore had been incorrect. From Java, he had passed through Singapore on his way not to Manila, but to Bangkok!

"How I have look for you, Fostair. I come back to Singapore and you are go to Borneo, and I come to Borneo and you are go to Manila, and from Manila I follow you to Japan, to Yokohama and Shanghai, and just now, twenty minute ago, I land in Hong Kong."

All the time I had thought I was pursuing him, he was pursuing me. His books in Italy had gone into the Nth edition, his publishers had finally sent him a check, and he paid me back the amount of my travelers' checks with which he had absconded.

"But your wife?" I asked.

"She is no more, Fostair. She have go away with another man like the chorus girl go."

"Then you didn't marry the chorus girl?"

"No, Fostair. I have marry one woman you know—Mrs. Rooney. But I am not fine big man like Rooney. I can not take her with one hand and throw her around like Rooney. We have one quarrel in Java, and she have say to me, 'I marry you because I pity you. You have long hair just like Sniffles.' You remember the dog, Sniffles, Fostair? All the time my wife call me 'Sniffles.' I do not like. When she go away, I say to myself, 'Nevair mind.' And I follow you to Hong Kong."

He had not changed a bit.

"Fostair," he exclaimed. "We are here where we have begin. We have the money. We can go to Siam, and have the dancing girl to jingle the brass upon the ankle. We shall be kings, Fostair—two kings in the jungle!"

But one experience had been enough, and I took passage on the first steamer for San Francisco. The poet escorted me aboard the ship.

"I hope you don't mind," I apologized, "if I write a book and call you the biggest fool in the Orient."

"No, Fostair. I do not mind. I also write one book and already I have call you the biggest fool."

Whereupon we parted before the Fool-Killer made another double killing.

THE END

DON'T MISS THESE OTHER EXCITING BOOKS FROM DIXON-PRICE PUBLISHING!

Down the Columbia — $19.99
Lewis R. Freeman   ISBN 1-929516-18-5

The Confessions of a Beachcomber — $17.99
E.J. Banfield   ISBN 1-929516-15-0

The Adventures of a Tropical Tramp — $17.99
Harry L. Foster   ISBN 1-929516-16-9

A Thousand Miles in the Rob Roy Canoe — $17.99
John MacGregor   ISBN 1-929516-06-1

By Reef and Palm — $11.99
Louis Becke   ISBN 1-929516-21-5

The Trembling of a Leaf — $15.99
Somerset Maugham   ISBN 1-929516-23-1

My Tropic Isle — $16.99
E.J. Banfield   ISBN 1-929516-22-3

Small Boat Building — $12.99
H.W. Patterson   ISBN 1-929516-04-5

Boat-Building and Boating — $15.99
D.C. Beard   ISBN 1-929516-17-7

AVAILABLE ONLINE AT
WWW.DIXONPRICE.COM